The Spirit of America

Chicken Soup for the Soul: The Spirit of America
101 Stories about What Makes Our Country Great
Amy Newmark. Foreword by Lee Woodruff.

Published by Chicken Soup for the Soul Publishing, LLC www.chickensoup.com
Copyright ©2016 by Chicken Soup for the Soul Publishing, LLC. All Rights Reserved.

The publisher gratefully acknowledges the many publishers and individuals who
granted Chicken Soup for the Soul permission to reprint the cited material.

Front cover artwork courtesy of iStockphoto.com/Andrew Rich (©Andrew Rich)
Back cover and Interior photo of Statue of Liberty courtesy of iStockphoto.com/
Delpixart (©Delpixart)
Back cover photo of American Flag courtesy of iStockphoto.com/blackred (©blackred)
Photo of Amy Newmark courtesy of Susan Morrow at SwickPix
Photo of Lee Woodruff courtesy of Stefan Radtke

Cover and Interior by Daniel Zaccari

Distributed to the booktrade by Simon & Schuster. SAN: 200-2442

Publisher's Cataloging-In-Publication Data
(Prepared by The Donohue Group, Inc.)

Names: Newmark, Amy, compiler. | Woodruff, Lee, writer of supplementary
    textual content.
Title: Chicken soup for the soul : the spirit of America : 101 stories
    about what makes our country great / [compiled by] Amy Newmark ;
    foreword by Lee Woodruff.
Other Titles: Spirit of America : 101 stories about what makes our country
    great
Description: [Cos Cob, Connecticut] : Chicken Soup for the Soul
    Publishing, LLC [2016]
Identifiers: LCCN 2016936475 | ISBN 978-1-61159-960-2 (print) |
  ISBN 978-1-61159-259-7 (ebook)
Subjects: LCSH: United States--Literary collections. | United States--
    Anecdotes. | Anecdotes.
Classification: LCC E169.1 .C45 2016 (print) | LCC E169.1 (ebook) | DDC
    973/.02--dc23

PRINTED IN THE UNITED STATES OF AMERICA
on acid∞free paper

25 24 23 22 21 20 19 18 17 16   01 02 03 04 05 06 07 08 09 10 11

Chicken Soup for the Soul

for the Soul®

The Spirit of America

101 Stories about What
Makes Our Country Great

Amy Newmark
Foreword by Lee Woodruff

Chicken Soup for the Soul Publishing, LLC
Cos Cob, CT

Chicken Soup for the Soul

Changing the world one story at a time®
www.chickensoup.com

Contents

❸

~Our Vast and Beautiful Land~

❹

~America's Heroes~

❺

~One People, United~

❻

~That American Can-Do Attitude~

❼

~Our Proud New Citizens~

❽

~American Traditions~

~Seeing America from Abroad~

Foreword

My breath caught in my throat. As we approached the highway overpass, hundreds of flags fluttered in the breeze, larger ones rippling from wooden dowels, the smaller versions fastened into the weave of the chain-link fencing.

Living overseas, this was our family's first visit back to America after the terrorist attacks of September 11th and we were nervous, uncertain of exactly what to expect and how we would feel. This was our generation's Pearl Harbor and the first time most of the people I knew had experienced anything like it.

Like the rest of the world, we had witnessed all of the horrible events on television from London, and as a reporter, my husband Bob had headed for Pakistan to report the story just hours after the planes hit the towers. Here we were, months later, back on our native soil, and I was overwhelmed at the magnificent sight that greeted us minutes after leaving the airport. Tears filled my eyes.

My deep love for my country and everything those flags represented hit me like a punch to the gut. In the immediate aftermath of the attacks I had felt so proud to be an American, even as I grieved. Here was my first, in-person display back home of how our country had knitted itself together to stand tall after such a personal and devastating loss.

The flags on the overpass were more than just symbols to me; they represented the essence of America in all its many facets: proud, undaunted, united and defiantly free. They might try to hurt us, to bring us to our knees, but we will always rise again, ready to uphold the freedoms our founding fathers fought for at the birth of our nation.

Bob would go on to cover the wars in Iraq and Afghanistan for the next five years, embedding with the military, losing journalist friends, and finally being critically wounded by a roadside bomb while reporting from Iraq. Bob began his recovery in the military hospital with the love and strength of family and friends. That experience — getting to know the many brave military men and women who saved his life, and their families — showed us a side of America that we hadn't known. It's a side of America that is well represented in this new collection of stories from Chicken Soup for the Soul, with dozens of fascinating and inspiring stories about active duty service members, their families, and veterans.

America is a vast and magnificent patchwork quilt of people, landscapes, experiences and beliefs, from sea to shining sea. And being an American means different things to each of us. That's the reason the stories in *Chicken Soup for the Soul: The Spirit of America* are such a wonderful representation of our country's inner and outer beauty. They are written by people from all walks of life and from every corner of our nation.

Author Amy Newmark has compiled 101 jewel-like examples of what makes America great. The book is a reminder that a country isn't just made up of ideals, but of people. And these stories are a cross-section of voices from the folks who make, and have made, this country the greatest nation on earth, exploring some of our hardest times as a country, some of our proudest memories, and the everyday moments of American life.

There is David Hull's touching story, "American Boots," about the black work boots his great-grandfather bought when he first emigrated from Germany. David keeps them by his door to remind himself to keep moving forward "one little step at time," the words his great-grandfather used to describe the way that he "made it" in America.

Some of the stories made me cry, especially the ones that involved a simple human kindness. Elizabeth Atwater's piece about the soldier's wife and newborn son who were stuck on a shutdown highway, unable to meet him at the airport for his short furlough, was one I'll never forget. A truck driver managed to convince a traffic-helicopter crew to land by the side of the highway and airlift the mother and baby to the airport in time, a great example of American ingenuity and compassion.

Enjoying our freedoms in America is a little bit like breathing. We don't regularly think about our right to speak our minds, to gather, to believe in a religion and to choose our own leaders. Most of us take these things for granted. But without them, we would not be the great country that we are today.

So it's inevitable when you talk about America that there would be a number of stories that deal with military families, legacy of service and reminders of the incredible Americans who wear the uniform every single day. I often think about the fact that my husband Bob is alive today, back to us as a father, husband and broadcast journalist due to the amazing actions and unflinching bravery of the soldiers and medics in his battalion. When the roadside bomb exploded near his tank, they did not hesitate to put someone else's life before their own. It was one of the many reasons our family chose to take our story and give back, starting a charity that would help veterans on the home front receive every opportunity that Bob had to heal.

It never ceases to move me when I think about the willingness of our service members to volunteer to go to areas of conflict and war so that the rest of us can make that choice. When they serve their country, they serve us as well. Many of the stories laced throughout the book are stirring reminders that the freedom we hold so dear in this country is not free.

One of the sadder legacies of war was our inability to understand the plight and needs of so many Vietnam veterans when they transitioned back to the home front. Renae MacLachlan's stirring account of watching a General salute a down-on-his-luck Vietnam-era Medal of Honor recipient made me think about what it really means to be a hero.

Catherine Ancewicz's story about witnessing an "Honor Flight," a wonderful program that flies World War II, Korean War and Vietnam veterans to Washington, D.C. to see the monuments, touched me because it was an unexpected moment in a reunion trip that ended up having the greatest meaning for her and her girlfriend.

There are many ways to serve your country and they don't all involve wearing a uniform. I loved Susan Mathis's story about jury duty.

She describes what most of us do when we get our summons — we grumble and talk about getting out of it. But Susan ends up serving, and to her surprise, she takes pride in being part of our country's judicial system and in serving her community. There is a lesson for all of us in that!

I loved the entire first chapter about the "red, white, and blue." Returning to America after September 11th, the sight of so many American flags reminded me how important our symbol of national pride is. Teacher Linda O'Connell's story about how she had her middle school students write their feelings on red and white strips of paper on September 11th, to create their own large American flag on the cafeteria bulletin board, shows the power of the flag for expressing our patriotism.

Pride and patriotism in our country is a little bit like a pilot light in a stove. It's always on, ever ready, but sometimes it needs a spark to make it catch and flare. This book is the match that will help you reignite your own passion for our nation. The people you meet in these pages, and the tales they tell, will remind you of your own stories about what our nation means to you, and why we are the most fortunate people in the world — Americans.

~Lee Woodruff

★ The ★ Spirit of America

The Red, White, and Blue

We identify the flag with almost everything we hold dear on earth, peace, security, liberty, our family, our friends, our home… But when we look at our flag and behold it emblazoned with all our rights we must remember that it is equally a symbol of our duties. Every glory that we associate with it is the result of duty done.
~President Calvin Coolidge

Flying the Perfect Flag

Ev'ry heart beats true 'neath the Red, White and Blue.
~George M. Cohan

"I'm ashamed to fly this flag," I told my husband. "It's faded and frayed. It's time to retire it."

He agreed. That worn-out flag had flown in front of our house every day for years. We displayed the stars and stripes because we love our country, because my dad, my husband, and three of my brothers served in the military, and because one of those brothers died in the mountains of North Vietnam.

"I'll just run out and buy another flag," I told my husband. Little did I know that I was at the beginning of a long and frustrating hunt for the perfect replacement.

I had a list of requirements for our new flag. None of the ones I saw measured up. Some were too flimsy. I knew they wouldn't fly gracefully in the wind. Others were cheaply made. I knew they wouldn't make it through one hot Southern California summer before they faded. And I wanted an America flag that was actually made in America.

I'd been looking for a flag for weeks and I was getting desperate. I'd visited all of the nearby stores without finding one that pleased me, so I drove a few extra miles to a shop that specialized in them. Most of their flags were ones that mark the seasons with pictures of bunnies or Santa Claus, or invited you to "Come in and Whine a Bit." Even their most expensive American flags didn't meet my high standards.

I thought about ordering one online, but I wanted to rub the material between my fingers. Was I becoming obsessive?

My search ended in my local warehouse store a few weeks before the Fourth of July. A display of American flags caught my eye. They were made of heavy material, each star and stripe individually sewn. The fabric felt crisp, thick and heavy in my hands. A gleaming flagpole that we could attach to our front porch railing was included. And right on the label was a notice: "Certified: Made in USA." I put the flag in my cart immediately and headed for the cash registers.

It seemed as if everyone had decided to check out at once. Carts were piled up as if there had been an accident on the shopping cart freeway. It was hot and it sounded as if every child in the building had decided to have a meltdown at the same time.

"It will take me forever to get out of here," I thought. My head and my back ached as I leaned on my cart. I considered putting the flag back and going home, but I'd finally found one I liked and I wasn't about to quit now.

"Let me pay for that," said a man.

"Are you talking to me?" I responded.

"Yes. I'd like to buy that flag for you."

"I can pay for it myself," I said.

"No, let me, please."

"I said no!"

What was going on here? Did I look as if I couldn't pay for my own flag? Was this some sort of clever way for a total stranger to get my credit card number? If he paid for my flag, would he hit me up for a favor? I was boxed in by all the shopping carts and couldn't get away from him. Should I call security?

"It just makes me happy to see someone flying the flag," he said.

And then I had a hunch: "Are you a veteran?" I asked.

"Yes. My name is Brian and I was in the first Iraq War." Tears came to his eyes. "I'm sorry. It was a long time ago, but it's still hard. That's my family over there in that checkout line."

Shame washed over me. When had I become so suspicious and distrustful?

I realized that it was easy for me to give, but I didn't want to receive. I didn't want anyone to think I needed anything. There was an icy block of pride where my heart should have been.

I gave Brian a hug and whispered in his ear: "I lost a brother in Vietnam. I will pray that God heals any pain you may still carry. And yes, I'd be honored to fly a flag that you bought for me."

Brian smiled, hugged me back, paid for my flag with his own credit card and left with his family.

The gift given to me by one of our country's heroes flies from my front porch as I write this. The stars and stripes gleam in the sunlight, and the flag floats in the air in the slightest breath of wind.

It is, indeed, the perfect flag.

~Josephine Fitzpatrick

Old Glory Flies Again

*Unity is strength… when there is teamwork and
collaboration, wonderful things can be achieved.*
~Matti Stepanek

My colleague Norris Kyles and I had been running on a steady diet of fast food and fear for almost a week, ever since May 18, 2013, when several rounds of monster tornadoes struck central Oklahoma. Moore, Oklahoma took the brunt of the storms, but many of the surrounding communities were severely damaged, too.

Norris and I worked as journalists at KFOR-TV, the NBC affiliate in Oklahoma City. He worked as a photographer; I worked as a reporter and anchor. During the endless days of breaking news, we'd both encountered things no one should ever see.

More than two-dozen people died from the storms, and hundreds more were hurt. Once the storms passed, many people had nothing left. Others tried to salvage what little of their lives they could still find. Hopelessness, anger, and despair were easy. Optimism, positivity, and resilience were not.

Indeed, as Norris and I approached Memorial Day, neither one of us felt very good. People across the country would go on trips, attend barbecues, and usher in the summer that upcoming weekend, but not us. The time for rest and relaxation would come much later. We had people who needed us. We had stories to tell. And we had a job to do.

That Friday found us doing it in the small town of Bethel Acres,

Oklahoma.

"What are you thinking?" Norris asked me, as he parked the car on what remained of a road that once led into a tiny subdivision. Storm debris, downed trees, piles of bricks, trash, and ripped up memories had replaced most of the homes. That morning, management at KFOR sent us to Bethel Acres in an effort to widen the TV station's coverage and make sure we didn't leave out some of the smaller communities.

Norris turned off the car. "Who do you think we should interview?"

"I don't know," I said. "I guess we'll just pick one."

Over the last week both of us had filed more "local family tries to rebuild" stories than we could count. Every day, and every story, had started to bleed into the next. So many people needed help. We could have told stories for a month and never told them all.

I scanned the neighborhood for someone who looked interesting and might put a different spin on all the sadness. "We need some…"

And then I saw him.

Alan Burch walked right in front of our car at that moment, dressed in his U.S. Air Force battle dress uniform. He was sweaty and tired, but he had a determined look on his face. More than that, he clutched an American flag to his chest.

"What's that about?" I said to Norris. "Let's talk to that guy."

Norris grabbed his video camera from the back of our news car, and I took the microphone. We stopped Alan, and he told us that he'd found the flag wrapped around what remained of a neighborhood tree. He didn't know who owned it, but he also didn't care. Despite enduring massive winds and tremendous pressure, the flag only had a few small holes. He took that as a sign.

"I had the fire department get their ladder out," Alan told me. "We pulled it out of the tree and folded it, and now I'm just looking for a place to hoist it up."

But this neighborhood in Bethel Acres didn't have standing homes, much less standing flagpoles. The mission looked bleak.

Alan didn't care.

"This flag means a lot to me, being a member of the U.S. Air Force," Alan said. He went on to tell us he wouldn't rest until he found a place to hang Old Glory. "It's a symbol of this community rising up and getting away from this tragedy."

For the next fifteen minutes or so, Norris and I followed Alan around the neighborhood as he searched for someone or something that would help him complete his effort. A small group of onlookers had joined him, all of them determined to see that flag fly again. Norris and I concentrated on getting as much sound and video as we could; we didn't have to tell each other that we'd found our story for the day.

When Alan asked David Meeks for help, the journey took another turn.

"We couldn't not help him. We couldn't say no. We couldn't turn our heads," David told me.

David and some of his fellow volunteers from Bread of Life Humanitarian Effort drove to Oklahoma from Paducah, Kentucky in the hours after the first round of devastating storms. The group had no idea what they'd find, or how they'd help, but that didn't matter. People needed them, and they wouldn't leave their fellow Americans behind.

"We don't let little things stop us from helping out," David said. "We're blessed to be able to do it."

In Bethel Acres, the volunteers put their skills to work, spearheading the effort to clean up what Mother Nature hadn't taken away. They had tools, generators, food, water, and skills. Most of all, they had hope.

The team from Bread of Life found a broken chain-link fence pole and straightened out the metal with cinder blocks. As the small crowd of grieving and downtrodden people watched, David and his team drilled two holes in the pole and cut two large swaths of chicken wire. They wrapped the wire through the holes and threaded the flag on to it. Then, with Alan's help, they jammed the pole into the ground and raised the flag in the middle of the storm-swept neighborhood.

By then, almost everyone around the community had paused to watch them raise it. Trash pickup, hammering, sawing, and sorting could wait. Many people cried once the flag flew again — including Norris and me. It was a moment of unity and strength at a critical time for all of us.

"Do y'all know what they just did? They took a fence pole and made a flagpole in like ten minutes," said onlooker Benjamin Jones as we gathered the final elements of our story. "I've never seen anyone do something like that in my life. Watching them join together and raise the flag like that, it made me proud to be with them. It made me proud to be an American."

I couldn't have agreed more. At that moment, we were all Oklahomans. We were all Americans. And we were all going to get through tough times together.

~Sara Celi

The Soul of Independence Day

In childhood the daylight always fails too
soon — except when there are going to be fireworks;
and then the sun dawdles intolerably on the threshold
like a tedious guest.
~Jan Struther

My son Nicholas is autistic. He is very sensitive to noise, so we avoided Independence Day celebrations throughout his early years. It wasn't just about the fireworks, but the full scope of chaos, crowds, waiting, and the traffic afterward.

I couldn't escape the feeling that my son was missing out on something extraordinary, though. For me, July 4th brings to mind happy memories of growing up in California. My family would come over to gorge on potluck fare, set off fireworks, and then from the front yard watch the big aerial show at the high school a mile away.

I had talked to Nicholas about the reason for the holiday. The facts were the easy part for him. He can memorize anything. He knows all fifty states and their capitals, the major dates in our nation's history, and even has the Presidents memorized by number. What I really wanted was for him to create his own beautiful memories of a day that meant so much to me.

Finally, when Nicholas was seven, my husband was able to take off the first week of July. We made the trip to my hometown so that Nicholas could fully experience Independence Day for the first time.

I kept thinking about the potluck and the fireworks. The big stuff. The climax of the day. My mom, though, knew to start with something even more important.

"Nicholas? Come here and get your sandals on," she called.

He set down the road atlas he was studying and ran over. "What is it?"

"You're going to help us put up the flag."

That was a task I used to help with at that age, too. I always felt like a big kid, carrying out that flag on its pole, standing on tiptoes to place it in its bracket.

My mom helped Nicholas lift the flag to its berth. My dad made sure it was angled just right.

"Fifty stars. Thirteen stripes," Nicholas said as he nodded in satisfaction. With him, everything came back to numbers. This was the kid who could recite every highway and exit number we had driven days before on our long drive from Arizona.

A few hours later, Nicholas went with my dad to buy a family pack of fireworks at a nearby fundraising stand. Evening came, and with it the potluck. Our numbers were few compared to the big celebrations of my youth — most of my aunts, uncles, and cousins are now scattered across the country — but one aunt and my grandma joined us. Nicholas's sensory issues keep him from touching or trying most foods, but he was excited that his grandma had bought his favorite potato chips.

As darkness fell, we sat in our customary chairs at the front of the house. I reminded Nicholas that if everything became too much, he could go inside, but that wasn't necessary. He wore his noise-canceling headphones and stared slack-jawed at the fireworks. Each blast of light illuminated the smile on his face.

"Wow," he said.

I stared at him, living vicariously through his delight.

We haven't been able to make it back to my parents' house every 4th of July since then, but we try. To Nicholas, that is where the holiday belongs. He knows the route there, and the alternate routes, too. He knows his favorite potato chips await him. He knows that he goes with his grandpa to choose the fireworks to set off on the lawn. He also knows he has a very important job to do on Independence Day morning.

On our most recent visit, Nicholas was a lanky ten-year-old. I stood there with my camera, ready to preserve the moment. He was hesitant to smile for the camera — a precursor of the teenage years to come. However, when the flag came out, he couldn't help but grin. My parents praised him as he set the pole at the right angle. Nicholas was tall enough to almost do it on his own. Morning light rippled along the flag and cast dancing shadows over Nicholas's head and shoulders.

"There!" he said. "Now it's the Fourth of July." His eyes suddenly clouded with tears. "On July 5th, we drive 538 miles back to Arizona. I'm going to miss my grandparents."

At that, he started to cry.

I gave him a tight hug. "I know. I'm going to miss them too, but we're here now. It's still July 4th. It's a happy day."

"Yes," he said, wiping his eyes behind his glasses. "A very happy day." The flag fluttered and ruffled his hair.

Nicholas could recite all the facts of our nation's birth, but now he understood the soul of the 4th of July, too. It was about family, joy, and togetherness, all bound together by red, white, and blue.

~Beth Cato

At The White House on 9/11

The red and white and starry blue is freedom's
shield and hope.
~John Philip Sousa

Our family had just purchased a restaurant with a full bar called The White House. I lived in a small apartment above the eatery and one Tuesday morning I was upstairs in the bathroom, showering and getting ready for another busy day at the restaurant, when there came a knock at my door. Since we didn't open until dinnertime, no one had ever knocked on my bathroom door that early in the morning and even though I found it a little odd, I happily sang out, "Who is it?"

"It's Paula," came the reply from one of my favorite waitresses. "You've got to come downstairs and watch the news."

"Umm, no I don't," I snapped back with doubt and suspicion. "I can't even remember the last time I watched the news. I have a restaurant to run."

"No, seriously," said Paula sternly. "You have to come downstairs right now and watch the news."

I threw on some clothes and shuffled down the back stairs.

I walked through the kitchen and as I headed for the bar, I saw Paula, my brother Dan and his wife Cindy standing with their eyes fixated on the television screen behind the counter. I could hear the steady drone of a newscast, but couldn't quite make out what the anchorman was saying.

The four of us stood there in complete bewilderment watching the North Tower of the World Trade Center with smoke billowing from a gaping hole in the side. Then the unthinkable happened when a huge, fiery explosion ignited the second tower, showering burning debris into the air, on to the adjacent buildings and the streets below.

"Oh my God!" we all said in unison.

At that horrific moment, no one really knew exactly what had just transpired. The first plane initially appeared as though it might have been some kind of freak accident, but what about the second strike? As reports flooded the news channels, there were even more planes crashing, one into the Pentagon and another in a field somewhere in Pennsylvania. We were under attack; the United States of America was under assault by some unknown enemy.

We watched for hours. And we wondered what we should do. Should we open the restaurant? Or would that be disrespectful?

"I'm calling Patti," I said as I darted behind the bar.

Patti owned a nearby coffee shop called The Pony Expresso, and they had already been open for hours, since long before these tragic events unfolded.

"I don't think we should open," I told Patti, "It just doesn't seem right."

"But you have to," she replied. "You own a bar; people might want to come out and talk about all of this, and they may need to process what has just happened. You have a responsibility to the community."

When she put it that way, we all agreed. We did open the restaurant on that horrible day, but no one came. Everyone was likely watching and re-watching the tragedy, as we all were.

As the afternoon wore on, we saw American flags flying at half-mast all over the country.

The flagpole! The empty flagpole that was in front of our restaurant. We had always said that we would fly the stars and stripes there, but the pulley at the top of the pole was jammed. In opening the restaurant just a few short weeks earlier, with everything else going on, we never got around to fixing it nor were we sure how to actually repair it since it was some thirty feet in the air.

Now we had to fix it. Right then. There would be a flag flying in front of The White House on this tragic day, no matter what.

So I raced to our local hardware store and purchased an American flag. I stopped by the fire station and begged a couple of firefighters to assist me with our dilemma. They agreed and followed me back to the restaurant in one of their ladder trucks.

Our own local, brave firefighters untangled the pulley at the top of the flagpole. I attached the stars and stripes to the chain, pulled the flag all the way to the large gold ball crowning the highest point on the pole, then slowly lowered it back down to half mast and tied it off.

~D.J. Sartell

A Devotion to Duty

He who does his duty is a hero, whether anyone
rewards him for it or not.
~George Failing

Tom Brokaw calls them "The Greatest Generation;" the men and women who came of age during the Great Depression and the Second World War and went on to build modern America.

But Baby Boomers like me didn't think of the men who answered the call of their country in the 1940s as the greatest generation; we simply thought of them as our fathers.

What was it that compelled these young men to willingly line up to enter the line of fire to defeat ruthless enemies? Men like Harlon Block. Block is in what has been called the most famous photograph ever taken: the iconic shot of the six flag raisers on Mount Suribachi at Iwo Jima. In the photo, Block is at the base of the pole planting it in the ground. He enlisted in the United States Marine Corps with all of the senior members of his high school football team. Why? Many reasons — but one in particular — a steadfast devotion to duty.

These men were rugged, self-reliant, yet, surprisingly reticent. They rarely spoke of what happened "over there." Seldom revealing and never broadcasting their individual roles or collective victories in this ugly war. This attitude is epitomized by John Bradley, also one of the six "flag raisers." (He is the second man from the right in the flag raisers photo.)

Bradley's son, James, author of *Flags of Our Fathers*, said this about his father in a speech commemorating the event in 2000 at the 55th anniversary of the Battle of Iwo Jima: "So there's my dad in the tallest bronze monument in the world, but that's about all we knew growing up. He wouldn't talk about Iwo Jima; he would always change the subject…. My father had kept his heroism a secret from his wife, from his family, and his community for half a century."

When our men came home from World War II they never looked back. Instead, they looked forward, to the future, and stuffed the memories of war so deep in the recesses of their minds that you couldn't distinguish a hero from a non-participant. They turned their attention from raising flags to raising families and shaping a great nation.

My father was a member of "the greatest generation," although he would scoff at that label. He too, volunteered to serve in the United States Marine Corps and his tour of duty included stints at Pearl Harbor shortly after the surprise attack, followed by brief stops at Guam, Saipan, Tinian, Eniwetok, and Kwajalein before engaging the enemy at Iwo Jima. He would fight on that tiny pork chop–shaped island until the flag was raised and victory secured.

So, what is it then that makes America great? Many things, but none more than an intense devotion to duty and a willingness to risk your life to keep others free. In his speech at the 55th anniversary of the Battle of Iwo Jima, Bradley struck this compelling comparison: "This was America's Battle. What else can you call a battle that in one day had more casualties than two and a half months at Guadalcanal? Normandy was terrible, but at the end of one day, at the end of twenty-four hours, you and I could have had a tea party on the beaches of Normandy. It was completely safe. Boys died on the beaches of Iwo Jima — on the beaches — for two weeks."

When the war ended in 1945, my father was honorably discharged and resumed his college education. He graduated with a bachelor's degree in finance in 1947 from Northwestern University. In 1948, he married my mother and by 1950 would have the first of six children over a ten-year span. I was the third, and growing up in the 1960s I watched many television shows glorifying the war. Invariably, my siblings and I nagged my father to tell us about his role in this conflict..

He wouldn't bite.

He dodged all our questions, including the ones that would have revealed his heroism. And he dismissed the Bronze Star we found buried in the bottom drawer of his dresser.

"They had a few left over after the war so they gave one to me as a souvenir," he said. It wasn't until I was an adult with children of my own that my then ninety-five-year-old grandmother set the record straight. Late one August evening, she dug out his letter of commendation for bravery in the line of duty at Iwo Jima. My father had nonchalantly enclosed it in a Christmas card he mailed her in 1944. He never mentioned the letter in the Christmas greeting he scrawled inside the card.

In 2008, at eighty-eight, he died after a five-year battle with Alzheimer's. After all these years, I remained curious about the details behind the Bronze Star so, at my sister Mary's urging, I picked up the phone and called a man who shared a foxhole with my father in Iwo Jima. His nickname was Ski and he was my father's closest friend during the war. Ski would later stand up for my father at his wedding. Ski had met me only once when I was a kid so I wondered how this ninety-one-year-old man would respond to my phone call seven decades after the war. I had one advantage. I was named after my father.

Ski was delighted to hear from me and warmly answered my questions about my father with joy, gentleness and grace.

"How did my father feel about being in this war?" I began.

"He simply accepted it," Ski replied. "He used to say, 'There's a war going on and we're in it. That's just the way it is.'"

"Did you have any close calls?"

"An enemy shell exploded on the edge of our foxhole late one night. For some reason the shrapnel exploded away from us. Had it exploded toward us we would have died together that night."

"My father had a Bronze Star in his drawer. Can you tell me how he earned it?"

Ski paused. I waited for his answer. "We both earned one," he said quietly. "And I don't remember how we earned it exactly."

"You don't remember?"

"No, but it doesn't matter."

I pressed him. "Why doesn't it matter?"

"Because at the time we both said we earned it for the same reason."

"What reason?"

"We used to say, 'we earned it for doing our jobs.' We were there to do a job. We did it. The war ended and we came home. That's it."

This calling to serve is not reserved only for our fathers. Today, our sons and daughters still answer this call to serve their country to keep us safe and free.

It all begins with a personal devotion to duty: a duty that has made great men and women — and a great nation.

~James C. Magruder

The Faces on the Mountain

*Let us place there, carved high, as close to heaven as
we can, the words of our leaders, their faces, to show
posterity what manner of men they were.*
~John Gutzon de la Mothe Borglum

We were on a road trip, taking our time and enjoying the incredible scenery in this country. It was kind of a National Parks road trip, staying a few days in each place. We had already been to the Grand Canyon, Zion and Bryce, and after making our way north we were now in South Dakota to check out the Badlands, the Black Hills and Mount Rushmore.

We were lucky to have a room in the historic Custer State Game Lodge, an old hotel in Custer Park that had served as the Summer White House for President Coolidge in 1927 and where President Eisenhower had stayed in 1953 when he was on a speaking trip. My husband and I had reserved the Eisenhower room, the very room the President had stayed in years ago!

We spent two days driving around the beautiful and diverse countryside and checking out the sites. We saw all kinds of wildlife too. Imagine driving down a small road in the park that is only wide enough for two cars to pass... carefully, and coming upon a herd of bison! That's exactly what happened to us. And what does everyone tell you to do when that happens? Pull over! Bison rule the road! They are huge. And they don't care if you have the right of way! They're bigger than you are. They just watch you for a while and then, when they decide it's time they amble on down the road. When they are a safe distance away, then, and only then, can you drive away… slowly.

The next day we had plans to visit Mount Rushmore. It was about an hour's drive from our hotel—more time for us to take in the scenery. It was also July 4th. When we told the concierge at the hotel that we had plans to visit Mount Rushmore the next morning she advised us to get there as early as we could. They were expecting huge crowds for the holiday and, although it had been almost two years since the terrible tragedy of 9/11, the security, while always tight, would be even more restrictive.

My husband and I are not early morning people but on that clear and sunny Friday morning we were up at the crack of dawn. After breakfast in the hotel dining room we started out for Mount Rushmore. We knew when we were getting close because, even early in the morning, there were lots of cars on the road. The line of cars in front of us, and in back of us, grew heavier and longer as we approached the entrance to the park. Like a parade, the cars slowly snaked up the hill toward the parking structure.

But first you had to pass through the entrance gates. There were soldiers with rifles and bomb-sniffing dogs stationed at each gate. Each car was stopped. Each person had to produce a picture ID. While one soldier checked IDs and looked into and poked around the car, another soldier, along with a bomb-sniffing dog, walked slowly around the car and used mirrors on long poles to check underneath. It was a slow process but they were not taking any chances. Thank goodness for that.

After we were cleared through security, we drove into the parking structure, found a place to park and walked toward the entrance. You walk up the stairs and down the Avenue of the Flags. There are fifty-six flags flying, twenty-eight on either side of the path: fifty state flags, one district flag, three territory flags and two commonwealth flags, all representing the United States of America. It is a very colorful and impressive sight.

In the background you can see the heads of the four Presidents carved into the granite face of the mountain. Of course we had seen pictures of the carvings in books so we knew what to expect, but everyone who had seen it told us that seeing it in person would be an unforgettable experience. And it was. You can't get the magnitude of the sculptures from a picture. It was beyond impressive and majestic.

We toured the Visitor's Center, looked at the exhibits and watched the movie on the history of the carving of the mountain. And then it was time to really view the sculptures. We walked out into the crowd standing on the Grand View Terrace. Everyone was looking up in awe, standing still and quiet. Even the children who were there seemed to sense that this was something special and were silent.

As we looked at our fellow visitors, we noticed something unusual. Almost without exception, these people were wearing red, white, and blue. Some people wore shirts with the American flag and the words "Proud to Be an American" printed on them. It was such a spontaneous outpouring of patriotism.

And then it started. Quietly. Kind of like humming. At first I wasn't sure I was really hearing it. Someone started singing "God Bless America." Then more and more people joined in until practically everyone standing and viewing this American monument was singing. It sounded amazing. Lots of people had tears in their eyes. Lots of people had smiles on their faces.

We are strong. We are proud. We are Americans.

~Barbara LoMonaco

Covering the Casket

Patriotism is not short, frenzied outbursts of emotion,
but the tranquil and steady dedication of a lifetime.
~Adlai Stevenson

I t took cancer more than three years to kill my father. You'd think that would have given the family enough time to plan all the details of his funeral. While his 6'1", 200-pound frame withered away to nothing, while his cheeks grew hollow and his voice weak, while he shivered uncontrollably even in the middle of August, you'd have thought we would have asked him what he wanted covering his casket.

But maybe you don't ask that question of a dying person. Because an answer is a confirmation of what you're not talking about.

When Daddy finally died on a cold January afternoon, Mother added "pick out casket spray" to the list of things we needed to do before the funeral. "Roses will cost about $500," she told me, wringing her hands. "Other kinds of flowers, a little less."

"That's a ridiculous waste of money," I said. "Why do we need flowers? Daddy was a veteran. He should have an American flag covering his casket."

"Oh, honey," Mother said, "I'm not sure he would have wanted that. He never liked to talk about his time in the service."

That wasn't entirely true. Daddy loved to talk about almost anything, including the Army. He told us countless times about how, because he had a college degree, he was assigned to Officer Candidate School after he was drafted in 1951. But a paperwork snafu got him shipped to Korea as a Private in the infantry instead.

He bragged, in a teasing kind of way, about what a fine ping pong player he'd become over there. He showed us how Korean players stood far back from the table and the odd way they held the paddle, with fingers curved like claws around its face instead of gripping the handle the way American players did. If he got any medals while he was in the Army, I never saw them. But he proudly displayed the ping pong trophy he'd won.

He talked about the genuine jade earrings he bought in Korea for my mother and the set of real china dishes he bought for my grandmother.

He told us about the time he went more than two weeks without taking his boots off. His commanding officer had warned the men that it was so bitterly cold that exposed skin would be immediately frostbitten, which could lead to amputations.

But when confronted with the inevitable questions that all children, sooner or later, ask a parent who's gone to war, Daddy was silent. "I don't want to talk about it," he would say in a tone of voice that my siblings and I knew meant the conversation was over.

As hundreds of mourners filed through our church's fellowship hall to pay their respects the evening before we buried Daddy, I was proud that the ultimate symbol of patriotism, rather than a spray of red roses, was draped over his casket. I was proud that, following a brief graveside service on a gray Tennessee morning, the flag was folded just so and presented to my mother, "with thanks from a grateful nation." I'm proud every time I pull out the photo album and see a handsome young soldier playfully saluting his buddy who was manning the camera.

~Jennie Ivey

Alien Persuaded

America, for me, has been the pursuit and
catching of happiness.
~Aurora Raigne

I t wasn't hard to get the point when I moved here. Patriotism was alive and well in this country. There were flags everywhere! Stars and stripes were mounted on brilliant white poles every few yards. Banks, schools, town halls, hospitals and office towers all made it clear I was in the United States of America. Every other house had a banner floating from its verandah. Most backyard gardens boasted at least one flag unfurling from a decorative post.

On the road it was like a party. Cars and vans, transport trucks and motorhomes displayed stars and stripes on license plates, bumper stickers, window decals and seat covers. Sailboats and surfboards proudly wore their badge of allegiance. Grandfathers wore T-shirts emblazoned with "proud to be American" while teeny teens on the beach wore stars and stripes bikinis.

Yes, it wasn't hard to get the point. Patriotism was alive and well in this country. Whether there was agreement or disagreement on war or global warming or politics. It was more than apparent that the ordinary American citizen truly was proud to be a part of this great country and in his heart believed in freedom and the protection and expression of it.

It was love that brought me to this country: marriage proposal kind of love. I did not know one soul here besides my husband. I did not know a street name or where the library was located. The landscape, the climate, the people were all foreign to me and it seemed every second sentence I spoke had the words "back home" in it. I was living here bodily but I had not really moved in.

Time passed. I settled in and made friends. We traveled through thirty-three more states, collecting memories and friends. I witnessed the beauty from the snowy peaks of Utah and the breathtaking cliffs of the Grand Canyon to the tropical beaches of Siesta Key and the gushing streams through leafy trails in Tennessee. I saw the sagebrush in Arizona, the peach trees in Georgia, the lobster boats in Maine and caught the aroma of freshly baked bagels from a New York City deli. I dipped my toes in the Pacific Ocean, the Atlantic Ocean, the Gulf of Mexico, Lake Mead and Passamaquoddy Bay. I met a chef in Georgia, a musician in Texas, and a teacher in Pennsylvania. I fed the ducks in Lake Arrowhead, California and bought cheese in Vermont. I experienced the sights and sounds, aromas and tastes of America. I felt the mist of waterfalls, tasted salty breezes, and inhaled the scent of gardenias. I did all this while still clinging to my legal resident status.

I was eligible to apply for citizenship but something seemed to be holding me back. I was falling in love with this country but was I ready to fully commit to it? From time to time I would contemplate the process but then let it slide to the back burner again. A friend called one day with an invitation. Would we like to go to Orlando with her to celebrate the Fourth of July? The Orlando Philharmonic Orchestra was performing a concert titled "Liberty Soars" at the Hyatt Hotel atrium of the Orlando International Airport. I was a bit hesitant, reminding myself I wasn't really an American. I heard her eagerness. "Come on. You'll love the music." So I agreed.

The seats filled up quickly and soon crowds were standing around the edges of the area. The Navy Color Guard brought solemnity to the occasion and the awarding of Medals of Honor to military personnel reminded us of the cost of freedom. As the orchestra played John Philip Sousa marches and other patriotic pieces the crowd sang heartily. A sea of flags waved constantly. Passengers from recently landed planes paused with their backpacks and suitcases to listen, watch and smile.

Suddenly I found myself choked with tears. By the end of the next Sousa march, I knew I was going to make a decision. I did.

A little more than six months later I walked into the courthouse in West Palm Beach. I stood beside forty-six others from twenty-seven countries and took my Pledge of Allegiance. I walked out as a new United States citizen. What did I notice all the way home? Flags! Flags everywhere! It seems to me that patriotism, and devotion to freedom and liberty that's worth fighting for, worth celebrating with fireworks, fanfare and famous orchestras, is the defining trait of the Spirit of America.

~Phyllis McKinley

The Feelings Flag

Tell me and I forget. Teach me and I remember.
Involve me and I learn.
~Benjamin Franklin

I stood in my living room and cringed at the sight of the plane hitting the first tower. I did not realize that the horror had only just begun. As I drove to school I listened intently to the reports. Then, I heard that another plane had crashed. I was as shocked, stunned and confused as every other adult in my school. No one was sure what was going on. Teachers were asking one another, "Did you hear about the plane crashes in New York? Is America under attack?"

It was like a punch in the gut, beyond our comprehension. Everyone felt winded, worried, and wounded.

My preschool classroom was on the lower level of an inner city middle school. What I remember most is the panicked youth in the hall changing classes who shouted at me as they passed my room, "America is at war!"

"Calm down," I said. "Don't jump to conclusions. Nobody knows for sure what's going on. This does not mean war."

They insisted they saw it on TV and that military jets were intercepting other planes.

I walked into my classroom and watched as my students went about their school day, unaware of the attacks. I knew they were okay.

My aide was capable, so I left her in charge.

I felt compelled to do something patriotic to relieve the mounting tension and confusion the middle school students were feeling, although I was not in charge of any of them. I cut twelve-inch by two-inch red, white and blue construction paper strips, the kind kids use to make paper chains. I did not consult the principal or counselor. I acted on impulse and intruded on each classroom teacher. I asked each if I might have a moment, then I said, "Nobody knows exactly what is going on. We've all heard rumors and news reports. It's a frightening time for all of us."

I passed out strips of paper to the students and asked them to write what they were feeling at the moment. Any fears, any words — anything would be acceptable. Some asked about spelling, and some asked if they should sign it.

"If you want to," I said.

I collected more than 200 strips and rolled them into loops; then I stapled them to the always-bare bulletin board in the cafeteria. I read an outpouring of emotional comments. "I am afraid." "I want to kick their butts." "Bomb them." "Why did this happen?" "What now?" "I want to go home."

I posted one after another, row after row, until an American flag took shape. Some of the comments were laced with misspelled words and profanity; some were smeared with tears. I did not censor. I stapled every single one. I stood back and gazed at our "feelings flag."

At lunch I stood against a wall and observed teens and preteens, who were usually destructive with bulletin board displays, as they searched for their piece of that flag. I listened to them read their words aloud, owning their emotions, giving voice to their fears and frustrations, initiating conversations.

On that horrible day, when America came under attack, I didn't know if my actions would do any good. It just felt good to do something. My friend Tammy said, "With that spontaneous action, you gave children a voice when no one knew what to say."

The bulletin-board flag stayed up for more than a week. Then the strips began disappearing as individuals claimed their sections... and their feelings.

~Linda O'Connell

Pulling Together

The union of hearts, the union of hands, and the flag of our Union forever.
~George Pope Morris

"HELP!" I screamed at the top of my lungs as the wobbly metal extension ladder slipped. I was on my tiptoes on the top rung, hugging the flagpole with all my might. Somehow I was the one chosen to make the final adjustment of the brass ball on the very top of the forty-foot towering flagpole as my husband and son steadied the ladder from the ground below.

Just weeks earlier we had learned that one of our sons would be deployed with the United States Army's 82nd Airborne Division to the Persian Gulf in Operation Desert Shield. This came on the heels of our other son's honorable discharge from his service with the United States Navy where he served on the USS Ranger.

We were obviously filled with mixed emotions — very worried about our son on active duty in the Gulf, but so proud of both boys. Our hearts were bursting with gratitude and respect.

As a family with deep military roots, we felt the need to vividly express our support for our troops and our sincere patriotism. My husband, a U.S. Army veteran himself, understood the meaning of commitment, and gave his all in whatever he did — it was either over the top or not at all.

So, it was no surprise when we decided to put up a flagpole that it would be the best and tallest one imaginable. However, we didn't realize the scope of the endeavor we were undertaking until we were well into the project.

After felling one of the tallest Douglas fir trees on our acreage, my husband and youngest son, Chris, dragged it out of the woods with the dozer to the front of the house. There, they removed the branches and painstakingly peeled the bark before sanding the wood to a smooth finish.

Finally, after days of working by hand with a post-hole digger and shovels, the hole was deep enough to support the primed flagpole. As we began to carefully maneuver our "pride and joy" to an upright position, reality set in — we were not going to accomplish this huge task alone.

Thankfully, our curious neighbors discovered our precarious predicament and came to the rescue with tractors and trucks. It was scary watching as ropes and chains pulled the pole from different angles in an effort to place it in the hole.

After a couple of hours, the pole was perfectly upright, towering in the deep blue sky. But the jostling had caused the brass ball top to tip too much to one side. When I pointed this out, it became my job to climb up the ladder and make the adjustments.

The crowd cheered for a job well done as I made my way bravely down the ladder. Once my feet were safely planted on the ground, I looked up at the beautiful sight — our glorious American flag blowing in the gentle fall breeze, expressing the heartfelt patriotism of an entire neighborhood.

Twenty-five years later, the mighty flag continues to fly in front of our home while our two grandsons, in keeping with family tradition, are serving in the United States Army.

~Connie Kaseweter Pullen

Memorial Day Volunteers

We come, not to mourn our dead soldiers, but to praise them.
~Francis A. Walker

My small town of Haddam, Connecticut has been commemorating Memorial Day with a parade and ceremony since the 1800s when the occasion was known as Decoration Day. Our event has always been organized by a team of veterans who, as they aged, passed the task on to the next generation of warriors. However, after the Vietnam War ended, the number of those serving in the military dramatically shrank, leaving us with fewer veterans to continue the tradition. With a diminished volunteer pool, one stalwart veteran took sole charge for a twenty-year period.

Eventually, by the mid-1990s, the observance had become stale and uninspired, primarily due to our speakers having difficulty appreciating the significance of the day. Attendance was suffering as well.

We always close our Memorial Day ceremony by somberly reading the names of our town's war dead over a soft drumroll. As the years passed and memories faded, the names of the fallen were becoming a blur and in some cases meaningless. Our older veterans were worried that if the townspeople continued to lose sight of military sacrifice that our Memorial Day observance would evolve into something unrecognizable.

Something needed to be done.

To reverse the growing concern, specially selected volunteers were sought to join the parade committee to help ease the organizational burden. It was an honor for me to be asked to assist, so I volunteered to give the next Memorial Day address.

The focus of my planned speech would be to change the reading of the names of our war dead from something routine into something of significance — something that would make it clear that these were genuine heroes who once walked among us. My talk simply consisted of each fallen soldier's branch of service, his rank, age, a personal trait and the circumstances of his death.

To gather the necessary information I solicited family members, distant relatives and old friends. Everyone I contacted shared so many fond stories of their loved ones that I began to feel as if I knew each soldier personally. As a result, it was a simple, gratifying task to put all those memories into a speech.

As an added bonus, relatives were so thrilled with the idea of a public remembrance that they felt compelled to give me old photos, newspaper clippings, letters, and in some cases, medals and other war-time memorabilia. The collected items were mounted in glass displays and unveiled at the close of the Memorial Day ceremony.

My speech was so well received, and the displays had such a historical and emotional impact, that our town officials asked that they be prominently placed in the town hall for all to see. Within a few weeks, citizens began asking where they could donate military uniforms, equipment, captured weapons, enemy flags and personal souvenirs from various wartime eras. Hundreds of items that had been gathering dust and taking up space in attics were offered because people did not have the heart to throw them away. It was obvious that our townspeople were still patriotic; they just needed to be reminded.

During the next few years, the collection grew so fast that parade committee members had boxes of wartime and home front memorabilia under their beds and stuffed in their closets. Our town officials were well aware of the artifacts we had amassed, so in 2001 we were granted use of a vacant firehouse and converted it into the Haddam Veterans' Museum. In less than two years, the building was filled to capacity. We also added an outdoor Veterans' Memorial Walk with large gray pavers engraved with the names of Haddam's war dead and small red pavers to honor specific veterans in a more personal way.

The museum became an immediate focal point, especially on Memorial Day, when hundreds of parade attendees spend hours reviewing the displays. During the rest of the year we get requests from local schools and civic groups for museum tours.

Prior to the reorganization of our parade committee, we practically had to beg people to give the Memorial Day address. Now we have a waiting list. The size of our parade committee has quadrupled and there is never a shortage of dedicated volunteers, both civilians and veterans.

On the Saturday before Memorial Day we place more than 500 new American flags on veterans' graves in ten cemeteries across town. In the past, this was an all-day undertaking. Now, the task is completed in less than three hours because our flagger ranks have tripled.

My speech may have been the catalyst that created our veterans' museum and got our Memorial Day observance back on track, but it was the selfless volunteers who banded together that really made it happen. Americans, once reminded, are happy to dive in and show their patriotism.

~Arthur Wiknik, Jr.

★ The ★
Spirit of
America

A Nation of Helping Hands

*Those who are happiest are those who do
the most for others.*
~Booker T. Washington, Up from Slavery

12

When Hearts Come Together

What's right about America is that although we have a
mess of problems, we have great capacity — intellect
and resources — to do something about them.
~Henry Ford

The slow traffic on the Interstate suddenly stopped moving altogether. After several minutes passed people began to blow their horns in exasperation. Two men in front of me got out of their car and walked forward past the row of idling cars to see if they could determine what caused the sudden halt. They returned several minutes later shaking their heads. I heard one of the men speaking to a small gathering near my car. "This row of cars goes on as far as we can see. We must have walked at least a half-mile. There must be a bad wreck somewhere up ahead. It looks like we might be here for some time."

People grew hot and irritable in their stuffy cars and one by one began to mingle in the road. Some people were grumbling about being late for dinner, an appointment at the hair salon, or some other dilemma that seemed important to them. Most were trying to make the best of the situation though, and they voiced their complaints with a wry smile. After all, we weren't the ones involved in the accident, so how much could we complain?

A frustrated young woman clutching a gurgling baby joined our small group. She was on the verge of tears. I gave her a sympathetic smile. "At least he's taking it well."

She swallowed hard. "Thank goodness for that. If he starts to cry, I will too."

I patted her arm. "Don't worry about a fussy baby. There are plenty of stranded mommies and grandmothers around who will be happy to help you comfort him if he cries."

She shook her head emphatically. "That isn't it. I'm supposed to be at the airport in thirty-five minutes to meet my husband. He's in the Army and is coming home from a stint in Iran. I'll only get to see him for a little while before he is taken away for debriefing before he can come home." She kissed the baby's soft cheek. "He's supposed to meet his son for the first time." Her lower lip began to tremble and the first tear cascaded slowly down her cheek.

A loud voice boomed out from our group. "That's a damn shame. When a soldier returns from overseas duty he ought to be able to see his wife and new baby before he is sent for debriefing. I served in Desert Storm and on my way back to the States all I thought about was seeing my wife and my little girl." All heads turned toward the burly truck driver who had a wad of tobacco tucked into his cheek. He had voiced what we were all feeling.

A loud chukka chukka sound came from the distance and grew louder by the minute. Someone shouted, "It's a helicopter. I bet it's the local news bird."

The truck driver's face crinkled in a smile as his eyes lit up. "I have an idea." He hurried back to his truck and grabbed his cell phone. The thick fingers on his huge hands flew faster than one would have imagined that they could. "I need the number of the local news station," he barked into the phone. He found a pen and a scrap of paper among the debris in his cab and jotted the number down. He insisted on speaking to the station manager and after a brief description of the situation his call was put through. We couldn't hear what the station manager was saying but judging from the argument that the truck driver put up he was not being agreeable. "It will be great publicity for your station," the truck driver said. "But it won't look so good if you let down a soldier who is returning home from serving his country."

"There's a field adjacent to where we are," the truck driver continued.

"You won't be putting anyone in danger at all. I'm telling you, this will be publicity that money can't buy."

The truck driver had his back to us so we couldn't see his face. When he disconnected the call and slowly turned around, his rugged face broke into a huge grin and he let out a whoop. He strode forward and placed one of his enormous hands on top of the baby's head. "Little fellow, you're going to meet your daddy today."

Tears of joy gushed from the young wife's eyes. She hugged the truck driver. "How can I ever thank you?" she whispered hoarsely.

"Your husband already has," the truck driver said. "He risked his life for me. This little favor I did for you and him is nothing compared to that."

A wild cheer went up from the crowd. Almost everyone close enough to realize that something special was happening had gotten out of their cars.

The helicopter landed in the field nearby and two men got out, one of them training a camera on the scene before him. They looked a little confused at their sudden new assignment but smiled as the crowd cheered again. "Where is the young lady and her baby that we are taking to the airport?" the one with the camera asked. She timidly stepped forward. "Well, come on honey," he said. "Your soldier will be landing in a few minutes and we have orders that you had better be there to give him a kiss."

Looking flustered, she pointed to a red Toyota parked in the inner lane. "But my car…"

The truck driver strode over to her car, climbed inside, and with a couple of deft maneuvers had the car safely parked on the grassy median. He jumped out, pulled a tattered handkerchief from his pocket, and tied it to the antenna.

"It will be fine until you can come back for it," he said, dropping the keys in her hand.

A middle-aged man stepped forward and handed her his business card. "Call me when you are ready to come get your car.

The crowd broke into spontaneous cheers, claps, and whistles as she cradled her baby and ran to the helicopter.

We all had wanted to see that young woman make it to the airport in time to greet her soldier. For just a little while we were all of one mind and one purpose and it was a beautiful thing.

~Elizabeth Atwater

13

Finding Purpose

*Start by doing what's necessary, then do what's possible,
and suddenly... you are doing the impossible.*

~Saint Francis of Assisi

September 11th started out like any other day for our family of five. My husband Jeff and I woke up early so he could take the commuter train to Boston's Logan Airport from our home in the suburbs for his 8 a.m. flight to Los Angeles. He would be attending a three-day conference for his fairly new job at Compaq Computer.

The night before as we were getting ready for bed, he did what he always did before he traveled — he rambled on about where the important papers were, which bills needed to be paid and which were still to come in the mail. He mentioned things like life insurance. As always, I only half-listened. Nothing was going to happen.

Jeff grabbed his bag from our bedroom that Tuesday morning and peeked into the kids' rooms. He had said goodbye to them the night before, spending time with each of them individually, making them laugh and promising to bring them something from his trip. As I drove Jeff to the train, he said, "For some reason I'm really tired this morning."

I replied, "Well, you have six hours to sleep on the plane."

We arrived at the station just a few minutes before the train pulled up. Jeff leaned over, gave me a quick kiss, and said, "I'll see you in a few days and we'll celebrate our birthdays then." My birthday is September 15th, and his was the 18th. We always celebrated together.

Instead of leaving right away, for some reason I sat and watched him walk down the platform. I had one of those fleeting thoughts—"We should have better goodbyes, because you just never know..." Then I pulled out and drove home to get the kids ready for school.

After the kids were off on their buses, I watched *Good Morning America* while sipping a cup of tea, waiting for a friend to pick me up to do a PTO errand. While Charlie Gibson reported that a plane had flown into the World Trade Center, I called my mother-in-law to tell her to turn on the news. We both talked briefly about how strange that was, and I said, "Thank God Jeff is on a plane to Los Angeles today," because he often attended meetings in those buildings and would have been there that day if not for the conference in California.

We hung up and I continued watching. With Charlie trying to explain what had transpired, a second plane flew over his shoulder and into the South Tower. At that moment we all knew this was no accident. Within minutes the news reporters began discussing terrorism and the possible airplanes involved, and American Airlines Flight 11 scrolled across the screen. I wasn't sure which flight Jeff was on, but after running the times in my head, I realized that Jeff could have been on that flight.

I made some calls and found out that he was booked on Flight 11 through his company's travel agency. I felt weak in the knees and sick to my stomach. My friend called and I told her of my concern. Several minutes later, she and numerous other friends, along with Jeff's family, began to fill our house. I called Jeff's cell phone repeatedly, knowing it was fruitless. But I had to hear his voice and I hadn't given up hope.

At 1:05 p.m. we received the call from American Airlines. I collapsed into the arms of my parish priest, and he tried in vain to comfort me. My life that morning, and my children's lives, changed forever. Nothing would ever be the same—for us, or for our country.

That afternoon, as word began to spread, the kindness also began. A local restaurant sent massive amounts of food over the next few days for all the friends and family that gathered at our house. People brought gifts for the kids. They brought food and flowers. A friend planted mums in our front yard and the local police stood vigil at our house to help control the media and others wanting to visit. Letters and checks, both large and small, filled our mailbox. A nine-year-old girl who shared Jeff's birthday sent her birthday money; our paperboy sent us his collections for the week; and a young girl around the corner made bracelets and sold them on the street corner to raise money to help my family. Friends and strangers alike contributed thousands of dollars to my children's education fund. We were overwhelmed by the generosity and thoughtfulness.

Two months later the kids and I were trying to adjust to our "new normal." We were still receiving letters, dinners on a regular basis, and expressions of condolences anytime we ventured out. I felt the need to do something to show our appreciation, so the kids and I planned a fundraiser to help other 9/11 families who weren't getting the same kind of support. We raised $50,000 in one afternoon with a yard sale and silent auction and gave every cent away to other families. It felt good to channel all that negative energy into something so positive, so we decided to create a foundation in Jeff's name. Now, nearly fifteen years later, the Jeff Coombs Memorial Foundation helps Massachusetts families with things like household bills, medical and funeral bills, camp tuitions for special needs children, grief counseling, and fulfilling wishes for sick and grieving families.

One of our favorite activities is the holiday party for military families that we've hosted for the last nine years. Many of the young men and women who served after 9/11 did so because of what happened that tragic day, so we felt compelled to do something for the true American heroes — our military. We have established a unique bond between our Foundation and the military families, and an understanding of their loss when one of their loved ones doesn't come home.

Losing Jeff affected our family deeply. We still miss him every day, and we draw strength from him with each new challenge life gives us. There were times we thought we would never be whole as a family again. But doing uplifting things through the Foundation in Jeff's name has given us purpose and a real appreciation for what it means to be a family. And while the terrorists attempted to bring us down as a country, we pulled together instead, showing the true spirit of America.

~Christie Schmitt Coombs

The Greatest Parade

Alone we can do so little; together we can do so much.
~Helen Keller

've always loved parades. As far back as I can remember, parades have meant fun and excitement, music, and goodies thrown from colorful floats. But on Friday, September 2, 2005, I joined a parade I hated to acknowledge, even as my heart swelled to see it.

The floats in this parade bore reflectors and hazard lights, rather than neon illumination. The only colorful headgear took the form of uniform caps and safety helmets. The costumes bore logos of utility companies and military units rather than sequins and glitter.

No bands marched with gleaming instruments to accompany this parade. The only music came from dashboard sound systems. The thump of tires on asphalt provided the beat, accented by an occasional automobile horn sounding.

These riders didn't laugh and call as they rode. They looked grim. Nobody stood along the way yelling "T'row me something, mistah!" Everyone who saw the parade pass threw kisses or salutes to them instead of asking for trinkets.

No king's float led the way. The line stretched as far as I could see in front of me and as far back as my rearview mirror could reflect behind me. The utility trucks, cherry-pickers, ambulances, civil defense vehicles, relief organization vans, fire trucks, military trucks, landscape service trucks and more formed a procession which I accompanied from northern Illinois to Jackson, Mississippi. These were some of the amazing people who answered the call for help issued from the Gulf Coast in the wake of Hurricane Katrina. I saw them and I cried.

Through tears of grief and gratitude, I spotted license plates from all over the U.S. and Canada. These were not the first folks to respond. Some of them had waited to gather supplies, personnel or equipment before embarking on the trip. Some had to be mobilized or wait for schedules to be arranged so that essential services at home wouldn't be disrupted. But they all left families and homes behind them and joined the parade of responders that had begun earlier in the week, a line measured not in miles but in days.

As we continued south, storm damage began to appear around us: twisted road signs, broken trees, and debris lined the road. At gas stops, I recognized the dismay in my fellow travelers' eyes as they contemplated what they might find at our destination.

I was in this parade because my mother was one of the many evacuees from Hurricane Katrina. I was collecting her from her evacuation site in West Monroe, Louisiana and taking her home to Illinois with me.

I left the southbound parade at Jackson to head west into Louisiana. Once I reached her, we headed back to Jackson to catch I-55 north to I-57 for the trip back to Illinois. As we headed north, my mother's tears joined mine. Across the dividing green of the median, we could see the parade heading south, still constant in its flow. Her amazement at the number of people coming to help left her unable to say anything more than "Oh, thank God."

But now we could also see the hand-lettered signs along the northbound exits, pointing evacuees to places of refuge and hot meals in towns from Jackson on north. With each sign, I said a prayer of gratitude, thanking God for the generous hearts of those people. They opened their homes and their larders to strangers fleeing a nightmare, and I loved them for it.

The convoy of people and equipment continued down the road toward the most heavily stricken areas of Mississippi and Louisiana and my prayers went with them. These folks and the residents of all those little towns along the interstate demonstrated the best of American spirit: the willingness to reach out to those in need. Every one of them was a hero in my eyes.

~Mary Beth Magee

15

1,000 Heroes

At times, our own light goes out and is rekindled by a
spark from another person. Each of us has cause to
think with deep gratitude of those who have lighted the
flame within us.
~Albert Schweitzer

We were city people until about five years ago, when we found ourselves in the midst of three major medical issues. My husband, our twelve-year-old son Holden, and I were all battling different forms of cancer. We decided to move back to my hometown in rural Nebraska to be close to my parents, who would help us with our treatments and the care of our other three children.

Holden adapted immediately. He was drawn to the hard work of a farmer and jumped right in to help his grandpa. He learned all he could and now helps with all aspects of the farm. He has even opened his own sweet corn business and took third place in proficiency at the state FFA convention. He didn't let his brain cancer slow him down.

When Holden's cancer returned for a third time, the neurosurgeons deemed it inoperable. My husband refused to give up and found a doctor in Boston who said she was confident she could remove the entire tumor. Unfortunately, our insurance company wouldn't pay for it. The hospital offered to discount the surgery, but we still needed $39,000. Years of cancer treatment for my husband and me had left us penniless. We had already cashed in our stocks and bonds, savings and both our 401(k) plans. We had no way to find that $39,000.

Holden's FFA advisor and our county 4-H leader decided to hold a fundraiser. The day of the event was cold, icy and windy, and yet people poured into the school and bid on silent auction items that covered all the cafeteria tables. Our country town of only 1,000 people raised more than $45,000! They sent the payment to the hospital and had enough left over to send my husband and me along for Holden's surgery. As I sat in the waiting room during the surgery, I logged onto Facebook and saw post after post from our town, with photos of everyone wearing their "Team Holden" shirts.

I am still humbled and amazed. It was an impossible task made possible by a small amount of people banding together in small-town America. Holden has been cancer-free for two years now. He works on the farm, plays football at his high school, and volunteers with his FFA chapter. He is very proud to be a blood donor and carries his donor card everywhere.

Once in a while I see a little kid run by me in a faded Team Holden shirt and I can't help but smile. I hope what people take from this story is hope, belief and inspiration. Our little town raised $45,000. Our son is cancer-free.

Miracles happen.

~Michelle Bruce

16

Military Bracelet Returned after Eighteen Years

Nothing is impossible if you believe.
~Author Unknown

"Mom, our neighbor found a silver bracelet on the beach with a name, service number, and USCG on the front, and 'With love, Babe' on the back. Since I'm in the U.S. Coast Guard he thought I could find a way to return it, because it may have sentimental value," explained my son, Steven.

"I checked the service number on the bracelet with headquarters and learned he was no longer in the military. When I contacted the National Archives and Records Administration they confirmed he was deceased. My search through countless records led to the unusual name in Massachusetts, but no further information to find his next of kin, so I paid $60 to obtain his full military records from them. The service member's file contained his records and military number, mixed with those of another service person from New York, with the same name but a different military number."

Years later, Steven was excited when he called from graduate school. "I've done several genealogy searches on the New York guy, and found the obituary of one of his granddaughters that referenced her two brothers living in Maine. One brother never replied to my letter, but I got the other brother's number from his church and called him. He was very skeptical about my bracelet story but agreed to let me send him a letter detailing my search, a photo of the bracelet, and copies of his grandfather's service records. I included my references, contact information, and emphasized I wanted nothing in return. He warmed up and said my research about his family revealed information he never knew."

Steven called with his final report.

"I mailed the bracelet to him. He's close to a niece and they were thrilled to have a keepsake from their grandfather/great grandfather. He sent me a $25 gift card as a thank you."

I told Steven, "I'm proud of your tenacity. It's an amazing story."

He replied, "Looking back, it surprises me how much time I spent on this while I worked on my master's degrees, established my military career, got married, and became a father. I was determined to return the bracelet, but I didn't know it would take eighteen years."

~Miriam Hill

Snowbound

*There is an emanation from the heart in genuine
hospitality which cannot be described, but
is immediately felt and puts the
stranger at once at his ease.*

~Washington Irving

The Malad Pass in southern Idaho can be treacherous in winter. Icy roads and windblown snow can close it down entirely, stranding drivers on either side of the route through the mountains. Such was the case one cold January day when I was driving home from the Salt Lake City airport to Rexburg, Idaho where I taught high school.

Christmas vacation had ended, and I had just returned from spending the holidays with my family in Southern California. I drove up Interstate 15 through a beautiful winter landscape, paralleling snowy mountain ranges. The miles passed swiftly, with the heater blowing warm inside my car and me humming along to the radio.

Then snow started to drift across the road. Just a few eddies at first, wispy and insubstantial as ghosts. Flurries began falling from the sky as well, and the wind swirled together the ground eddies and snowflakes into whiteout conditions. I could barely see the road ahead of me, and by the time I reached Malad City, the pass north of town had closed.

All traffic was directed off the highway into a small town with a population of 2,000 people. No one knew when the pass would reopen.

My beginning salary as a teacher kept me on a strict budget, and the expense of a trip to California coupled with holiday gift buying left little money to spare for lodgings for the night. And those lodgings were filling fast with other stranded motorists.

However, I had a "clever" idea. I would drive to the sheriff's department to wait out the storm. It was bound to be warm and dry, and they could tell me as soon as the pass opened. If all else failed, I even had a backup plan.

I can't imagine what the sheriff thought when I unveiled my backup plan: "If the pass stays closed, can I spend the night in an unused jail cell?"

There I stood, a twenty-something in the open-toed shoes I'd been wearing since my flight from sunny California, asking if I could sleep with the prisoners if the storm continued. I may have been naïve, but I had nerve.

The sheriff said to wait and see if the pass opened, and he let me stay in his office all afternoon, listening to the reports of spun-out cars and snowbound big rigs.

By nightfall it was apparent that no traffic would be allowed over the pass until the next day. By then every room in town had been booked. Would I be spending the night in jail?

Fortunately, the sheriff had a better plan. Instead of giving me a spare cell, he called his ex-wife, who agreed to put me up for the night. She offered a warm bunk, a pizza dinner and an unquestioning welcome to a young woman sent to her doorstep by her ex-husband.

After breakfast, I returned to the sheriffs' department to wait for word. By mid morning the good news came that snowplows were leading convoys of twenty cars at a time over the Malad Pass. I could get in line on Interstate 15 and wait my turn.

Once again, I was heading north, dressed in more sensible shoes than the day before, warm and dry and well rested because of the hospitality of small town America.

~Susan Lendroth

American Spirit Soars at Lowest Times

*Unselfish and noble actions are the most radiant pages
in the biography of souls.*
~David Thomas

"I t was the best of times, it was the worst of times." Charles Dickens was writing about London and Paris in *A Tale of Two Cities*, but on Patriots' Day 2013, the familiar opening line from his famous novel perfectly described Boston. Indeed, it was a "City of Two Tales."

The worst of times was the two evil bombs, designed to kill and maim and cause terror, exploding near the marathon finish line and succeeding on all counts.

But even before the second sinister explosion went off twelve seconds after the first, the best of times were underway and the spirit of America was on display. Watching the breaking news videos on TV for the first time, my son saw this best instantly, turning to me and saying: "Look at all the people running toward the explosion and going into the fray to help!"

Within three terror-and-adrenaline-fueled-racing heartbeats, the first responders in bright-colored vests were bravely running toward the blast, toward the smoke, toward the chaos and danger to help victims in an American city suddenly turned into Baghdad or Tel Aviv, into a war zone.

Yet even more remarkable was to see the heroes without vests, the race volunteers and runners and spectators without special emergency and disaster training, hurrying into harm's way to help.

As with 9/11 and Hurricane Sandy and on and on, it was a vivid example of the wisdom of the late Fred Rogers — famously known as Mr. Rogers — who told his TV viewers that if they saw a scary thing, "Look for the helpers. You will always find people who are helping."

"Helpers" by another word are "heroes."

The best of times was to see images of a burly man "helper" carrying an injured woman away from the blood-wet pavement.

The best of times was to hear a woman praising a "helper" for rushing her to safety in a wheelchair and then racing back to aid another person in need.

The best of times was to learn of a Good Samaritan being, in truth, a Great Samaritan by using his belt as a tourniquet to try and save a life — and a runner doing the same with his T-shirt.

The best of times was the marathoners who crossed the finish line and continued running two more weary miles to Massachusetts General Hospital to donate blood.

The best of times was Patriots' Day becoming a day of true patriots.

In the early aftermath the most popular hashtag on Twitter was #PrayforBoston. But people did more than pray — they acted. Restaurants opened and gave free meals; coffee shops provided free Wi-Fi for runners to contact loved ones; on social media message boards local residents offered beds to those who could not return to their hotels.

Feeling a desire to connect in some small way, I posted my own #PrayforBoston tweet: "Today we are all runners."

Even three thousand miles away from the mayhem in Massachusetts, as a marathon runner myself I soon experienced the outpouring of a unified community. Mere moments after this 21st century Boston Massacre, a knock came on my front door: it was my concerned neighbor — with whom I have only a wave-in-passing relationship; usually when I am running and he is driving — checking to see if I was home and not racing in Boston.

Too, I received a number of phone calls, texts and e-mails asking the same question. One came from a friend I had not heard from in more than three years; another was from a fellow runner pointing out that the finish-line clock read 4:09 when the blasts went off and, accounting for our delay in the pack of runners getting to the actual starting line of the race four years ago, that is about when we triumphantly ran down Boylston Street — with my wife cheering me on precisely where the second bomb went off.

During a twelve-mile run later on this horrific day, as I tried to settle my thoughts and also honor the victims, three pedestrians — one I know and two unfamiliar faces — yelled out: "Glad you weren't in Boston today."

On Boston Marathon Monday 2013 we were all runners.

More than that, we were all neighbors.

~Woody Woodburn

All Hail to the USO

*If you haven't got any charity in your heart, you have
the worst kind of heart trouble.*

~Bob Hope

As I was growing up, I often watched documentaries about the USO. They always showed members of the military dancing and being entertained while they were in the service.

For quite some time, I thought that was all that the USO did — entertain.

Then a USO center opened in my city, in the retired airport terminal of the Ontario International Airport in California. I went on one of their free tours and learned the remarkable facts about this great organization that does so much for our military.

This local center, as are some other USOs, is named after Bob Hope, who spent forty years entertaining our troops during Christmas holidays, often taking his group of starlets, comedians, and entertainers into dangerous war zones to bring laughter and happiness to our military.

I was shown around the impressive, large facility, located in the West Wing near the new airport Terminals Two and Four. As I toured, I learned that the USO is a valuable home away from home between flights for military personnel and their families. It provides a place to rest, sleep, and recharge.

And what they also provide is impressive: meals, snacks and drinks. No military person goes hungry there. In the Library Room, I saw bookshelves lined with all types of books, to read there or take as the service members choose. There are computers with full Internet access. The recreation room is fully stocked with a pool table, air hockey and basketball games, puzzles, musical instruments, and more. The media room contains comfortable recliners and TVs.

There's even a room for those traveling with families so they can have all the comforts of home, with child-size beds, cribs, games, and toys. Even diapers are provided. And for those who want to enjoy the California air, there's an outdoor patio.

At the end of the football season, a group of Marines was treated to their own Super Bowl party. To help raise funds, this chapter holds a large car show once a year, plus other activities.

I was also impressed with the helpful staff — many of them retired military men and women themselves. Instead of sleeping in, playing golf, or attending a movie, they're at this center from morning until night, tending to the needs of those who are now making a sacrifice for our country like they once did.

"We take care of them like they're our own families," said John, my tour guide, an Army veteran. He added that the staff also provides transportation, hotel stays, and other services whenever they're needed.

My eyebrows went up in surprise when John told me that before the USO opened at our airport, military members who had an overnight flight had to sleep on the airport benches, and worse yet — would often sleep on the grass outside!

"But why did the government let them do that?" John explained that before the USO center opened, there were few other options.

Further explanation revealed that the USO, chartered by Congress, is a private, nonprofit 501(c)3 and relies on the generosity of corporations and individuals for funding day-to-day operations.

Another volunteer tour guide named Chris told me about the special place he has in his heart for the USO. "When I was in the service," he said, "March Air Force Base used to have young women come and dance with us to keep us occupied during training. That's where I met my wife, and so I have this organization to thank for my wonderful wife and family." But his experience with the USO did not end there. Once he was out of the service, Chris went into studio work. "I ended up working on some of the shows that Bob Hope himself produced."

Kristen, a local USO manager, went on to say that more than 180 locations worldwide provide a temporary haven for those who give so much to protect this great land of ours. Her own daughter, who's in the military, often uses the services of the USO in Guam, where she's currently stationed.

Later that day, I met Frank, now retired from the Navy. He often used the USO in Norfolk, Virginia, and what he told me was equally remarkable. He added that some USO funding also comes from the Combined Federal Campaign, an organization where the veterans themselves donate to help keep the USOs running. Former military not only staff the USOs, they also fund them! They do this to repay those centers for the support they once received.

By now, my heart was completely swelling with American pride. I am so grateful that I took the time to find our local USO and discover the wonderful work they do around the world.

~Kay Presto

Home from Haiti

September 11 is one of our worst days but it brought
out the best in us. It unified us as a country and
showed our charitable instincts and reminded us of
what we stood for.
~Senator Lamar Alexander

All I wanted in the aftermath of 9/11 was to get home to my husband Ken. The United States Embassy assured me I'd remain safe in Haiti, where I'd finished staging an HIV/AIDS prevention seminar for Peace Corps volunteers and their counterparts.

"Reagan National will remain closed indefinitely," the ambassador's aide explained. "You can get on your flight for Miami Sunday, but once there, you'll be stuck. All the rental cars are long gone. People will wait days to grab a seat for Dulles or BWI."

"I understand," I said, "but I'll risk getting delayed. If worse comes to worst, my daughter-in-law's parents live there and might put me up for a while."

My husband had still been asleep in Silver Spring, Maryland, that Tuesday morning when, a dozen miles away, a hijacked jet smashed into the Pentagon. He hadn't learned about the day's events until the early afternoon when one of his sons phoned to check on him.

I'd been 1,500 miles away, in a rustic hotel in coastal Montrouis, two hours north of Port-au-Prince. Still newlyweds, we'd grown used to separations during our first year of marriage, since I traveled overseas frequently for my job. This, though, was different. I needed to be with Ken right now for mutual solace.

When the news reached us in our hotel conference room, we'd taken a break. We'd poured into the adjacent bar, where the manager had switched on a generator-operated black and white television. We stared in disbelief as CNN showed reruns of the collapse of the Twin Towers.

"We should cancel this training," a few volunteers suggested through tears.

"No," others countered. "People are travelling here from all over the country. Some have to hike miles to catch a tap-tap. We can't disappoint them."

Tap-taps, the gaily-painted vehicles that provide public transportation in this Caribbean country, follow fixed routes on rough roads. Some of the counterparts might walk for most of a day or more in torrid heat to reach the nearest pickup site.

The Haiti Peace Corps health programmer and I exchanged glances. We had not even considered canceling. Though HIV/AIDS prevalence rates had diminished from the horrendous highs in the 1980s, mother-to-child transmission rates remained shockingly high. This long-planned event would be Peace Corps' first training effort here.

We somehow struggled through the conference. The Peace Corps nurse, an energetic Haitian woman, drove from the capital to counter the myths that had sprung up about the disease. In Creole she set her superstitious countrymen straight that voodoo played no part in selecting victims. The volunteers translated for their counterparts and engaged them in the interactive skits and scenarios that are the hallmark of Peace Corps trainings worldwide.

Most volunteers reported their counterparts now had a better understanding of the disease and would spread the word back in their villages. We were happy with this positive outcome.

Sunday morning, the embassy drove me to Toussaint L'Ouverture International where I boarded an American Airline flight for Miami. The flight attendants all wore black armbands to honor their colleagues who had died on 9/11. They informed us we needed to remain seated for the entire flight. Everybody seemed uneasy at takeoff, some Haitians weeping. Air conditioning couldn't mask the acrid odor of perspiration.

Once in Miami, I buzzed straight for the American Airline desk. I produced both my return ticket to Reagan National and my government passport.

"Sorry, we don't have any seats available on any flights right now," the check-in agent said. "Wish we did. We have one flight diverted to Dulles tonight at 11:00, but the last economy seat got taken about ten minutes ago. All I can do is put you on a wait list."

I went to a nearby pay phone and called Ken. I knew he'd be relieved that I'd at least made it back to the mainland.

"I'm here at Miami International," I said when he answered. "Might be here for days. Things don't look good."

"Call me again tonight, baby," he said. "I miss you so much. I've been on the phone with all my sons today. We're all hoping you get home safe… and soon."

I sat down near the gate and began to read Herbert Gold's *Haiti: Best Nightmare on Earth*, when a young man sat down beside me. He looked exhausted and angry. I realized that nearly everybody in the waiting area wore similar expressions of anxiety and defeat. It had been a terrible week for us all.

"Haiti?" the man said, peering at the book in my hands. "Why bother to read that? That country's done for."

"Not quite," I replied. "I work for Peace Corps and our philosophy is a positive one. I've just come from conducting a health training there."

His scowl faded. He blinked. He shifted his gaze to my face.

"Tell me more," he said. "I'm in pharmaceuticals and we're always looking for new markets."

I explained a little about how HIV/AIDS had devastated the country and what efforts had been made to counter the disease. Soon he was telling me about his family in Virginia, and how lucky he'd been to get on the 11 p.m. flight there.

"I got the last seat," he crowed.

"Oh, it's you. I came ten minutes later." I fished in my purse and hauled out my wallet.

"Here's a photo of my husband. We've been married a little over a year. He's alone in Silver Spring, and I've been yearning to get back to give him a hug. I've never missed anybody more."

He studied the photo. "Looks a lot like my dad. He died a few years back. I always could go to him for honest encouragement. Your husband has the same kindness in his eyes."

I nodded, and smiled.

Soon the man rose and walked to the check-in desk. I returned to my book. First class had already boarded for that last Dulles flight. I pictured my companion settling into his seat.

The loudspeaker crackled. "Will passenger Elders come to the check-in desk?"

I approached, steeling myself for the bad news about how many hours or days I'd have to wait to get a seat on a flight.

"Here's your boarding pass. You're in the last row, but you'll be home tonight."

"But…"

The clerk smiled. "The guy who had this seat upgraded. He said to tell the lady who had been trying to do some good in Haiti to give her husband a hug."

Finally I released the tears I'd held back all week.

I phoned Ken from Dulles. "Not everything is a nightmare. Prepare to be hugged in a couple of hours, thanks to a stranger's kindness."

"I'm ready," my husband replied.

~Terri Elders

21

Hands Across America

*It's easier to accomplish the impossible than
the ordinary.*
~Ken Kragen, organizer of Hands Across America

t was May 25th, 1986, and our family of six was packed into
our Chevrolet Monte Carlo, heading to a mountain crest just
outside Johnstown, Pennsylvania. Crowds of people were cheering along the road as we approached our destination. That day,
millions of Americans were doing the same thing, heading to different destinations to create a chain from New York City to Long Beach,
California.

I was only eleven years old, but I was pretty sure this was going
to be an unforgettable experience. As far as my eyes could see, people
frantically scurried to form a makeshift line along the shoulder of the
highway. My brother Garrett, who lugged our boom box from the car,
hastily loaded the six D batteries into their compartment.

"Hurry, we're gonna miss the song," I yelled anxiously while taking
my place in the row.

Scowling at me, he quickly tuned the radio into local station WCRO.
The DJs were already buzzing about today's events and that a member
of a popular Sixties group would be stopping in Johnstown to join our
line. Suddenly, the crowd started to count down the last seconds to
the three o'clock scheduled time. Everyone hastily joined hands. Then,
in unison, several radios from different places up and down the line
blared "We Are the World," then "America the Beautiful," and then our

theme song and reason for the day, "Hands Across America." Smiles stretched from ear to ear as our human chain swayed to the music. We raised our clasped hands as we sang along to the familiar melodies.

Six and half million people formed a path across the continental United States. Many paid $10 each to reserve a place in line and the event raised $34 million for the USA for Africa charity. It was part of a larger effort that raised money not only to fight famine in Africa, but also to fight hunger and homelessness in America.

I believe the experience of participating in Hands Across America left a lifelong imprint on our family. Most of us chose vocations where we could help people in our communities. My twin sister, Melina, is the Program Director for a county program that provides food, nutrition counseling, and access to health services under a supplemental nutrition program for women, infants, and children. Gina, my younger sister, is a Youth Support and Data Specialist for a youth mentoring program. I spent over a decade as a Chemical Dependency Technician Supervisor and Residential Program Manager for several transitional living facilities and group homes across Western Pennsylvania.

Our country is still struggling with issues of hunger and homelessness. I believe individually we can all do great things, but together, linked, we can do even more.

~Carisa J. Burrows

22

A Hero's Welcome

*We often take for granted the very things that most
deserve our gratitude.*
~Cynthia Ozick

"**A**ttention Ladies and Gentlemen, we apologize for the delay,"
announced the Southwest Airlines attendant at gate 12
in the Baltimore/Washington International Airport. "The
flight you are waiting for has been delayed in Florida due to
severe thunderstorms. We will board for Manchester, New Hampshire
as soon as it arrives. Again, we apologize for the inconvenience."

My lifetime friend, Jane, and I were finally taking the trip we had
been talking about for several years. We were both anxious and excited
to be on our way. My frustration regarding the delay was mounting
by the minute.

"I can't believe we are finally doing this," said Jane.

"I know! I wonder if other people have ever planned a neighborhood reunion with the kids on their street after forty-nine years." I
shook my head in disbelief.

"It really is a special trip. I hope everyone comes to the picnic
next Wednesday."

"They will," I assured her.

We sat next to each other at the gate. I was quietly lost in my
own thoughts of the week ahead and my memories of our childhood
in the old neighborhood.

Jane and I reminisced about our favorite childhood memories.

"Remember the Fourth of July parades every summer that started downtown and ended at the park at the end of our street?" Jane asked.

"They were so much fun. Everyone dressed in red, white, and blue."

"We even decorated the spokes and handlebars of our bikes with red, white and blue streamers." We laughed at the memory.

"Our parents were certainly glad when the night was over. They had been at the park since early morning helping to set up tables and chairs for the picnic."

The airline attendant interrupted our conversation. "Ladies and Gentlemen, our flight from Florida has arrived and is taxiing to the gate. I have a special surprise for all of you. The flight is carrying veterans from World War II, the Korean War and the Vietnam War. It is better known as 'The Honor Flight.' These veterans will be visiting the war memorials in Washington, D.C. for the very first time. We ask that you give each of them a hero's welcome as they are brought to the gate area. When they come through the open door let's applaud and salute these American veterans."

Jane and I looked at each other in surprise. Jane exclaimed, "Can you believe this? I've heard about this, but never thought I would have the privilege of being part of something so patriotic."

I nodded in agreement. "These veterans are the unsung heroes of America. Your parents and my dad served in World War II. Some of the boys from our high school fought in Vietnam. Some of them never made it home."

"I remember," Jane said sadly.

We heard the door open. Everyone in the gate area turned and faced the doorway in quiet reverence and anticipation. The first veteran emerged in a wheelchair pushed by a volunteer. Tears came to our eyes as we clapped. One by one they appeared. We continued to applaud them. Some walked with canes and some were in wheelchairs. All came forth with their volunteer guardian beside them. Tears rolled down my face.

I looked at Jane. Through her tears she whispered, "I wish our parents had lived long enough to do this."

"Me too."

We walked in silence as we boarded the plane. I was lost in thoughts of my dad. I thought of the photos of him proudly smiling in his Army uniform. Jane had photos too — showing her mom and dad in their Army uniforms. They were hung on her living room wall with an American flag folded between them. It was given to Jane at the cemetery during her dad's funeral service.

Our reunion trip was even better than we had hoped. We toured our old high school, much expanded now. We gathered at the beach where we all learned to swim. We shared photos and memories of our childhood on a quiet little street in a small city in New Hampshire.

We wrapped up our trip with a visit to the cemeteries where our parents are buried. Witnessing the Honor Flight in Baltimore gave me a newfound admiration for my dad. He never talked about his years with the Army. History books told me what I needed to know. I prayed a silent prayer thanking God for the parents He gave me, and for the sacrifice my dad gave for his country in World War II. We left that cemetery and drove to the one where Jane's dad was buried. She had brought her mom's ashes with her to be scattered on the plaques given to each of her parents by the U.S. Army.

"That was quite a week!" Jane said to me as we buckled our seatbelts for the long flight home.

"It sure was, and to think it started with the privilege of witnessing the Honor Flight veterans, that made it even more special."

When the plane was at cruising altitude, Jane turned to me with misty eyes and said, "This trip can never be repeated."

"What do you mean?"

"It started with the Honor Flight and ended with visits to the cemeteries."

"Okay, but I still don't get your point."

"Without our parents, who served in World War II, we would not have any of these memories to carry with us. Your dad, and my mom and dad, served and they survived. Without them we would not be here."

I thought about that for a few minutes. She was absolutely right. I tapped Jane on the shoulder. She looked up from the book she was reading and turned to me. With a grateful heart I simply said, "God bless America!"

~Catherine Ancewicz

23

How Mr. Hawkins Changed My Life

*Never bend your head. Always hold it high. Look the
world straight in the eye.*
~Helen Keller

When I was a child my family moved from Indiana to Texas. Already on the shy side, I quickly became the subject of ridicule in my new school. I had a strong accent and only one pair of pants. On my first day at my new school it was clear to me that I would never be given a chance to fit in. The other students referred to me by my full name, spitting it off their lips like it was foul. I accepted the fact that the best I could hope for was to be ignored. Most of my classmates lived in houses. I was one of the "apartment kids," who were considered to be a lower life form.

There was a homeless man who all the apartment kids called Mr. Hawkins. The apartment manager would pay Mr. Hawkins to do odd jobs around the complex, such as picking up trash and cleaning the laundry rooms. It wasn't uncommon to stumble upon him in the late afternoons passed out in the laundry room with a brown bag in his hand. The kids would poke their heads in the door to catch a glimpse of him. We all took interest in Mr. Hawkins because, as harmless as he actually was, there was an air of danger and mystery about him.

My mother had told me that under no circumstances was I to talk to Mr. Hawkins or go near him when he was passed out in the laundry room. Being what they called in those days a "latchkey kid," I spent most of my time alone. Even when my mother was home I was still left unsupervised or ignored most of the time, and as long as I didn't get into any trouble and was home when the street lights came on, I came and went as I pleased.

One hot, summer evening I found a quarter lying in the parking lot across from our front door. The back of my shirt was wet with sweat and my hair clung to my forehead and neck. It was nearly time for the streetlights to come on, but if I ran all the way there and back, I could make it to the soda machine in the laundry room and still be home on time. I ran around the building and down the walkway through the complex and through the doorway of the nearest laundry room to the vending machines in the back. I wiped the sweat from my eyes and put my money in. I smiled as I held the icy-cold can in my hand and popped it open, taking a long drink as I turned around.

There he was, Mr. Hawkins, standing between the door and me. I looked past him through the windows and could see that it was almost dark. "Excuse me, I have to get home. It's almost dark." I pointed past him out the windows.

"What's wrong with you?" he asked.

"I need to get home or I'll get in trouble."

"That's not what I mean. What's wrong with you?"

"I don't know."

"Yes you do. You do know. Now answer me, what's WRONG with you?"

"Nothing."

"That's right," he said, "nothing IS wrong with you. So why do you act like it?"

"Act like what?"

"Like something's wrong with you."

"I don't know."

"There ain't nothin' wrong with you, but you walk around with your head down like there's somethin' wrong with you. Who told you there's somethin' wrong with you?"

"Nobody."

"Someone did. A pretty, little girl like you don't walk with her head down for no reason. Somebody done told you there's somethin' wrong with you, didn't they? Maybe they didn't say it with words, but they made you believe it."

He took my chin between his thumb and his fingers and gently lifted my head as a tear ran down my cheek.

"You walk with your head up and look people in the eye so that they know there ain't nothin' wrong with you. You understand me? You don't listen to what them kids say and don't you start believin' it. They don't know you. They don't even see who you are. All they see is someone they can hurt, and that makes them feel powerful. When you walk with your head down, it tells them that they're right about you, there's somethin' wrong with you. Don't you let their words matter. You know who you are. You know there ain't nothin' wrong with you, so act like it. You understand what I'm sayin'?"

"Yes, sir."

"Good. Next time I see you I don't want to see you lookin' down. I want to see you walk with your head up, and when someone speaks to you, look them in the eye and respond with confidence."

"Yes, sir."

"Alright, I'm gonna be watchin' you to make sure. You hurry on home now so you don't get in trouble with your mama."

I ran home as fast as I could and quietly slipped in the back door. I couldn't get his words out of my head that night. I felt happier than I had felt in a long time. There was nothing wrong with me, and Mr. Hawkins knew it.

The next morning I noticed the apartment manager and all the kids gathered around the laundry room. I ran over to see what was going on. Mr. Hawkins had died in that laundry room and I realized that I was probably the last person he had talked to, and he spent his last moments being kind to me, helping me. From that day on, I walked with my head held high, and when I caught myself looking down, I remembered Mr. Hawkins' words. He'd be watching me.

My world changed after that night in the laundry room. When I went back to school in the fall the other kids looked at me differently.

They commented that I had changed. One girl said, "You were such a loser last year, but now you're really cool." I closed my eyes and thanked God for Mr. Hawkins, and I knew that he was up there watching me and smiling. Mr. Hawkins may have seemed like "a nobody" to everyone else, but to me, he was my angel; and the lesson he taught me changed my life.

~Lisa P. Tubbs

★ The ★ Spirit of America

Our Vast and Beautiful Land

The winds that blow through the wide sky in these mounts, the winds that sweep from Canada to Mexico, from the Pacific to the Atlantic — have always blown on free men.
~President Franklin D. Roosevelt

24

Fifty States — One Nation

Experience, travel — these are as education
in themselves.
~Euripides

W hat's the best way to experience America? One step at a time. And that's precisely what I set out to do in 2006 when I endeavored to visit all fifty states in fifty consecutive days. Oh yeah, and run a marathon in each of them while there.

Yes, you read that correctly. Starting on a warm and balmy day in September, I began my quest of running fifty marathons, in fifty states, in fifty days with the Lewis & Clark marathon in St. Charles, Missouri. It seemed like a fitting place to embark, given it was the 200th anniversary of the Lewis & Clark expedition.

After Missouri the plan was to head west across the country, stopping in each successive state to visit, explore and run a marathon. As you might imagine, the logistics, scheduling and research were every bit as challenging as the running itself. Given the awkward timing of various marathons across the nation we weren't always able to follow a straight line from one state to the next, but rather zigzagged across the country in a complex web of travel.

A complex and glorious web of travel — and one that was made all the more meaningful by the presence of my family. My wife, a dentist, had adjusted her schedule to join the procession, and our two children — Alexandria (age eleven at the time) and Nicholas (age eight when we began the trip) — would be taking fifty days off school to travel with us. Well, not exactly off school. My mom, a retired school teacher, would also be part of the crew and the children's respective schools would send her the weekly lesson plans each Sunday night so that she could "road school" the kids as we ventured. My father also came along because, well, we're Greek, and where one family member goes the others are soon to follow.

It might be easy to conclude that seeing the country so quickly would be an indistinguishable blur, but just the opposite was true. I remember every single state with amazing clarity, even to this very day, nearly a decade later. Because we traveled so quickly, the differences between geographies, cultures, climate and cuisine were markedly pronounced. There was no dilution of memory as there may have been had we toured various regions months or years apart from each other.

The first thing that was readily apparent was how vast and unexplored the West still is, even now, two hundred years after the Lewis & Clark expedition. Driving from Missouri to Colorado, for the Boulder Backroads Marathon, (via Memphis, Tennessee; Gulfport, Mississippi; Little Rock, Arkansas; Wichita, Kansas; Des Moines, Iowa; and Lincoln, Nebraska) the open spaces along the highway became broader and broader, and the humidity dropped lower and lower. This dynamic became even more pronounced as we moved from Colorado through Wyoming, the Dakotas, Montana and Idaho, eventually arriving in Seattle for our first seafood fest!

I watched the kids marvel as the fishermen hurled massive salmon from their coolers to awaiting merchants at Pike Place Fish Market. Soon we would be making one of those our dinner, along with freshly caught crab and clam chowder, the thick fresh smell of saltwater drifting in off the Pacific as we sat at an outside table watching the sun go down.

From Seattle we would fly to Alaska, only to encounter an early-season snowstorm! Thankfully our expedition was sponsored by the outdoor clothing company The North Face, so we had plenty of warm clothing. Not that we needed it for long, because the next day we found ourselves in the tropical splendor of Hawaii sipping Mai Tais (well, at least we adults were) and slathering on the sunscreen. Thankfully my body was holding up to the daily marathon routine so I was able to enjoy the great diversity of people and places we were experiencing, along with the colorful Hawaiian umbrella in my drink.

After Hawaii we flew back to the mainland and resumed our land-based travels eastward through the Southwest and Texas. Not only had the landscape changed, but so had the language. I remember the race director of the Dallas Marathon greeting us in a thick Texan drawl: *Howdy y'all!* Thankfully my in-laws from Lubbock had joined us so we had interpreters. By the time we departed for the Midwest my language skills had become quite adept: *We're fixin' to go. See y'all later.*

We arrived in Green Bay, Wisconsin on October 24th, which corresponded with Nicholas's ninth birthday. Unbeknownst to any of us, they had a big party planned for him. Just as unexpectedly, Nicholas announced that morning that he wanted to run the final nine miles of the marathon to celebrate his ninth birthday. You've been hearing a lot about my experiences traveling across America, so I thought it would nice to get the perspective through his eyes, too. Nicholas is now eighteen and tells his side of the story like this:

As a nine-year-old kid, not much really sticks with you. You hope to get enough time to play at school and you generally live your life without thinking twice. More than half my life has passed since that frigid October day in Wisconsin, but the memories are carved in my mind like writing in stone. I awoke in the early morning buzzing with nervous anticipation. It was my ninth birthday and I decided to run the last nine miles of the marathon with my dad. I revered my father as a god, as most nine-years-olds do, and I wanted to be just like him. The only problem was my four-foot frame would only take me so far.

There I was, a sight to behold, a nine-year-old running down the streets of Green Bay with a chase vehicle in tow and a wide grin on my rosy face. The run itself was memorable but the destination was amazing. I have been a fan of football my whole life, from playing in the sandy beaches of Southern California as a kid, to under the lights as a high school senior. Football has always been my athletic endeavor of choice.

I joined up with my dad and the rest of the runners a few blocks from the finish line and we turned onto Lombardi Drive and I saw the holy shrine of football: Lambeau Field.

Our course took us around a lap of the field itself — which they had opened exclusively for us runners — and I couldn't help but imagine all the plays Brett Favre had made not twenty yards from where I was running. After the run, my father and I were given a private tour of the locker room and team facilities and I was given my very own happy birthday signed football by some of the Green Bay Packers.

At the conclusion of our tour, the Mayor of Green Bay presented me with a massive green and yellow cake, with nine burning candles the size of hot dogs to top it off. It was more than enough to feed all the runners and volunteers alike. For a wide-eyed nine-year-old, it was more than a dream come true.

I am eighteen now and preparing to go off to college, but I still reminisce about that magical fall day in Green Bay.

Eventually the procession of cross-country gallivanting brought us to the fiftieth and final state for the New York City Marathon. It had been a most extraordinary journey, one in which we saw firsthand the tremendous diversity of people and cultures across this great land of ours, and in that final marathon of running through the five boroughs of New York I got to experience it all over again, only this time it was compressed into 26.2 miles.

Crossing the finish line that November day in Manhattan, I was struck by how varied and eclectic we are here in America. We wear different clothes, eat different foods, speak with different accents and enjoy different pastimes. Yet in some fundamental way we are also all very much the same. We believe in freedom and liberty, and we continue to harbor the hope for a brighter tomorrow, a better future for us all. Walking through Central Park, draped in a Mylar finisher's blanket as volunteers rushed around to tend to all the runners, I realized that while America may be comprised of fifty states, we remain united as one nation.

~Dean & Nicholas Karnazes

25

The Man of the Van

We travel not to escape life, but for life not to escape us.
~Author Unknown

On September 11, 2001, my husband Mike and I gathered our kids Adam and Dana, then thirteen and ten, to tell them three things: They were safe and loved; America was strong; the world's people were good. The last point was important to us because our kids have been traveling the world since they were babies. Respect for all people is part of their upbringing, and we'd allow no terrorist act to steal that.

As the numbing slowness of the weeks after September 11th yielded to relative normalcy, I regained enough focus to give the future some thought. That future had us traveling again, but this time, we'd see our America. On a June day nine months after 9/11, my kids and I set out on a 12,000-mile cross-country journey. We'd be gone for the summer, driving a southern back-road route from our Boston home to the Pacific and a northern route back. We kissed Mike goodbye, climbed into our minivan (named New Paint as it was the successor to Old Paint, a workhorse with a decade of service), and left to explore America's towns and byways and confirm the strength and resolve of her people.

By the time we'd crossed Connecticut, New Paint was transformed. The family van became a comfortable home — a secure haven, a full member of the expedition. The kids settled in with pillows and books, I eased into the rhythm of the road, and New Paint purred confidently westward. We were four travelers — three with legs, one with wheels.

Of the memories made that summer, the most enduring are of the people we met. People like Scotty, a Kentucky motel janitor who moved his broom over the same spot as he listened in wonder about our trip, and who washed New Paint with the motel's hose so she'd gleam. Scotty said our journey into the healing country was important. He seemed proud of us, and I realized that his opinion mattered to me. On the morning we checked out, Scotty was waiting outside to see us off, waving as we pulled away.

We'd meet more people like Scotty — in parking lots, post offices and diners; at gas stations, parks and fishing docks — who asked about our trip and shared stories of their own cross-country journeys or their dreams of future ones. They told us how lucky we were, a mom and her kids, to spend such rich time together. Indeed, as we tucked more miles under our wheels, we felt the ties between us and our appreciation for one another strengthen. At times the power of our connection took my breath away.

People asked about other parts of the country and how folks were faring. That summer, the simple act of one family's trip across the nation was enough to unite the Americans we met in a certain, knowing bond. We were there, on the road, traveling freely, robbing terrorism of its ability to scare us. I realized that people were cheering us on and that we represented them as we continued. Perhaps they couldn't make the trip themselves, but we could make it for them, touching the country's corners and middles, confirming that things were all right. We — Adam, Dana, New Paint and I — were messengers that summer. We were a cord, a thread. We had the capacity to sew patches of the vast American quilt together simply by threading our way through it and talking to people we met about its remarkable beauty, vastness and resilience. The revelation that this trip was important not just to the trio making it but also to others was a gift from Scotty and the scores of people we spent time with in the twenty-one states we rolled slowly through.

Fifty miles from Tucumcari the orange and adobe-colored land began to thrust itself upward into buttes and mesas of ochre and cinnamon, and the wilder red rock in the distance promised utter majesty. The patient hand of time had sculpted the earth into art. This was a powerfully beautiful world where the ordinary seemed extraordinary. The bewitching headlights of a hundred-car Union Pacific train created a shimmering mirage as it curved toward us through the desert. We were in a place where a freight train becomes a magnificent thing.

In Santa Rosa, New Mexico we took in a collection of vintage cars and Mother Road memorabilia at an auto museum on Route 66. Adam and I dashed around photographing the gleaming Mustangs and GTOs, DeSotos and Impalas, Bel-Air Nomads and Dust Bowl–era panel trucks. I asked Dana to take a picture of Adam and me in front of a tomato-red 1950s convertible. Dana found us in the lens, then put the camera down, exclaiming, "Adam's taller than you!"

At least once a week over the past few months, before excusing himself from the table, Adam would look at me and say, "I'm taller than you," which required me to stand up and prove him wrong. I knew the day would come when he'd be right. We always stood eyeball-to-eyeball because we enjoyed looking into each other's eyes, his pair saying something like, "I'm not a kid anymore," and mine something like, "Hold on bud, I'm still your mother." I'd been winning by a hair until then. Now, hearing Dana's pronouncement, Adam turned to me, grinning. He was taller than his mother. If Dana, chief competitor in almost everything in life had said it, then it must be true.

We stood eye to eye. I disregarded the fact that Adam wore Nikes with massive rubber soles that lifted him two inches off the floor. I'd be conceding height to him soon enough. Why not now, while we were on an incredible journey that allowed him to be a boy most of the time, but called on him to be a man some of the time? I'd left Boston with a newly minted teen. I was standing, thousands of miles later, next to a beautiful young person I knew I could count on to take off his headphones and pitch in to help us through bumps in the road or add to our appreciation of this mighty adventure. On this trip, Adam was the man of the house — or van, or tent, or motel — for 12,000 miles. "You are taller than me. When did that happen?" We all grinned. Dana lined up her sights again and snapped the photo.

Later, we pitched our tent between fragrant cedars at a Route 66 campground. The manager, from Massachusetts, gave me a discount to celebrate our journey and applaud my having driven so far. I took canned beans, corn and tomatoes from the car top carrier, and Dana made chili over the campfire. The kids reconnoitered the game room for other kids, and I strapped on a headlamp and wrote in my journal. That night we fell asleep to the distant whistles and steady hum of long trains and the light drum of blessed desert rain over our heads.

~Lori Hein

26

Free a Marine to Fight

Marines everywhere can take pride in their
contributions to our great nation.
~General James L. Jones, USMC

Mom could hardly contain her excitement as we packed the car. We were headed to Washington, D.C. to visit my sister Marie. This family get-together had been planned for months. Mom had baked for the past two days. I'm pretty sure we loaded more food storage containers than luggage into the car that day.

Mom's dedication to being prepared was no surprise. She had been a United States Marine during World War II.

At the tender age of twenty, as President Roosevelt implored all Americans to do their part, Mom heard the call and took it more seriously than most young women. A poster she saw on the subway wall convinced her to join the U.S. Marine Corps. The sign read, "Be a Marine. Free a Marine to Fight." In the picture a young woman smartly dressed in uniform stood holding a clipboard in front of a military plane. By the end of the day, Mom had signed on the dotted line.

Her decision met with enthusiastic negativity on the home front. Mom's younger brother had already quit high school and joined the Navy. He was headed for the South Pacific. My grandmother was, to say the least, perturbed to learn that her only other child was leaving home for the military. Hiding her feelings was never my grandmother's strong suit. She pitched a fit. My grandfather, on the other hand, cried.

Mom stood her ground though, and in March of 1943 she headed off to Hunter College in New York where the first platoon of United States Marine women recruits gathered to train.

By the end of the war she had been promoted to Sergeant and served in Washington, D.C. and Philadelphia. She put her secretarial skills in high gear so that she could "Free a Marine to Fight." That's exactly what she would tell you if you asked why she enlisted.

Fast-forward about fifty years and her own platoon of children was plotting to surprise her with a tour of the National Museum of the Marine Corps.

"Where are we going?" she said, as we all piled in the car.

"Thought we'd take in some sights, Mom. You must know your way around Washington."

"I haven't been here in fifty years!"

"That's okay, Mom. I heard they haven't moved any of the important stuff," I said.

She rolled her eyes at me. "Oh you! Behave yourself."

The National Museum of the Marine Corps is located in Triangle, Virginia, so Mom began to get suspicious as we left D.C. and were passing through Arlington.

"Okay, give it up," she said. "Where are you taking me?"

"Um… We found a neat restaurant we thought you'd like. It's in Triangle, Virginia."

"Oh," she said. She didn't believe a word of it.

When we pulled into the museum parking lot she was dumbstruck. "Whose idea was this?"

"Ours," we said in unison.

"Can we go inside?"

"Sorry Mom, it's only for active military. We just thought you'd like to see the parking lot."

"You're not too big to smack, Annie! Now get out of my way. I can't wait to get in there."

My mom's new hip replacement slowed her down a bit, so while my sisters helped her out of the car and up the steps I scooted inside to purchase tickets.

Down the hall a bit and off to the right sat the reception desk with a fine looking Marine behind it.

"Good afternoon, how can I help you?" he said.

"I'd like to purchase tickets to tour the museum please. That's my mom and sisters coming through the front entrance. My mom was with the first class of United States Marine Corps Women's Reserves in 1943."

"She was?"

"Yes, indeed!" I said. "She read 'Free a Marine to Fight' on a poster and she decided to do it."

"What is her name?"

"Back then her name was Marie Sherin. She was a sergeant."

He grinned at me and said, "There's no charge for the tour Ma'am. I look forward to meeting your mother."

Then he watched Mom, with her slight limp, slowly make her way to the reception desk. When she stepped up to the counter the young Marine stood at attention, snapped my mother a crisp salute, and barked in drill sergeant style, "The National Museum of the United State Marine Corps is ready for your inspection Sergeant Sherin!"

Slightly stunned, Mom saluted back and told him to stand at ease. Then we watched as a shy smile crept across her face. I think she had trouble coming to grips with being recognized.

The young Marine emerged from behind the desk to shake her hand, but Mom would have none of it. Instead she hugged him good and strong with a force that transcended time. Marine to Marine, they embraced. She held him fast in thanks for his genuine kindness and respect for her.

"Semper Fi, young man."

"Semper Fi, Sergeant Sherin. You get the royal treatment when you've freed a Marine to fight."

For a second I really think she had the notion he was psychic until she caught a glimpse of me winking at my sisters.

My mom smiled. "Oh, that was a long time ago," she said.

"A Marine is a Marine, Ma'am — forever. We never forget our own."

I still tear up when I remember the look on my mother's face and how touched she was by that young man's sincerity. Without his recognition of her service, she'd have walked through that museum and never mentioned that she was with the first class of the United State Marine Corps Women's Reserve in 1943. Mom would've spent the entire time pointing out everything that related to my Dad's United State Marine Corps enlistment. She'd have talked about nothing but how proud she was of him. That was always her way.

Her new young comrade in arms ignited a flame, a sense of pride, and a willingness to share her experiences with us as we made our way through the exhibits. I'll always be grateful to him for making her feel so special and appreciated.

I have often heard my mom's age group referred to as the "greatest generation." I don't believe she ever felt that way until the kindness of a single Marine from the current generation honored and recognized that she did her part when she answered the call and "Freed a Marine to Fight."

~Annmarie B. Tait

Taking Root

*My garden of flowers is also my garden of thoughts
and dreams. The thoughts grow as freely as the flowers,
and the dreams are as beautiful.*
~Abram L. Urban

never thought I would miss dirt. I had imagined that when we moved from the northern tip of Illinois to the northern tip of South Carolina, I would miss snow more than anything. But it was dirt that I pined for... the black rich soil of the Midwest.

I am by no means a master gardener. But back in Illinois, the month of May always signaled the return of the flowers. After the long and often harsh winters, those colorful beauties always lifted my spirits. I would purchase bedding plants and then spend a happy afternoon planting them around our yard. The moist scent and texture of the soil made patting it down around a fragile new plant satisfying. It was like tucking a small child into bed. I trusted that soil completely; I knew that it contained everything my small flowers needed to grow and thrive. All that was required of me was adequate water.

During our two-day drive to South Carolina, I remember watching the changing scenery with interest. When we left Illinois, it was the last day of February. The trees were bare and the skies were gray. There was little to indicate that spring was on its way. But as we drove southeast, a transformation slowly took place. The first thing I noticed was the grass becoming greener. And then the trees began to show signs of budding leaves. Farther south, the trees were already flowering.

I was stunned to see tulips and daffodils already in full bloom in our new neighborhood. The bird activity was exciting too, as if they were scolding me: "You're late! Get busy!"

At the garden center, I eagerly filled my trunk with trays of my usual favorites. I also purchased a few unfamiliar plants that weren't hardy enough to grow up north. That was a bit intimidating. I thought about the bluebirds and the lizards that I was seeing for the first time in this southern climate. "I'm not in Illinois anymore," I thought to myself, feeling a bit like Dorothy in *The Wizard of Oz*.

I couldn't wait to spruce up our new yard, but first I had to contend with this strange orange soil that was hard as rock. I was able to dig down a bit but was dismayed that conditions didn't improve as I went deeper. I was dealing with clay now, and it resisted my shovel.

I glanced at the many trays of plants that I had carried home with such confidence. There was nothing to do but proceed. They weren't going to plant themselves.

Two hours later, I stiffly stood up, grabbing the fence for support. The battle was over, but I couldn't claim victory yet. The plants were in, but I worried about them. The soil hadn't enveloped them in the snug and cozy manner of the black dirt I was used to. The plants looked different, too, against this orange backdrop. I sprinkled them well and crossed my fingers.

While Illinois offered fertile soil, South Carolina offered warmth and sunshine. As the bluebirds busied themselves with their nests, my flowers began to flourish. They grew fuller and stronger. I even had success with the unfamiliar varieties, and I photographed these "new friends" with delight. I spent many afternoons on the patio, watching as hummingbirds and bees inspected the garden.

I've embraced the new environment, and I too am flourishing. South Carolina feels like home. That orange clay soil is part of the landscape that I now recognize and cherish.

America is a vast, wide and welcoming country. What an amazing array of natural beauty surrounds us, from the mountain peaks to the sandy shores. The terrain may change from state to state, but roots can still be established no matter where you plant yourself.

~Marianne Fosnow

28

Abandonment

*At the end of the day, a loving family should find
everything forgivable.*
~Mark V. Olsen

t was one of the highlights of my childhood, the year my parents
took the four of us on a cross-country trip from the East Coast
to the West in a station wagon and a trailer that we shared with
our cousins. The trailer at night was transformed into a little
house including a kitchen, storage and bedrooms for six and a dog.
Bathrooms, electric and water hook ups were supplied by the camp-
grounds for a nominal fee.

While we were camping in northern Kentucky our dog, who was
mostly Beagle, made a friend. She was a black, white and brown puppy
who seemed to have been abused and then abandoned by her owner.
The poor little thing was afraid and had been hiding out in a drainpipe.

Our family decided to save the pup. We offered her food, water
and a bed but she still wouldn't come out of the drainpipe. Eventually
my father frightened her at one end of the pipe so that she would run
out the other side, into our open arms.

After both dogs sniffed each other, the puppy, who we named
Kentucky, joined our family. I got the honor of sleeping with her the
first night.

We drove on, fighting with each other, complaining of boredom,
and tiring of the scenery outside as it turned into mostly farmland.
Finally, at the Illinois/Indiana border, we stopped for gas and a break.

As we all slid in, my mother asked me to count everyone to see if we were all there. Since I was the oldest at age twelve I took my job seriously.

Barry, eleven, was sitting in the back row, reading. Beth, five, was sitting next to the dogs, and Brian, seven, had already fallen asleep (a habit he seemed to be a master at) in the well with a blanket over his head. In those days station wagons came not only without seat belts in the back seat, but also with a "well" — the space between the second row and the rear facing third row.

"All accounted for." I told my mother.

And off we went. We passed the border and drove deep into Illinois, passing fields of corn and wheat. We stayed pretty quiet since Brian was sleeping. In fact it was a very quiet trip. Finally we reached a mountain scene and it was breathtaking. A waterfall fell from the top of a mountain, cascading along the rocks and producing a brilliant full rainbow. My father wanted to take a family photo in front of it.

We all left the car and posed in front of this colorful majestic sight. But Brian was still sleeping. "Wake him up; this is too beautiful to miss. Besides how long does he need to sleep?" my father asked.

I went to wake Brian up in the well and discovered there was no Brian under that blanket.

Within two minutes we were all in the car heading back to the gas station. We were speeding and were a bit afraid when we kept noticing police cars heading in the opposite direction. They didn't seem to notice our hurry. Yet as we crossed the border back into Indiana, a police car materialized in front of us. He pulled us over.

"Did you abandon your kid in a gas station a few miles back?" he asked accusingly.

"FORGOT my kid!" my mother corrected him with indignation. "Is he okay?"

The police officer followed us back to the gas station, where we found Brian having a blast. The gas attendants had shown him how to pump gas and lift up cars on the hydraulic lift; and they had given him an ice pop. He was having a great time and had no interest in coming with us.

Since the gas station had only written down the license plate of our trailer, which had our cousin's New York plates and not our New Jersey plates, the police never noticed our speeding station wagon as we had raced back to the Indiana border. Only when the police saw both the station wagon and trailer did they know who we were.

Although my parents (particularly my mother) found it to be a harrowing experience, Brian still remembers the day fondly.

And we got to see a little more of America.

~Tziyona Kantor

29

National Parks — America's Best Idea

*Nature's peace will flow into you as sunshine flows into
trees. The winds will blow their own freshness into
you, and the storms their energy, while cares will
drop off like autumn leaves.*

~John Muir, Our National Parks

whipped the vehicle to the side of the road, put it in Park, and jammed on the emergency brake. I jumped out and joined about fifty other people along the banks of the Madison River. We watched a pair of trumpeter swans gliding gracefully through the ripples of water, guarding six cygnets. Although I had seen swans before, rarely had I encountered so many babies with their parents.

My excitement matched the other Yellowstone National Park tourists. I really wasn't a tourist — I had lived at the park's west gate in West Yellowstone, Montana for more than a year, and I had resided in the region for nearly seven years. Even though I was a local, each time I traveled to America's first national park it felt like the first time.

Geysers, grizzlies, and mountain goats all fascinate me. Bison, eagles, swans, and elk stir my soul, and I love watching paint pots bubble and translucent water pools sparkle.

National parks are America's best idea, preserving unique lands and conserving wildlife for the public's enjoyment; Yellowstone was the first, set aside in 1872.

I began visiting national parks during the 1960s, when my parents and I drove from our Iowa home to the western states. Mom and Dad were like 1800s pioneers, envisioning vast landscapes and anticipating natural marvels; so we trekked west. Our family vacations were spent in Yellowstone, Teton and other forested and plains areas. I guess I caught the "park bug" from them for, after college, I moved to Montana and lived in Yellowstone country for more than fourteen years.

I took a job as a reporter for the *West Yellowstone News*, and within a year became editor. I witnessed and wrote about the release of wolves into the park, photographed bison and snowmobilers, and reported on the increasing number of tourists who traveled to this unique area. I hiked trails, took snow coach rides, and observed Sandhill cranes conducting their spring love dances. I even watched a pair of such cranes taking on a mama moose who was leading her gangly-legged youngster to a pond and must have ventured too close to the cranes' nest. That led to amazing sights and sounds, from flapping wings to deep-throated bellows. Parents fiercely protect their young, no matter their species.

Yellowstone never ceases to surprise me: a golden orb of harvest moon in October breaking through the steam at a geyser basin; the sound of elk bugling in September as fountains of water shoot up; a massive, wooly bull bison taking a siesta under a pine tree — an even greater surprise when you unknowingly encounter that great creature as you round the corner of a walking trail!

The smells of America's first national park are also incredible, from the sulfurous geysers to the fields of blue flax, yellow sunflowers, and purple lupine. Canvases of colorful wildflowers mingle with hues of greening grasses and all wave in the pine-scented breeze, stirring the senses as an artist stirs his paints. Yellowstone is magical, mystical, and vibrant.

Photographs from the early days of Yellowstone and other parklands speak to the acceptance of the world's first national park and of the importance of every one created thereafter. From Yosemite to the Grand Canyon, from Zion in Utah to Glacier on the Montana-Canada border, each park represents a unique environment with different species of wildlife and plant life. From red-rock deserts to alpine glaciers, from ocean coasts to prickly-pear plains, these environs beckon humans to return to a historic time, whether that's the cliff dwellings of Mesa Verde or the rainforests of the Olympic Peninsula. Every national park calls to the human spirit.

Despite the vast numbers of people who visit, one can find solitude in America's natural treasures. Perhaps that's by a lake or on top of a mountain; perhaps that's by the seashore or in a canyon. Sometimes the tranquility must simply be created by slowing down, even stopping, not racing through like one is driving an interstate.

The National Park Service turned 100 years old in 2016. America's best idea — to preserve, to conserve, to welcome and to educate the people about their public lands — began with visionaries. It remains because Americans and others value and appreciate the concept, the outcomes, and the opportunities these landscapes provide for recreation, refreshment, and replenishment. Even before the Park Service was established as an agency, history notes those who saw value in setting aside lands for the enjoyment of all the people, not for simply a select few who could afford to buy vast lands.

Since that day on the Madison River in Yellowstone, I have spent time in many of our nation's special parks. I've hiked dirt trails at Bryce Canyon in Utah, photographed fields of white bear grass in Glacier, and heard elk bugle during misty autumn mornings in Rocky Mountain National Park. I've camped in Olympic, fished in Teton, and picnicked at the Grand Canyon. Many generations have benefited from the visions and visionaries of 1872 and 1916, including me, and future generations will continue to do so. The spirit of America reigns in our national parks, for they remain America at its natural best.

~Gayle M. Irwin

30

Trucking Across the USA

*May the sun in his course visit no land more free, more
happy, more lovely, than this our own country!*
~Daniel Webster

glanced over at my husband's sturdy hands as he effortlessly
maneuvered the forty-ton, eighteen-wheeler along the icy pavement of Interstate 80. We were headed to Maine with a load of
lumber from the West Coast. The weather would continue to get
worse as we traveled east, but we were always warm and toasty in our
new Mack semi with a comfy walk-in sleeper.

I felt safe traveling across the country with Larry at the wheel; in
his thirty-year over-the-road driving career, he'd never had an accident.

Larry was a company driver for several years while the kids were
growing up. He worked hard and we diligently saved enough money
for a down payment on a new truck so he could live out his dream
as an owner-operator and have more control over where and when
he traveled. An added bonus was that I could go along with him now
that the kids were older.

We were truly living the American dream. There's no better way
to see our beautiful country than through the windows of a huge
semi-truck. When I first started tagging along, I noticed how we flew
right past exit signs for places I'd always dreamed of visiting, such as
Niagara Falls, Washington, D.C., Graceland, Nashville, Disney World,
Miami Beach, New York City, Las Vegas and Hollywood.

With a little arm-twisting, I eventually persuaded my husband to take these exits so we could see some of our country's well-known tourist sights. After all, he had worked hard for many years—it was time to slow down and enjoy our lives while still earning an income. Not everyone is so fortunate.

We had some awesome experiences, and some—well, not-so-awesome experiences! But, I wouldn't take back a single one of them. I could, after all, live with Larry's I-told-you-so annoyed looks as long as I got my way!

One of my suggested exits led us directly to the White House via Pennsylvania Avenue. "Honey, stop the truck!" I was so excited to take photos that I couldn't contain my enthusiasm.

"I can't just park in the middle of the street unless you want to end up in jail," he scowled!

"Of course you can! Just do it!" I commanded.

Having no choice, as I leapt from the truck during a momentary halt in the traffic, Larry stopped.

"I can do this in one minute," I shouted back as I ran toward the tall rod iron fence.

I was having the time of my life capturing awesome shots of the White House in all its glory. A nice couple offered to take a photo of me standing in the foreground, and I was the proudest American ever, until I glanced over to see the truck surrounded by what looked like the entire White House police force on and off their motorcycles. One officer had climbed up the steps and was leaning in the driver's window obviously questioning my terrified husband.

I grabbed my camera, quickly thanked my photographers, ran across the street and slithered into the passenger side of the truck quiet as a mouse.

"Like I said, officer, my wife insisted on getting a picture of the White House," my husband reiterated, pointing his finger directly at me.

The officer shook his head as if he understood wives, then told us in no uncertain terms that we had to leave the area immediately because semi-trucks can never, under any circumstances, stop in front of the White House. Relieved, we thanked him profusely, before the entire force escorted us out of the area. (They have since closed that portion of the street to all traffic.)

When we got to our delivery site at the U.S. Navy base in Coronado, California, we were horrified to learn we'd been hauling two large crated torpedoes under our tarps. YIKES!

My husband didn't talk to me for a week—I don't know if he was mad or just couldn't catch his breath.

Need I say, we didn't take another gratuitous exit for quite some time?

I did eventually get to see most of the sights on my list. Niagara Falls was breathtaking—so powerful! We were able to drive the truck right up to the parking area and it was just a short walk to the falls.

We also loved the warm waters of magnificent Miami Beach, and there is nothing comparable to the brilliance of Las Vegas in the distance on a clear night.

Two of my favorite side trips were to visit our sons who were in the military. What an honor to be able to spend Family Day with Darren at Fort Benning in Georgia. We took our two young grandsons, Timmy and Elijah, along on that trip. It was an awesome experience for them. The fact that we continued on to Disney World made it even better.

We visited our son Tim twice; once in Illinois while he was training at Great Lakes Boot Camp, and again at Coronado Naval Base when his ship, the USS Ranger, was in port.

It was an awe-inspiring decade traveling with my husband throughout the United States. Regardless of the season, the landscapes were breathtaking.

Our country's natural beauty is surpassed only by her people. We met so many wonderful new friends. I'll never forget eating lunch one fall afternoon at a lovely quaint restaurant in Vermont when two precious elderly ladies engaged us in conversation; we ended up spending a good portion of the afternoon chatting with them. They were very eager to hear about life in Oregon, and they told us about their lives in Vermont.

We never once had to experience being stranded when the truck broke down on the highway. Some thoughtful person always came to our rescue.

Whether traveling from Miami, Florida, to Seattle, Washington, or from San Diego, California, to Portland, Maine, my observation was continuously reinforced—Americans are the kindest people in the world.

We are a melting pot of many different races, religions, and ethnicities; but, we all have one thing in common—we love our great country!

~Connie Kaseweter Pullen

31

Traveling Human

Travel and change of place impart new
vigor to the mind.
~Seneca

At a rest stop on Interstate 80 somewhere in Iowa, I ended up in a conversation with a crusty old character from Nebraska. "Nebraska," he said, "is so wide open that just about anywhere you go, there's nothin' between you and anyplace else 'cept hundreds of miles of cows."

Seated on a picnic bench, he leaned back against the table and said with a chuckle, "Yep. Some of our state troopers will patrol up to 500 miles. When one pulls you over, it's not to give you a ticket. It's to have someone to talk to."

Neb, as I called him, made me laugh out loud. I met him about eight hours into a two-day road trip my husband Terry and I were taking from Detroit, Michigan to Custer, South Dakota where my father lived.

Normally, that conversation would never have occurred. Trips in the past had meant racing to every possible touristy thing in record time. But there was nothing like a life-changing blow to force you to slow down and open your eyes. A recent acquisition and reorganization at work had cost me my job. Seven years of proving myself were wasted, apparently. So this trip was different.

A few hundred miles before I met Neb, at a rest stop in Illinois, a man had strolled past me walking a strange little dog. Then I realized it was no dog, but a baby raccoon. Intrigued, I wandered over to where they had stopped.

"That's a baby raccoon," I said, pleased with my cleverness.

"Yep. His name is Buddy," the man answered. He explained that a car had killed Buddy's momma.

"Can I pet him?" I asked.

"Sure!" he replied. "He loves it."

I crouched beside Buddy and started stroking him. He seemed to be enjoying it when suddenly he went rigid and keeled right over.

I jerked back, horrified. "What did I do?"

The man laughed. "He wants you to scratch his belly."

Tentatively, I reached down and scratched. Sure enough, Buddy stretched out with delicious languor, his little eyes closed.

It was a timely encounter with a man and his baby raccoon, a strange and wondrous sight that I saw as I took my time exploring a part of our great country.

A few days later we were in Custer, South Dakota, staying in a little hotel called the Bavarian Inn. Every morning at breakfast, Terry and I would see this same big man seated alone at a corner table. He was a huge, imposing fellow with a goatee, an earring, tattoos, and a jet-black Mohawk ponytail. No sensible person would want to irritate this mass of a man.

One morning after breakfast I took a stroll to investigate the outdoor pool at the back of the property. The big man was in it, lazily backstroking. I turned to leave when a deep voice said, "Hi!"

I turned around. The big man swam to the edge, smiling, extending his enormous mitt at me.

"Jason," he said.

I mustered the courage to accept the hand and watched mine disappear inside of it.

It turned out that Jason, a mix of Choctaw and Cherokee, was living there for the summer while teaching at a school on a nearby reservation. He was also in the process of obtaining his doctorate in English. English had been my major. Jason and I were kindred sprits with the same love of the written word. More amazingly, this dangerous looking man's dissertation was on, of all things, female

Native-American poets.

Over the next week, Jason, my husband, and I breakfasted together, enjoying many lively conversations. One favorite thing about Jason was how he would raise a massive fist and say "Right on!" whenever he really liked something, though the phase has been long extinct. We sometimes honor our memories of Jason by mimicking him that same way.

A few days later, I met Linda. Linda owned a small grocery in Pringle, South Dakota, with a population of eighty. That day, we were meeting my father and his wife there for lunch.

Arriving a little early, Terry and I waited outside on a porch, seated in a row of eclectic chairs. A dusty truck pulled up and two burly fellows who looked alike climbed out, eyeing us as they shuffled past and into the store.

A minute later, one of them stuck his head out the door.

"You here for Al Kopka?" he said.

"Yeah," I replied. "He's my dad."

He came over. "Remember me?" he asked. "I'm Warren Schwartz."

I remembered him then. The other guy, his twin, was Lawrence. They were the locally famed handymen "The Schwartz Brothers." I'd met them several years earlier when my sister and I flew out for a visit. I realized I should have known them in the first place since they looked to be wearing the same clothes as last time.

Warren invited us inside. We followed him through the store to the back where several mismatched tables and chairs were arranged. Several other locals seated inside smiled at us as we timidly came in and took a seat with the brothers. To one side was an open kitchen area where a woman somewhere in her forties moved around like a tornado.

Within a minute, the tornado was setting plates of food in front of us. Warren and Lawrence dug in. My husband and I looked at each other. We hadn't ordered yet. We hadn't even seen a menu.

Seeing our baffled expressions, the woman said, "You're here to eat, right?"

"Uh... yeah," Terry said.

"Well, enjoy," she said with a smile and whirled off.

Apparently, if you were there, you were there to eat whatever Linda, the owner and cook, was making. That day it was ham steak, corn, potatoes, biscuits and lemon meringue pie. For six bucks, everyone got the same meal, made from scratch, and more delicious than anything in this world.

I managed to have a conversation with Linda afterward. She had purchased the store a year ago and business had been so poor she would cry herself to sleep some nights. Then she got the idea of serving a meal every day to attract more customers, so she renovated the back and built her little café. Word got around and people came — including a couple of tourists from Michigan.

Linda made me want to follow my dreams.

I discovered treasures of all sorts during that trip, mainly because I thought I'd lost everything else. I still encounter treasures now because now I know where they are. I even became grateful to have lost that job. Away from the chaotic commutes and corporate politics that can turn you cold, I was reminded of what I was part of — a great land filled with heart. The spirit of my home and its people helped me find my way again.

~Karen DeVault

32

I'm Not the One with the Accent

The accent of a man's native country remains in his
mind and his heart, as it does in his speech.
~François VI, duke de La Rochefoucauld

"The snow in Rome falls slowly on the Pope. The snow in Rome falls slowly on the Pope. How'd I do?" I asked my boyfriend, Tim.

"It still needs work," he replied, grinning.

Not even close! Rats!

It was 1979, and I'd traveled 3,000 miles across the country to attend the University of Oregon. I winced when one acquaintance after another asked, "Where are you from?"

I usually answered their question with, "How can you tell I'm not from around here?"

They would shrug their shoulders and ask again: "Where are you from?"

It was frustrating. I was from Wilmington, Delaware, and wanted to blend in with the students at the University of Oregon.

The previous year, my brother John's friend had joined my family for Thanksgiving and described his studies and travels beside the sparkling waters of the Willamette ("Wil-lam-et") River in Oregon ("Organ"). He encouraged me to explore the National Student Exchange Program, as he had. Always ready for adventure, I applied right away and was admitted for the following fall.

When I arrived in Eugene in August, I introduced myself around. I met good-natured but egocentric Westerners who insisted that I was the one with the strange accent. Imagine that! But when I assured them that they were the ones with the weird pronunciation, their eyes met and they stifled a laugh.

I noticed that a hint of a smile appeared around people's eyes whenever I said a word with a long "o." I didn't think anything of it at first. But one night, hanging out with some new friends at the local pizza parlor, I realized that it was later than I'd thought. I leapt up from the table and said loudly, "Oh, no! It's time to go home!" My "o" was a blend of half a dozen vowels. There it was again, only this time there was no mistaking it.

That night, as I lay awake, Eliza Doolittle came to mind. In *My Fair Lady,* an English professor, Henry Higgins, bet a friend he could cultivate the speech of young flower girl, Eliza, and pass her off as a well-bred, high-society lady. Higgins taught her to practice her a's by repeating, "The rain in Spain stays mainly in the plain." She did it. She pulled it off. So maybe, just maybe, I figured, if I practiced a phrase with one or two long o's, I might fit in with my new friends.

So I gave it a go: "The snow in Rome falls slowly on the Pope." I repeated it on my way to Catholic Mass each week; on my way to campus, the city bus windshield wipers swish-swish-swishing; in the coin-operated laundromat; and even in the Autzen Stadium football bleachers, where it rained as much as it did on the plain in Spain, apparently.

What did I know about Rome? Nothing. I'd never been outside the United States. The farthest from Delaware I'd ever been was the Poconos in northeastern Pennsylvania, where there was lots of snoeauw. No. Wait. Lots of snow.

I noticed that classmates chuckled and repeated my words, emphasizing the middle sounds, like t's in "spotted," "plotted," and "rotted." I found out that they pronounced everything more "laid back," as they called it, and used softer consonants. When my roommate told me that we were required to take a three-class riding series, I did a double take. Had I stumbled upon the Wild West I'd seen in the movies — saddles, stirrups, and reins? We had to take riding lessons? Didn't pioneers travel the Oregon Trail over a hundred years ago? Who still rode horses, for crying out loud?

She chuckled and explained that everyone enrolled in Bachelor's degree programs on campus had to take the writing classes.

I enjoyed Oregon so much that I transferred there and completed my Elementary Education degree. And, despite his funny way of saying things, I fell in love with Tim. We were married a year after we met. I taught Language Arts and English as a Second Language in public schools and as a private tutor for more than thirty years.

We raised three kids — Ben, Andy, and Emily — in Portland. They ran around town on roads like Couch (rhymes with "pooch") and Glisan ("Glee-san"), passing through towns called Aloha ("Uh-LOE-uh"), Tigard ("Tiger-d") and The Dalles (which, of course, rhymes with "the pals").

Today I call Oregon home. I live in a neighborhood that boasts families from around the world: Mexico, Ukraine, Romania, Russia, Japan, and Vietnam. All kinds of marvelous, multicultural stories are lived and told every day at my library, elementary school, waterfront market, and favorite restaurants. Many of those stories are told with accents. But, I am certain, most of the speakers would tell you they are not.

After thirty-seven years, I've adopted the Pacific Northwest and its peculiarities of speech as my own. Truth is, I wouldn't want to move anywhere else.

Not even to Rome.

~Lynn Hare

★ The ★ Spirit of America

America's Heroes

*Every good citizen makes his country's honor his own,
and cherishes it not only as precious, but as sacred. He
is willing to risk his life in its defense and is conscious that
he gains protection while he gives it.*
~President Andrew Jackson

33

Heroes in Plain Clothes

National honor is national property of the
highest value.
~President James Monroe

"'ll warn you — he's really rough around the edges. Gruff, with strong opinions. He's had a hard life," the visitor said. "But he's special, you'll see. And he's wanted a tour of Gettysburg his whole life. I told him I knew just the person to show it to him."

I wasn't so sure.

The visitor was a man who had been on my tours of the Gettysburg battlefield before. As a licensed battlefield guide here, I'm part of a century-long tradition of showing visitors the fields where the bloodiest battle fought in the Western hemisphere took place — a battle that served as a major turning point in the American Civil War.

People of all ages visit us from across the country and around the world. They come from all walks of life, all levels of education. All of them hunger to understand how our country came to blows with itself not so long ago, and how we managed to go on and become world leaders today in spite of it.

My visitor pressed me again, saying his acquaintance was one of these people, despite his downtrodden appearance and difficult demeanor. I'd already done many tours that day, but something in my visitor's eyes convinced me to take him and his friend on a tour.

"Great!" he exclaimed. "I'll take you to the truck."

We walked to the parking lot, where I met Medal of Honor recipient David Dolby. A big, burly fellow with a bushy gray beard, he smiled as he struggled out of the pick-up truck with his cane. His clothes had seen better days and his swollen, bruised feet were clad in flip-flops. But his sky-blue eyes twinkled, and from his neck hung the Medal of Honor suspended from a ribbon with its field of blue with white stars — absolutely spotless.

I knew that decoration immediately, because the Medal of Honor is a specialty of mine. It's the highest military decoration a soldier can receive in the United States — most of us know it as the award for bravery "above and beyond." Of the millions who have gone to war under our flag, fewer than 3,500 have received it. Dolby, who was awarded the medal for his actions in Vietnam, was the first recipient I'd ever met — the privilege of a lifetime.

As we drove through the battlefield, it became clear that Dolby knew a lot about Gettysburg but had never seen it before. Like so many of our visitors, he was astonished at its size and scope. He talked nonstop: about the horrors of Vietnam, how the government let the returning veterans down, how some officers didn't know what they were doing, how the war destroyed his health. I didn't expect the dour talk, but this man was about to teach me what real patriotism sounded like.

As we wound our way through sites like the Peach Orchard and Pickett's Charge, his attitude changed. He couldn't contain his admiration for the soldiers and the sacrifices they made to defend their ideals. At our stop in the Wheatfield — a bloody cauldron nicknamed the "Whirlpool of Death" by the soldiers who fought there — he tearfully said, "Good God, those boys were one of a kind."

I reminded him that he'd seen some serious combat himself.

It was May 1966 near An Khe, and Specialist 4th Class Dolby was serving his first tour of duty when his platoon walked into an ambush. In a flash, the enemy killed six and wounded several others, including his platoon commander. In the four-hour battle, Dolby took command, carried comrades to safety under fire, assaulted enemy machine bunkers until he ran out of ammunition, and marked enemy positions so that air strikes could stop the attack once and for all. One of his wounded comrades, who was quoted in Dolby's obituary, said that Dolby was "the bravest man I ever knew, maybe the bravest that ever lived. He saved all of us." Dolby volunteered for four more tours of duty after that battle, which earned him the Medal of Honor. He also received more accolades: the Silver Star, the Bronze Star, and the Purple Heart.

During our tour together, though, he brushed off his service and heroism. After the war, his fortunes sank; he fell on hard times. So when I had suggested that he, too, had fought bravely, he shook his head, looking down. "I'm just a normal person. I did what had to be done. But the ones who fought here..." his voice broke, then he composed himself and lifted his cane, gesturing across the Wheatfield, "They're the brave ones. We walk in their shadows."

We piled back into the pick-up and headed to the Devil's Den. I pulled into a parking place, and noticed a familiar face getting out of a van beside us: Brigadier General Harold Nelson, a West Point graduate who had served in Vietnam, too — a prominent instructor of future officers and author of many texts. He waved to me and smiled, so I introduced him to Dolby.

As Dolby hobbled out and around the truck, I said, "David, this is General Harold Nelson."

All the negative talk about his service melted away, duty and affection for his country emerging in its place, for not only did Dolby immediately come to attention as straight as his broken body allowed — but the retired general, upon seeing the medal around Dolby's neck, assumed a ramrod straight posture as he saluted him slowly, reverently. There were large groups of tourists around us, and they stopped, spellbound at the sight.

One young man said to me, "What's going on? I heard you say the one guy's a general — why did he salute that shabby guy first?"

I told him that when members of the armed services see another wearing the Medal of Honor, it's their duty to salute him or her first — no matter their rank — to show their regard for the medal-wearer's bravery and patriotism. The boy said, "That's cool. A brave guy doesn't need a bunch of stars on a uniform to be brave — right?"

I'll never forget that day or that moment. Two modern American men, two modern American warriors — ranks apart and thousands of miles from their battlefields — heroes in plain clothes standing on a long-ago American battlefield, bound by respect and a love of country for which they both, in their time and in their place, gave their all... for us.

~Renae H. MacLachlan

34

The Only Easy Day Was Yesterday

This nation will remain the land of the free only so long
as it is the home of the brave.
~Elmer Davis

"ISIS isn't even very close, Mom. They're fifteen to twenty miles away."

"Thanks. I feel so much better."

Such is the mentality of a Navy SEAL and the life of a SEAL mom.

The SEAL motto reads "The Only Easy Day Was Yesterday." When my son joined the service, I learned the truth of this motto, for my journey has been every bit as hazardous as his. Landmines lay ahead, emotional explosives capable of detonating at any time.

The journey started early. At the end of his junior year of college, my son felt God was calling him to the teams — the SEAL teams. Cream of the crop of the special ops community. The dropout statistics alone were staggering. He'd kicked the idea around before. But now, he trained in earnest. His upper body regimen alone made me shudder. I told him that his dad and I needed the year to prepare, too. He gave me a blank look and asked, "Why?" I couldn't find words to answer him.

A SEAL contract enables a sailor to go directly to SEAL training following boot camp. To earn one, a potential candidate must pass a battery of tests, one of which involves a timed swim, pushups, sit-ups, and pull-ups, ending with a timed run. Hence, the extreme exercise routine. When he tested in January, his scores were good, but we both knew he wasn't quite there. Awfully close though. Two weeks later, he tested again, and I knew he would nail it. He did. I was so excited for him. I shared the news at church that night — and promptly burst into tears. Reality hit like a two-by-four to the head.

My son and I had planned to hike the Grand Canyon the weekend after his graduation from college. He left for boot camp instead. Leaving him at college for the first time paled in comparison to dropping him off at the recruiter's office. I tried not to cry in front of him. His poor dad got stuck with mascara streaks, a runny nose, and a heartache that has never quite healed — even as Dad choked back tears of his own.

From then on, anytime I saw a uniform, my head turned, and my heart twinged. I wrote letters and scrambled any time the phone rang, fearing I would miss a precious five-minute phone call. Eight weeks passed, and we flew out for boot camp graduation. Our baby was a man in uniform now. We couldn't hug him enough. Still the same, but different too. We left for home while he stayed to prepare for the first half of SEAL training in California.

Special ops present unique challenges both for the wannabe and for the family. Trainees endure the joys of BUD/S, specifically Phase 1, the infamous weed-out phase for potential Navy SEALs. Salt water, sand, and suffering. For families? Lots of prayer and lots of waiting. If you want to improve your prayer life, this will do it. Hourly we wondered if our son had survived another day or had added his green helmet to the long line of those who dropped. A short text would tell us he was still in.

I've read more Navy SEAL books than any mom should. I scoured Dick Couch's *The Warrior Elite* daily. In the book, Couch, a former SEAL, tracks a class through BUD/S. It became my other Bible. In Hell Week, SEAL trainees receive about four hours of sleep over a five-day period. At home, we played, "What Do You Think He's Doing Now?" because we knew he was up. Still. Pray without ceasing took on new meaning. During Hell Week, no news is good news. Half of our son's class quit that week. When the news finally came that he'd made it we celebrated. He slept.

When our son came home at Christmas, the only time we saw him during BUD/S, he looked like a human action figure. We stared at him in awe. Who was this person?

BUD/S graduation passed with little fanfare, and SQT, Part 2 of training, initiated. Jump school. Cold-weather training in Alaska. (They also ran a marathon there — just for fun. It takes me three months to train for one.) My heart swelled with pride. No one receives better training than potential SEALs and that helped this mom sleep a little better. Until…

Until someone has an accident, and you're reminded that, with SEALs, even the training can kill you.

It was a cold day in San Diego when Class 298 graduated. Walking on the legendary Grinder gave me chills. Little white flippers stared at me from the blacktop, and I wondered which spot had been his. We heard stories from friends in his class. One told of how our son had saved his life in a medical close call during Hell Week. Class 298 rang the famous brass bell to celebrate their graduation, and nineteen of the original 167 class members received their Trident.

Now we await the end of his first deployment. Birthdays and holidays have piled up like wrapped gifts as we wait. We know where we think he is. And what we've been told he's doing. But even when he's stateside, we don't see him nearly enough.

Military life is tough. Distance is no friend to family. The job demands much from spouses too. As we trekked to San Diego for his wedding, the bride and groom sections were decidedly lopsided. Half of the groomsmen couldn't make the ceremony. They were active duty SEALs who had to work, though our youngest son was more than willing to take up the slack and escort two young ladies down the aisle instead of only one.

With all of its flaws, the big machine of the U.S. military turns by the blood, sweat, and tears of the awesome men and women who serve and that of the families and friends who support them. Our children shed the blood and sweat, and we at home make up the difference with tears.

My shipping guy knows me when I come in. Last time, as he printed labels for Iraq, he asked me to describe the contents of my boxes.

"Cake."

"And this one?" he asked.

"More cake."

He smiled.

As for support, it's been humbling. Relatives deluged our son with boxes at Christmas. Many more have prayed for him. Those closest to us check in often, especially during deployment. Then there are those who have never even met him. World War II vets. DEA agents. Dance moms. Soccer moms. Friends from church.

This is the America that makes me proud. The America that values service and sacrifice. The America that understands that if it's worth having, it will come at a cost. The America that fights from its knees in prayer, while its sons and daughters take their weapons into the fray.

This America stands for something, and I'm proud to be a part of it.

~Gayle Veitenheimer

35

And Justice for All

Let gratitude be the pillow upon which you kneel to
say your nightly prayer. And let faith be the bridge you
build to overcome evil and welcome good.
~Maya Angelou

The sound of the helicopters reverberated against the mountains, filling the canyon with a deafening noise. It was almost one in the morning, but the normally quiet streets were bustling.

I was standing outside my house, tears streaming down my face. I had been crying for hours, but it felt like a minute; I had no concept of time. Earlier that night, I had returned home from work to find my mother lifeless. She had been killed during a heated argument with a family member and her killer had fled, leaving me to find the grisly scene.

In those excruciating hours, friends and family arrived and filled our suburban street. I cannot recall everyone who showed up; their faces meld together in my mind like a collage of love. All I know is that I eventually made my way to a neighbor's home; the owners were longtime friends of my mother's, and they had graciously opened their doors to the circus outside.

I sat on their couch, being comforted and awkwardly hugged by people coming in and out. They said all the right things, but their words sounded empty and my heart ached too much to believe them. Eventually, a man I had never seen before entered the room and sat down with the crowd that had gathered.

"Hi Amy. My name is Detective Michael Valento," he began. "I'm here to bring you and your mother justice."

Justice. It sounded like such a familiar concept, one I had been brought up to believe was around every corner in America. Our country was built on justice and fairness... but nothing about that night seemed just or fair to me. Despite fully knowing its meaning, in that moment I couldn't fathom ever feeling that justice had been served. My mother could not be brought back to life.

"Th-thank you," I replied. I didn't know what else to say.

A few months later, Detective Valento was a regular part of my life. Our phone calls became an almost weekly occurrence. Each time we spoke Mike vowed that he would do everything in his power to ensure my mother's killer would be sent to prison as expeditiously and as permanently as possible. I believed him at the time, but as the months wore on, and the number of hearings grew, I lost hope.

Despite my emotional struggle, I grew to know and care for Mike. He was a kind, gentle man with a heart of gold. His intentions were of the purest, and he symbolized the hope I once had. He was a wonderful advocate. He continued to call me often, checking in to see if I was okay, asking how my wedding plans were going, updating me on everything that was happening.

Alas, the months turned into years, and very little happened. Justice and the American way were not prevailing. My hope morphed into anger. I was angry my mother's killer hadn't been accorded his punishment. I was angry my mother was gone. I was angry that a system I had been reared to respect was so clearly failing. My mother's murderer was playing the system, and he was getting away with it. Or so I thought.

One particularly hard day, nearly four years after my mother's death, I came close to losing it. I had been in court all day and I was mentally, as well as physically, drained. Mike had been in court with my fiancé and me, sitting by our sides the entire time. I turned to him and pleaded, "When will this end? Why is he being protected? Why hasn't he been convicted? Life needs to go on."

Mike thought carefully for a moment. He looked at me kindly

and said, "I know it doesn't seem like it, but this is all for you and for your mother. You have to understand that our legal system, although at times seemingly imperfect, is protecting you. If we didn't cover all of our bases right now he could appeal and possibly be free one day. So, for now, we must be patient. I know it's hard, but in America good things come to those who wait." Again, my heart was so heavy I couldn't quite grasp his words, but this time I accepted the situation. I waited patiently for another year.

Five years and two days after my mother's murder, a judgment was delivered. My brother was given a sentence of fifteen years to life. I was as relieved as I could be. Justice had finally been served and I could begin to repair my own life, which had been shattered that horrific night. I remember as we fled the courtroom for one final time, Mike had leaned in for an embrace.

After our hug he pulled back and said, "See. I told you all would be right in the end."

At that moment my heart filled with warmth that it had not felt for a while, warmth ignited by someone who had been a complete stranger a few years ago. This man, despite knowing nothing of the content of my character, dedicated a large portion of his life to fight so I could regain control of mine. Mike's actions showed me the camaraderie and strength America instills in its citizens. His upstanding dedication to his country and position of service helped change my life for the better.

Detective Mike Valento of the Los Angeles County Sheriff's Department exemplifies everything that is right in our country and with our police force. And although there is no reason left to carry on a relationship with him, my adoration, respect, and gratitude for him will never diminish. For, it's men and women like Mike who gave me my strength, hope, and life back, and I can never be thankful enough.

~A.B. Chesler

Shorty and Me

Heroism is the divine relation which, in all times,
unites a great man to other men.
~Thomas Carlyle

t was early morning when I pulled into the parking garage at
Cleveland Hopkins International Airport. I located the baggage
carousels and noticed a banner that read, "Welcome Veterans."
I found the registration line for "Guardians" and received an
information packet and two T-shirts: one for me and one for my hero.

While I was getting organized and putting on my T-shirt, the
veterans on the August trip with Honor Flight Cleveland started to
arrive. As a guardian for the day, my job was to make sure my veteran
was safe and fully enjoyed himself on his trip to Washington, D.C.

I finally located my hero among the sea of handsome faces in wheelchairs. Before I could crouch down and introduce myself, Shorty — his
nickname — quickly stood and took my hand. I was delighted when
he looked me square in the eye, as I am six feet tall myself, and we
laughed as he told me the story behind his moniker.

"I used to be even taller, but age does that to a body," Shorty
stated and then introduced me to his son who was dropping him off
that morning.

Shorty was in the Navy in World War II and had been stationed
stateside, in Texas, as a supply officer. He was a pleasant man, not too
talkative but bright and cheery nonetheless. We hit it off from the start.

"Let's get this T-shirt on you, Shorty, so everyone will know it's your day today, okay?"

We said goodbye to his son and I wheeled him over to the men's room. All the veterans are required to ride in a wheelchair whether they need one or not. It's for safety reasons but, truthfully, it makes it a bit easier for us guardians to keep up with some of these guys.

There were a lot of us — enough to fill a large plane — and the excitement mounted as we paraded through the airport to the cheers and applause of our fellow travelers.

The guardians sat at the front of the plane, while the veterans sat together and shared stories with each other. I wished I could have heard some of them, but the point was for the vets to be with each other.

When we landed in Washington the fanfare was even louder, and a number of servicemen stationed in the area had turned out to shake the veterans' hands. It was so heartwarming that I had a difficult time keeping my composure.

The staff of Honor Flight Cleveland were spectacular and worked with amazing precision to get the veterans on and off the buses at every stop we made. Their hard work and competence made everything go smoothly.

When we pulled up to the National World War II Memorial, the gasps were audible. It is a breathtaking sight. I waited as Shorty stepped off the bus and into his wheelchair and then we slowly wheeled our way inside.

As we entered, it was evident this was going to be a special moment for Shorty. He was quiet and clearly overwhelmed by the enormity of it all as we walked around to read each marble panel. We finally had to sit and take it in as a whole.

"Do you feel like this monument is for you, Shorty?" I asked.

"Yes, I do, I truly do. For all us guys."

"I think you should claim a part of it, just for you. How about that piece up there?" I said, pointing up toward a corner of a panel that said "Freedom."

"Perfect," said Shorty. And then he asked me: "What made you decide to become a guardian?"

"Well, my father was a World War II vet. A Coast Guardsman in what you guys called the 'Hooligan Navy' back then. He died before I could bring him here to see this beautiful place, so I thought, since it's his birthday this month, I'd help another veteran in his honor."

"I'm so glad you did. I'm enjoying your company."

"And I, yours, Shorty."

We sat in silence for a while longer and then he had his picture taken standing next to the part of the monument that was marked "Ohio" and we boarded the bus.

We visited all of the Washington monuments that day. They honored the sacrifices that our servicemen have made, and they served as memorials and as healing places. The healing was in full force when we watched the changing of the guard at the Tomb of the Unknown in Arlington Cemetery. I was honored to take the arm of one of our frailer veterans who was trying to stand and salute when the guard passed. As he began to teeter a bit I whispered in his ear, "He feels your presence, Sir," and helped him back to his seat.

After a very long, emotion-filled day, we returned to Hopkins Airport in the late evening. A bagpiper led the way back down to the lower level as well as, much to Shorty's surprise, several of our Navy's finest in their starched dress whites.

When we reached baggage claim we were reunited with Shorty's son, but before we left we made sure to get our picture taken with a group of those Navy men and women, each one making Shorty feel so very special and honored.

It was difficult to say goodbye to Shorty and tears of gratitude flowed down my cheeks as I watched him walk away. I mean, who but God could orchestrate the perfect hero for me, right down to his six-foot frame?

Driving home, I couldn't help but reflect on the Will Rogers quote that graces the back of my Honor Flight Cleveland T-shirt: "We can't all be heroes, some of us get to stand on the curb and clap as they go by."

And some of us, by God's grace, get to be Honor Flight Guardians.

~Cathryn Hasek

37

The Cell Phone

True heroism is remarkably sober, very undramatic.
It is not the urge to surpass all others at whatever
cost, but the urge to serve others, at whatever cost.
~Arthur Ashe

My husband and I were having a good night. We had just seen a comedy, emptied an entire large bucket of popcorn and a bag of M&Ms, and laughed like two carefree kids. As we crossed the parking lot and contemplated our next high caloric activity, I noticed something on the asphalt.

"Oh, wait!" I said, and broke free from his hand. "What's that?"

"Looks like a wallet," he said, jangling his car keys and watching as I inspected it.

"Nope. It's a cell phone." But, not just any cell phone — it was the most expensive model on the market. When I opened the case, the phone was locked, so I couldn't scroll through the contacts to find the owner.

"You want to leave it at the ticket booth?" he asked.

"Are you kidding? No way! I'd rather keep it safe and find the owner myself."

As we walked to our car, my husband was grumbling about the responsibility I was taking on. But I had seen the picture on the screen, and it was of a young soldier — probably the owner's daughter. I wanted to reunite this phone with its owner.

Once we settled in and drove off, the cell phone vibrated. When

I opened the case, the smiling soldier background lit up again. It was an incoming text, but I couldn't respond because the phone was locked.

Instead of driving straight home, we went to a nearby gas station to fill up, which was clearly my husband's way of killing time. He really wanted me to get rid of this phone. And then it happened. The phone rang, the screen said "Home" was calling, and I would finally find the owner.

"Helllooooo! I have your phone!" I said happily, secretly excited to give someone the news that a Good Samaritan had found his phone.

The gentleman on the other end of the line was ecstatic and thanked me for finding his phone. He asked if we would return to the movie theater, where he would meet us. I agreed, and he thanked me repeatedly. With a light heart, I ended the call.

"I told you it was the father of a soldier," I said triumphantly. I smiled to myself as we turned out of the gas station's parking lot and headed back toward the theater. Getting an idea, I reached into my purse and found a scrap of paper. On it, I scribbled the sentence "God bless your soldier" and drew a heart beside it. I slipped the note inside the cell phone case.

Back at the theater, we found a big, burly man waiting for us. "Thank you so much," he said with relief when I approached. "I thought I was going to have to turn it off, cancel it, the whole thing!"

My heart swelled with joy from making him so happy. Privately, I couldn't wait for him to read my little blessing for his soldier.

"It's my pleasure," I said, and then watched as the man waved happily and fairly skipped to his own car. He thanked me at least three more times.

The man drove in one direction and we drove in the other. "You can tell he's a good person," my husband said as we headed toward the freeway, his tone suggesting that he'd surrendered to the rightness of what we'd just done.

"Yes," I said sighing, allowing myself to feel good as I remembered the man's grateful smile. I don't know what it is about doing a good deed, but the person doing the deed always seems to feel even better than the beneficiary.

We hadn't driven four blocks when we heard a horn blaring. I pressed the button to roll down my window, and it was the same man, speeding to catch up with us. He had his window down, too.

"Thank you so much for your note!" he hollered as he drove alongside our truck.

I absolutely beamed. "Oh, you are so welcome!" I yelled back, giving him my best Forrest Gump wave.

If happiness manifested itself as helium, I'd have floated right out the window.

He continued. "I appreciate it so much! The soldier is my daughter," he yelled out his window. "She died October 1st, so thank you so much for that message!"

In that instant, my helium was gone. All the previous euphoric feelings I experienced morphed into unspeakable grief and love for a total stranger.

"I am so sorry," I yelled back, my smile gone, my eyes filling with tears. It had been just six months for him.

"Thank you! She was twenty! Thank you!" He waved, still smiling, and drove off.

I stared out the window until my husband quietly pushed the button to close it from the driver's side. We were both too stunned to speak.

Inside our car, if it weren't for the road noise, the only sound would have been my soft weeping, caused by the quick and profound grief I experienced through a stranger's loss. We have a twenty-year-old, and I put myself in this man's shoes.

"Wow," my husband finally said. "Why do you think he needed to tell you that?"

I knew. As a mother, I knew.

"It's his way to keep her memory alive," I said, wiping the tears off my face with both hands. "He wanted to talk about her. It's his way of dealing with the grief."

And, in that moment, I knew why I'd found the cell phone. It was a reason so much bigger than saving someone $500. I was directed into this man's circle of healing — a stranger — through a lost cell phone, and reminded again of the sacrifices of those who serve our great nation.

~Dana Martin

38

Good Soldiers

What are the values of a Good Soldier? Freedom and
courage. Freedom is what makes us fight, and courage
is what keeps us from running away.
~Roger Nye, The Challenge of Command

'**ve** lost track of how many people around town have stopped
me or phoned after they read that story — my story — in the
newspaper. I have even received thank you cards. All this
attention is a little overwhelming," confided the ninety-year-
old World War II Navy veteran.

In the Pacific Theater, he had participated in ten invasions on
board a big battleship, the USS Colorado. However, to the community,
Charlie Ripper had been regarded as our retired barber and former
councilman, just another well-respected senior citizen.

Summing up the surprise of his Central Texas friends and neighbors when they learned of Charlie's story, Lou Ann Adcox said, "Who
knew?" She was right. Before the article appeared, who indeed knew
about Charlie's wartime exploits?

"You know what I wish?" Charlie said. "I wish all the boys in this
county could tell you their war stories. You could write them down
and share them just like you did mine."

I had read that 500 U.S. World War II veterans are dying every
day, so Charlie's suggestion was compelling. All too soon, there would
be no veterans left to interview. When I discussed the idea with others,
they cautioned me that World War II veterans were reluctant to talk,

plus many were in poor health.

Nevertheless, The Fayette County Record's publisher Regina Keilers and editor Jeff Wick were enthusiastic about the opportunity. We agreed that I would listen to as many war stories as possible and put them on paper. Then I would go back to each veteran and read him his story to ensure its accuracy. Our goal was to publish a special insert to mark the 70th anniversary of the end of World War II.

I listened to Dennis Rudloff, an Army Air Force sergeant, who was a crewmember onboard a B-24 bomber stationed in England. On his first mission to Germany in 1944, one of the aircraft's bomb bay doors was damaged by enemy shrapnel, leaving a 500-pound bomb stuck half in and half out. As the bomber headed back to England, Dennis and the bombardier crept out on a six-inch ledge to release it. They were thousands of feet above the ground without parachutes. When Dennis dropped his screwdriver somewhere over Germany, he resorted to beating the crimped metal of the bomb door with the barrel from a 50-caliber machine gun. Finally, over the English Channel, the bomb dislodged, hitting the water with a spectacular splash. Had they not been able to release the device, the crew would have had no recourse but to parachute out of the plane and ditch it.

Ted Wolfram, an Army Air Force second lieutenant, fretted at having to serve as a flight instructor in West Texas before finally being assigned to fly a C-46 transport, the largest two-engine aircraft of its kind at the time. For one year, he flew The Hump, an aviation route over the eastern end of the Himalayan Mountains between India and China, transporting diverse cargo such as bombs, food, Jeeps, spare parts, engines, gasoline and tents. Although his aircraft was high above the fog and clouds and the dreaded updrafts and downdrafts, Ted was all too aware that below was the Aluminum Trail, a string of C-46s that had crashed during missions just like the ones he was flying.

Frank Stastny, a ninety-seven-year-old who had been a private first class in the 339th Ordnance Depot Company, vividly remembered the events of his first German air raid on New Year's Eve 1942 in Casablanca, Morocco. There was so much gunfire that the American soldiers could see their shadows, but Frank couldn't desert his post as a guard to take refuge in an air raid shelter. He recalled seeing fire and smoke coming from the tail of a German plane and watching it spiral down into the sea.

Charles Mazoch vividly reminisced about spending 119 days on the island of Luzon in the Philippines where his unit traded shells with the enemy every day. The Americans had been pulled off the front line for a rest in mid-August 1945 when they received the good news that the war had ended. On the day Charles arrived home in November 1945, he accompanied his sisters to a dance down the road. Later that evening, he marveled at how little the world had changed for his family while he had been fighting for his life in the jungle half a world away. He gave thanks to God that they had been spared.

A technical sergeant in the Third Army, Eugene Hollas recollected not only the hand-to-hand combat in battles during his wartime service in France and Germany but the noise, the destruction and the stench of dead men and rotting livestock. As the Americans pushed toward Germany in battle after battle, Eugene was wounded three times and awarded three Purple Heart medals. A lesson he learned from firsthand experience is how much abuse a human body can withstand. Eugene will never be sure whether he was just lucky to come home or if a guardian angel was looking out for him.

When he was drafted, Johnny Kobersky was forced to sell the cattle and poultry on the family farm, as well as find somewhere for his invalid widowed, adoptive mother to live. When Johnny was inducted in 1942, he left behind his eighteen-year-old wife of five days, Hazel, with her family. Johnny was assigned to the operation of a howitzer gun that fired shells measuring five inches in diameter. It was a very accurate but deafening piece of equipment that he frequently blasted as the Army's 84th Infantry Division moved across France, Holland and Germany.

* * *

These veterans — and others I listened to — were articulate, yet humble. Several shed a few tears as they talked, but talk they did. Some stories were poignant. Others were upsetting. Still others were amusing. The bottom line was that each man still believed in the freedom that his country had called upon him to defend. It was a privilege to spend time with them and save their stories, which otherwise might have been lost.

Charlie's wish to see his buddies' war stories in print came to fruition when "Veterans' Voices" was published in *The Fayette County Record*. The special newspaper section featured forty World War II veterans and more than 100 photos, as well as clever, nostalgic advertising purchased by area businesses and organizations.

The community reacted with unbridled excitement. Overnight, the World War II veterans were regarded as heroes, although they scoffed at the description. Their phones rang, they received countless hugs and handshakes and notes arrived in the mail as family members, friends and neighbors — and even strangers — thanked them for their service.

"It was fascinating to learn what each of these small-town boys did in World War II that has produced such a tremendous legacy for our country," said Erin Wied, who has known some of the veterans all her life. "By finally sharing their war stories, they always will be remembered."

For a veteran of any war, there is no greater honor.

~Elaine Thomas

39

A Change of Command

Where liberty dwells, there is my country.
~Benjamin Franklin

I had ventured on to what was then called McGuire Air Force Base, a mere twenty miles from my home in New Jersey — but a place that seemed a universe away. The base was teeming with activity, with uniformed men and a few women. I felt like an alien.

I had come to hear a lecture. Although I can't recall the subject I do recall vowing to go back someday and learn more about what it meant to be in the military.

"Someday" finally happened when I had received a personal invitation from a man with whom I'd corresponded for several years, but had never met. Colonel U.K., as he was affectionately known, was moving on in 2015. He was leaving the unit after serving as Commander for four years, and was off to a different base in Atlanta.

And there was to be a Change of Command ceremony to which I was invited. Even the event name sounded impressive!

"Change of Command" is far different than a civilian job title change. It has a ring of authority and great responsibility about it, certainly not lost on this civilian babe in the military woods.

Because I write a column for local papers, the Colonel had occasionally alerted me to events at the base, now known as Joint Base McGuire-Dix-Lakehurst, but somehow I had never gone to any.

I admit that there was something intimidating to me about these vast places where regimentation and order ruled. This civilian is known for her general lack of order — just ask my family — and I typically feel out of place when surrounded by those who know how to look spiffy and perfect.

But I was indeed curious.

That's because this colonel had sometimes surprised and delighted me by responding to some of the personal essays that I frequently wrote. I was amazed by his warmly human side.

My assumption was that these high-ranking military guys were pretty tough cookies, and he'd shown me otherwise. I loved his insights and his generosity of spirit, and decided it was high time to meet this Colonel U.K.

I went to the base for that Change of Command ceremony with my husband Vic, who had served as an officer for two years in the Air Force before we ever met, back in the days of ROTC commitments.

Vic had loved the Air Force, but it was a chapter of his life we didn't share. Suddenly, those days were coming back to him as we drove on to the massive Joint Base where I felt it again — that instant intimidation. Uniforms and military lingo — not in my comfort zone.

We passed muster and went on to a pre-reception for Colonel U.K. Standing in blue dress uniform with military ribbons and commendations marching all across his chest, was the colonel with a broad smile. A warm and wonderful smile. In some way, he seemed to me like the modern version of a knight in shining armor — one willing and eager to defend his country. That notion became very real to me as I watched him and heard what people were saying about him.

I'm 5'2" on a good day; the colonel is toweringly tall. There we were, an awed civilian and this imposing, seasoned leader of 2,500 men and women who clearly admired and adored him.

My general sensory overload continued at the sight of hundreds of those uniformed men and women gathering soon in a giant hangar. Up on the stage, with a huge American flag behind them, was an imposing Major General, the new commander of the Wing, and of course Colonel U.K.

There's nothing fancy about an Air Force hangar, but it somehow felt like a sacred space as we stood to hear "The Star-Spangled Banner" as I've never heard it sung before. It was not just the airman's voice, but the setting, that instantly had me choked up.

I think I'd almost forgotten that once upon a time, when I was a kid, patriotism was the norm, and men in uniform (back then we seldom saw women) stirred something easier felt than explained. Something like reverence.

Yes, that's what I felt as the Major General straight out of central casting talked about the colonel's magnificent leadership, his airlifts and medical support missions and humanitarian relief operations.

Who knew that this man, my South Jersey neighbor, had flown combat missions during Desert Storm, been Chief of Safety at a Royal Air Force base in England, and somehow also managed to fly missions to check out tropical storms and hurricanes?

When Colonel U.K. himself got up to speak, his emotion was palpable. Even though he smiled a bit, and generously thanked so many others, it was clear that this was a tough and bittersweet moment for him — and for all of us in the hangar.

His two handsome teenage sons sitting in the front row listened to their dad apologize to them for missing so many of their games and events; he thanked his wife for doing what military wives do: handling the home front.

By the end of his remarks, I was drowning in the mascara I should never have worn, and thinking how ironic it was that my first meeting with this man was likely to be my last as well. In that one summer afternoon, I had leaped over some of the intimidation, but not the awe.

I don't care how corny it sounds — sitting at that Change of Command ceremony thirty-five minutes — and light years from my home town — I came to understand the real meaning of the three words that flowed that day about service to this country: "Pride." "Professionalism." "Passion."

And to deeply respect them.

~Sally Friedman

Living to Serve

*When you are running away from an emergency, first
responders are the ones running toward it.*
~Bill Bierbaum

t was a sunny day, but the man lost control of his vehicle. His
pickup truck, stuck under a larger truck in the accident, was
dangling inches away from going over a high embankment, held
by a guardrail that was close to letting go.

The man was alone, incredibly scared, and pinned to his seat,
unable to get out. But then a paramedic with nerves of steel and a
heart of gold decided to climb into the passenger seat to keep the man
calm until he was rescued. Although the paramedic was being called
by his crew, and told that it was dangerous, he stuck with the man and
kept him talking — and even laughing — through the entire ordeal.

This man was saved, suffering only some bruises and scrapes. He
called the paramedic a hero. Later, during an interview, the paramedic
was modest, saying that this is what people in his line of work do.
They do everything they possibly can for those who need them. To
me, they sound like real-life guardian angels.

The paramedic in the story is known in our community as a hero.
Personally, I call him Dad.

~Samantha Harmon-Thompson

Freedom Fighter

How important it is for us to recognize and celebrate
our heroes and she-roes!
~Maya Angelou

As the wife of a veteran who battles post-traumatic stress disorder, I had just finished a very fulfilling speaking engagement to other wives of warriors battling PTSD. Now I was ready to relax and unwind on my flight home. I was thankful to be sitting next to a pleasantly quiet young lady, who did not say a word, the entire flight, but seemed to be elsewhere as she gazed out the window.

The plane had barely gotten off the ground when behind me came a vulgar streak of profanity in a piercing female voice (which I'm certain carried throughout the entire plane). This lady let it be known that she already had a few drinks and was on her way to party in San Francisco for the weekend. Woohoo!

Nosy person that I am, I had to sneak a peek. She was young, tall, wearing very short shorts, had lengthy tan legs, long golden hair, and a face that would sell a million magazines. Stunningly attractive by most standards. What was missing, I realized later, was a smile.

As hard as I tried to tune her out, I could not. Every sentence out of her mouth featured the words "I" or "me." I have never heard one person talk for so long about herself... so loudly, and with such foul language. And it was not even interesting. She was consumed with bars, places to go, men... all about what SHE liked, where SHE lived, what SHE wanted to do and what SHE wanted to see. Me. Me. Me. So empty! So annoying! So sad.

And still not a peep out of the lady next to me.

Finally we landed, but were informed that we had to wait on the tarmac for the gate to open up. All those who had connecting flights panicked! Passengers were abuzz with anxiety. Including the lady next to me. From the corner of my eye I saw her texting her mother asking for prayer. Would she make her connection?

Still no movement by the plane.

So we talked.

It turned out this quiet, amazing lady was in the Navy — a warrior — and was going for a three-day weekend to meet her Navy warrior husband in Hawaii, for the first time in a year and a half! And then they would have to wait another sixteen months before they could be together again! Wow!

I expressed my heartfelt gratitude to her and her husband for their service and sacrifice. And what a gracious smile she gave me. It truly was an honor to meet her!

Finally the plane arrived at the gate and everyone scrambled. I watched as the first female (hardly a lady) took off running to catch her flight for three nights of partying in San Francisco, all the while spewing offensive expletives.

And turning, I saw my seatmate, truly a classy lady, running to catch her flight for three days of celebration and closeness with her warrior husband.

As I walked on, I felt overwhelmed. I managed to pray for both women, and gave thanks for one. The one who ensured the freedom of the other to unthinkingly head off to her party, totally oblivious to what that freedom has cost millions of our best.

~Welby O'Brien

42

Sacrifices

America was not built on fear. America was built
on courage, on imagination and an unbeatable
determination to do the job at hand.
~President Harry S. Truman

I felt like my heart was being torn in two! My daughter, Michele, bought tickets for me to attend a Christian Women's Conference in Minnesota with her and my granddaughter, Katie. Around the same time Katie would be turning twenty-one years old and I really wanted to be there for that special celebration.

The problem was that I couldn't leave my husband, John, at our home in California alone. He is 100% disabled due to PTSD contracted after his service in Vietnam, which left him with nightmares and depression. He has epilepsy and the seizures occur randomly. The seizures have gradually affected his brain until he has very little short-term memory. He is waiting for carpal tunnel surgery for tremors in his hand and has therapy for fall prevention due to a loss of balance and several bad falls. He has to wear a CPAP machine at night for sleep apnea and needs help hooking it up. He can no longer drive and I have to administer his pills morning and night so he won't forget. How could I leave him?

John's psychologist at the VA told us about a respite program where caregivers can leave their loved ones twice a year for fifteen days to give them a break. She called the program for us and found out that John more than qualified for the program and asked the social worker to call me.

Monique, the social worker, called to ask me when I needed to leave John and I gave her the dates in October. "Oh," she said, "we are booked through January. I'm so sorry."

"Do you have a waiting list?" I asked her.

"No, I'm sorry, we don't, but you can check back from time to time to see if there have been cancellations."

"Okay, thank you." My heart was heavy when I called Michele to tell her I didn't think I would be able to come.

"You should just get your ticket in case something changes," she suggested.

I waited a few weeks and then called Monique at the VA. "Have there been any cancellations?" I asked her.

"No," she replied, "and now there are no vacancies until February."

I talked it over with John and he kept telling me to just go — that he would be fine at home by himself. I didn't feel like I could leave him alone for twelve days. What if he had a seizure or fell down the stairs? No one would be there to help him. There was no way he could skip his medications even once and I knew that although he tried hard to take care of himself, he wouldn't remember to take his pills on time.

"Just get your ticket and go," he begged me. "I'll be fine."

I was so uncertain about what to do. I really wanted to visit Michele and her family. It had been three years since I had been there for Katie's graduation. I prayed, "God, I feel so confused. If You want me to go to Minnesota, please help me because I don't know how to make this happen."

The very next morning, Monique called me. "Don't get too excited," she began, "but some dates have been freed up in October. Tell me again what dates you wanted to go on your trip."

My voice was shaking as I told her, "I wanted to leave on the seventh to be there for Katie's birthday and return on the nineteenth after the Christian conference." There was no answer from Monique. "Are you still there?" I asked her.

"Yes — yes," she replied. "Those are the exact dates that opened up! That is so weird!"

"No," I told her. "That is God at work." I told her about praying for God to work it out since I didn't know what else to do myself. "How does it feel to have God use you and the VA to make someone's dream come true?"

By the time we hung up, we were both crying. I thanked God then, still in disbelief that He had worked this all out for us. "You are amazing, God. Now, if you can help me convince John, I will be even more thankful!"

I explained to John that the dates had opened up and he could stay at the VA while I was gone.

"No, I don't want to stay there! I can take care of myself!"

Trying to be patient, I told him, "I know you might be fine, but you also might have a seizure or a fall and no one would be here with you. Will you please stay at the VA to give me peace of mind? I would feel so terrible if something happened to you while I was gone. I would worry about you the whole time."

"I don't need someone to take care of me!" he protested. This once able-bodied soldier had received a Purple Heart and a bronze cross for his service. He didn't want to be "taken care of" like a child.

"I know you MIGHT not need help, but you can't drive either. If you stay at the VA, they will take you to your appointments and therapies so you won't miss any. You will have other veterans to talk to and they always have something fun going on for the residents."

"Okay," he finally agreed. "I'll do it for you, but I don't need the help."

John told everyone I was leaving him at a "kennel" while I was gone! Although he would not admit it, John got along fine. He was very popular with the nurses and became quite a Bingo shark! He also found new friends to talk with.

I enjoyed my time in Minnesota and got to spend a lot of time with Michele, Katie, my son-in-law Tim, and grandson Kris. I was able to meet Katie's boyfriend and Kris's girlfriend. The weather was cool and the fall leaves were spectacular. I came home with precious memories ready to pick up my role as caretaker again.

I realized that where we end up in life is not always in the future we planned. We pass people on the streets who don't look like heroes as they move along with the aid of a walker. We go through our days caring for our loved ones with our lives revolving around their needs and appointments resulting from their service to our country.

Yet, when I see my husband struggle to his feet when the national anthem is played, I also know we live in the most wonderful country in the world. Despite his limitations, my husband is still proud to be an American and proud to have served.

~Judee Stapp

43

I Love You More

Only in the agony of parting do we look into
the depths of love.
~George Eliot

t was one of those days in Kansas when the cool morning air tricked us into jeans and long sleeves for our 11 a.m. arrival at the Battalion parking lot. Now the hot sun beat down on us. Families popped their trunks and sat in the back of their vehicles with their soldiers, dreading the moment when they would announce it was time to go. I remember praying that every moment would last forever, at the same time I was praying that we could just get it all over with. We watched as our three-year-old daughter and eighteen-month-old son played with the other children. We had prepared with snacks and games, knowing that this is how deployment day works. Hurry up and wait.

It was 3 p.m. when a soldier came to our van. "Hey man, it's time for formation." The words stung. My husband turned to me like it was just another day, "Okay, let's go." We loaded the kids into the double stroller and walked toward the motor pool in silence. We stopped at the top of the hill as other families walked toward the bus. This is where we would stop.

It was our fourth deployment so I knew the routine. This time I would stand on the hill. We would say our goodbyes here and I would watch him walk away.

This was it. My husband turned to me and said, "I'll call you when we get to each airport to let you know we are safe, just like I always do. Okay?" His words were strong and certain. Until that moment I was strong and certain too, but the heart can only take so much before it breaks.

I wrapped my arms around him, burying my face into his stiff camouflage top. I took a long deep breath, attempting to memorize the smell of his cologne. It would be a year before I smelled it again. I felt the hot tears rolling down my face.

The kids sat in the stroller oblivious to what was going on around them. It was time for him to say goodbye to them. I rubbed my face in his top to wipe away the tears and turned to the kids. "It's time to say goodbye to Daddy," I said in the happiest voice I could muster.

My husband knelt down to the kids and told them how much he loved them and to be good to their mommy while he was gone. They cheerfully replied, "Okay Daddy, love you," and opened their arms for a hug. I could see that he didn't want to let them go. He stayed there, kneeling on the ground with his arms around our kids and whispered into their ears. I could hear them laughing. This is the moment I would remind them of when they started to notice he wasn't coming home. When they realized what it felt like to miss someone.

As my husband started to stand up I could feel myself taking a few steps back. I didn't want it to be my turn. I didn't want to say goodbye. He smiled at me and opened his arms: "Come here, babe." I walked toward him, taking a long, deep breath, attempting not to cry. But as his arms wrapped around me again I began to sob.

"Please don't go. Let's turn around and flee the country. They'll never find you," I begged.

He laughed. "You know that's not how this works. You can do this. We'll talk as much as we can. I'll be home before you know it."

I squeezed him tighter, knowing that he was wrong. This year would feel like a lifetime. It would be a year of worry, of missed holidays, of children's milestones that he could never get back.

"I love you. I love you so much it hurts."

"I love you more," he said softly.

I loosened my grip on him and looked up at his face. We kissed and again I did everything I could to burn this moment into my brain. I knew on the hard days I would need to close my eyes and remember this feeling.

My husband grabbed his large green military bag and threw it over his shoulder. "I love you guys. I'll talk to you soon. Be good for Mommy."

"We love you, Daddy," I said, now standing by the stroller. He smiled, turned away and began walking down the hill to the bus.

"Please don't go!" my head screamed, but we stood there, silent, watching him walk away. As he got near the bus he turned one last time and waved to us. I could see the pain on his face. The pain he tried to never show, the pain that proved he knew how difficult this year would be. The three of us waved back and then in the sea of camo and tears, he was gone.

Two of my friends and their children walked over to us as we stood there on the hill. Our three families watched until the bus drove our soldiers away. We would get through the hardest days of that year with each other and the memories of those hugs, kisses and I love you more's.

~Katelynn Stream

44

Above and Beyond the Call

A single act of kindness throws out roots in all
directions, and the roots spring up and make new trees.
~Amelia Earhart

The movie was nearing the end. That's when my daughter showed me the text: "Please come home now." My heart began to beat fast as I realized my son-in-law would never ask my daughter Jill to leave a movie unless it was an emergency. As a former police officer and captain in the Army reserves, Josh was skilled in first aid and problem solving. He also loved his kids and was happy to spend the afternoon with the younger two. Something must be terribly wrong.

Jill left immediately. I stayed behind with the grandchildren and their aunts. I tried to distract myself with the movie but it was no use. I silently began to pray. I asked God to prepare us for what was to come.

Then I got the text from my daughter: "Please pray. Audrey was run over."

Oh God no! With trembling fingers I texted back: "By who?"

Jill's one-word response filled me with dread: "Dad."

Oh God have mercy! Audrey had just turned two. Her older sister Avery was sitting on my lap and I hugged her close as I rocked back and forth. I felt paralyzed in grief.

I wanted to rush home to be with my husband Tom, but I knew it wasn't wise to take the grandchildren home to the scene of the accident. At that very moment their sister and cousin lay unconscious, perhaps hovering between life and death in our driveway.

The movie ended and I rushed home with my other two daughters and grandchildren. Grateful that the ambulance had already whisked Audrey to the emergency room, we made arrangements for the other children and headed to the hospital.

On our way, my devastated husband relayed his story. "I was pulling around Josh's car and heading into the garage. I saw that Josh had the baby and I didn't see Audrey so I assumed she was still in the car. I didn't know she had been let out of her car seat and was walking around the front of their CRV to go wait on the porch. I began to cut the wheel when I heard Josh yell, 'Tom, you just ran over Audrey!' I never saw her. I never felt the hit. But I immediately stopped the truck and jumped out. When I saw her lifeless body I ran inside to call 911. When I came back out I stood over Josh, who was desperately trying to awaken her. I did the only thing I could: I prayed."

Firemen, paramedics and the police officers arrived on the scene. Expertly they secured Audrey's tiny frame to a stretcher and loaded her into the ambulance. My daughter accompanied her to the hospital.

Officer Chris McBane was the first to arrive and the last to leave. He was instrumental in helping my husband deal with the situation. Filling out an accident report was necessary, but he did it with care and concern for my husband's emotional state. After collecting all the facts, he reassured my husband that it wasn't his fault. The truck was large; Audrey was small. When they collided it was truly an accident. It was impossible to have seen her. Thankfully, she had been hit by the edge of the tire, and not actually run over.

The police officer stayed until my husband collected himself. His reassurance that it wasn't Tom's fault laid the foundation for my husband to start healing.

When we arrived at the local hospital, Audrey was being prepared for a life flight to Children's Mercy Hospital. While they were securing her in the helicopter, Officer McBane pulled up in his squad car. He got out of the car and slowly approached us. Carrying a small, stuffed lamb in his hand, he headed straight for my husband. As soon as my husband spotted him he walked over to meet him. His concern for my husband was written all over the officer's face as he inquired about Audrey's condition. He had come to reassure my husband again. My husband was grateful for this thoughtful gesture.

We were surprised and very comforted by this act of kindness from the officer. He could've filed his report and gone home. Instead, after working his shift, he stopped at the hospital. The lamb, intended to bring comfort to my injured grandchild, gave him an opportunity to bring comfort to my husband. After a short conversation he handed Tom the little lamb and he was gone.

Time seemed to move in slow motion as we waited for the flight to take off. It was a long night as we waited for the results of scans and tests. Audrey's ear was ripped and the back of her skull was shattered. She had shoulder fractures, a partially collapsed lung, and road burns on her face and back. But she was alive. A long recovery lay ahead, but we had much to be thankful for. Despite the head trauma, Audrey had no brain swelling or bleeding.

Audrey was released from the hospital three days later to recuperate at home. The ache in my heart was ever present: for little Audrey, her parents, and my husband. Support poured in from our neighborhood, our church family, and friends. Grass was mowed, gift cards given, and meals brought. Slowly but surely life began to take on a normal rhythm once again, although it took my husband a week to be able to return to work.

Two weeks later, there was a knock on our front door. Opening the door, Tom was surprised to find Chris McBane on the other side. We welcomed him into our home. Chris was pleased to hear about our granddaughter's miraculous recovery. I suspect his real reason for the visit was to check on my husband. The relief on his face showed his care and concern for Tom. Stopping by our home was above and beyond the call of duty.

The media today is filled with negativity and disrespect toward police officers. Daily, officers put their lives on the line for us. We need to respect our boys in blue. Thank you, Officer Chris McBane, for being a shining example of all that is good and right about law enforcement.

You serve our community well, and we are eternally grateful for your care and compassion in our time of crisis.

~Cindy Richardson

45

My Father's Footsteps

The veterans of our military services have put their
lives on the line to protect the freedoms that we enjoy.
They… deserve to be recognized for their commitment.
~Judd Gregg

Crunch-slide. Crunch-slide. Crunch-slide.

My father's footsteps announced his arrival.

"Why is your Dad so loud when he walks?"

"He isn't!" I snapped.

But he was.

My father was a veteran of World War II.

On an icy day in France, in January 1945, shrapnel sprayed my father's infantry unit.

Tiny bits of metal ripped through the soldier next to my father, his body shielding my father's.

The young soldier was killed — his death saved my father's life.

Just not my father's leg.

Crunch-slide. Crunch-slide. Crunch-slide.

My father's footsteps announced his disability.

"Why does your dad walk funny?"

"He doesn't!" I shouted.

But he did.

As a result of his injuries my father's left leg was several inches shorter than his right. His leg was permanently mottled black and purple, and metal oozed out of him years after that bomb exploded.

Between his injuries and his diabetes, the threat of amputation hung over him.

Crunch-slide. Crunch-slide. Crunch-slide.

My father's footsteps announced his differences.

"Why is your dad's shoe so weird?"

"It isn't!" I screamed.

But it was.

My father's shoes were another thing that made him different. One shoe was normal. Black, leather, lace up. The other one was bulging.

Bulbous.

Heavy.

Crunch-slide. Crunch-slide. Crunch-slide.

Throughout my childhood people asked me about my father's differences — focusing on the sound of his footsteps, focusing on his disability, focusing on his shoes.

And I focused on lashing out against the questions instead of focusing on what was important: my father was brave.

He was a hero.

He was a veteran.

Crunch-slide. Crunch-slide. Crunch-slide.

My father's footsteps sounded different because he was a courageous young soldier who marched straight into unknown dangers and witnessed unimaginable horrors when he was only nineteen.

My father walked differently because another hero saved his life by losing his.

In a twist of horrific fate another family lost a son, but my father kept his life, though forever changed.

And my father was grateful.

My father's shoes looked different because of his commitment and sacrifice to America. They were an outward sign of how he changed on that battlefield — a true testament to his survival.

What I wouldn't give to hear my father's footsteps again.

Crunch-slide. Crunch-slide. Crunch-slide.
So I could say, "Thank you, Dad."

~Bridget Magee

46

An American Mother

Military parents have the Honor of loving a hero,
the Courage to let them go, and the Commitment to
Support them.
~Author Unknown

thought I knew what it meant to be an American, what it felt like to be proud of this country and those who serve and have served in its armed forces. Silly me, I thought it was the goose bumps I got when I heard the national anthem or the comfort I felt when crossing paths with a soldier or a sailor.

The truth is I didn't know what it meant — not really. It wasn't until my firstborn son voluntarily joined the United States Navy in 2013 and was deployed to the North Arabian Gulf and the Red Sea aboard a guided-missile cruiser in 2014 that I truly appreciated what it meant to be an American, not to mention what it meant to be a mother.

It meant sacrifice in the highest form.

I remember the day I saw my son's ship steaming into the fray on CNN, one of the first ships to be sent to the front lines. I had never been more proud or more frightened. I was torn between the two heaping emotions, so much so that I could hardly breathe! The little boy with big, green eyes who I tucked into bed every night, the same boy who was afraid of fireworks on the Fourth of July, was headed into harm's way for the sake of his country, for the sake of something much bigger than himself. Not once did he hesitate or show fear in the face of danger. And so his bravery became mine.

Like the day he was born, I will never forget the moment I held him in my arms after he returned from serving nine months overseas. Nor will I forget the handsome, young man sporting a United States Navy uniform, my "little boy" with the big green eyes, getting down on one knee in that same airport terminal and proposing to the woman he loved. It was one of the proudest moments of my life, as both an American and a mother.

Now when I hear the national anthem or I cross paths with a soldier or a sailor, I feel deep in my bones what it means to be an American and a mother. I know how it feels to love your country and your son so much that you would bravely, and without reserve, watch the one you once guarded with your life steam into the fray for the sake of something much bigger than himself. That is the truest spirit of America... and motherhood.

~Natalie June Reilly

★ The ★
Spirit of
America

One People, United

*To survive in peace and harmony, united and
strong, we must have one people, one
nation, one flag.*
~Pauline Hanson

An American Home Town

*Even the smallest act of service, the simplest act of
kindness, is a way to honor those we lost, a way to
reclaim that spirit of unity that followed 9/11.*
~President Barack Obama

I n western Pennsylvania, September 11, 2001 dawned blue and
gold, my Shanksville-Stonycreek High School colors.

I called Mom that morning. She still lived in the house where
I'd grown up. I'd been planning a visit but was overwhelmed
with work. "I think I'd better wait till Thursday, if that works for you."

We chatted a while, and then I headed to the shower and Mom went
to start some laundry. I was still in the shower when my phone rang.

"Oh, Susan, the world is coming to an end!" My editor from the
local weekly started reeling off facts faster than my brain could absorb
them. I snatched at fragments, trying to make sense of them: two
planes had hit the World Trade Center, one hit the Pentagon, another
came down in Somerset County.

My heart jolted. "Where in Somerset County?"

She didn't know.

"My mom lives in Somerset County."

"Wait a minute." She quickly checked. "Does your mom live anywhere near Indian Lake?"

The world stopped.

"About five miles away." I later learned that the plane had come
down a lot closer than that.

My editor had wanted me to start making phone calls for an article about the response of our local school districts to the terrorist attack. But at that point, all I could think of was Mom. I dialed her number with fumbling fingers and got a recording: "This call cannot be completed…"

Why? Had the plane crash disintegrated the phone line? Or had it destroyed the house with her in it?

For the next few hours, I dialed and re-dialed, praying until I finally got her.

It turns out that the plane crashed barely a mile and a half from her house. It left a huge crater, black not from coal dust, but from incineration. My cousin called her from work, to ask if his house was still there. His was the last call to get through before all lines in and out of the county were jammed.

For the next several hours, she told me, vehicles streamed past the house on our backcountry road — rescue vehicles, news units, and military.

Growing up, I'd felt safe in our little town where everybody knew everybody — and most were related to each other. Just a few houses, a small church, woods, and fields. I'd often told my kids, "If anything happens, we'll head for Grandma's house. We'll be safe there."

But now, the world and its problems had gotten there ahead of me.

Once reassured Mom was safe, I went back to work for the newspaper, making my calls and writing my article. A while later, the phone rang. My three kids were in the high school office and my daughter was crying. The principal had initially refused to let them use the phone, not realizing how very close that crash had been, which contributed to my kids' growing panic.

"Is Grandma all right?"

I was so glad I'd gotten through to Mom before they called, and was able to reassure them. I resisted their request to come straight home, said I'd see them soon, and then asked to speak to the principal. I still needed quotes for my article.

The next two days were a national nightmare. The skies were empty, apart from military aircraft. The enormity of what had happened, the massive hole that had been ripped through all our hearts, was impossible to process.

But suddenly, we weren't so conscious of our pigeonholes. We weren't so much a certain race, religion, or ethnicity. Not so much urban, rural or suburbanite. Not wealthy or homeless, liberal or conservative. Not Californians, New Yorkers, Southerners, or Midwesterners. We were Americans. Many people, I suspect, woke up for the first time to the realization of how much they loved this country. We loved each other. We crowded into prayer services. We drew together, mourned together, and together pulled the torn pieces of our collective heart back over that gaping hole.

But how had this atrocity changed my hometown? It had always been a good place, with good neighbors who looked out for each other. I wondered if our little town, where everyone knew everyone, could ever survive this. Nonstop international news coverage posted updates from New York, Washington, D.C., and Shanksville. Could my father or grandparents — all in their graves for years at that point — ever have imagined something like this?

The third day, I went to see Mom. When I got off the turnpike in Somerset, and turned toward home, even the road seemed weirdly empty, like the skies. The Armory parking lot was full of military vehicles, though. It had been turned into a temporary morgue.

All along Route 281, and the pull-around in front of Friedens Elementary, flags flew. Handmade signs said, "God Bless America." Handwritten messages of sympathy for family members cropped up all along the way.

In this surreal new world, I felt a rush of warmth and pride. I knew — although everything had changed in an instant — we were still the same here.

A strange car sat in my mother's driveway. My sister-in-law Wendy, in New York City on business, had been staying in a hotel near the World Trade Center. She'd been scheduled to leave September 11th. With all planes grounded, and car rental computers down, she'd finally convinced a rental agency employee to hand-write a contract for her, so she could get home. She'd taken an overnight break at Mom's on her way back to Dayton, Ohio.

Wendy offered to ride with me to a news briefing at the site, and help gather information. Where I used to catch the school bus there was now a security checkpoint. I shared my credentials and was passed through.

We followed the school bus route for another mile to a field being used as a staging area. Behind the sunflowers blooming along the edge of the road, satellite trucks and Red Cross tents sprouted like some kind of alien crop.

Sitting behind reporters from CNN, a stone's throw from a farmhouse where I used to babysit, and another where we'd had 4-H meetings, I felt another disconnect. Until I heard the Somerset County Coroner, Wallace Miller, speaking. Until I heard emergency workers thanking the neighbors for not only accepting the disruption, but also offering food and coffee and bathrooms — and even leaving their house keys when they went to work. Everything shrank back to human scale again, and I was home.

Whatever was taken from us as a nation — and specifically from families and friends who lost loved ones — they hadn't taken our souls. Nothing has given me greater pride in the years since 9/11 than hearing the bereaved family members say they feel a bond with the people of Somerset County. My heart swelled when I read a Red Cross account that said: "When the buses carrying family members to and from the crash scene went by, adults and children lined the roads, shoulder to shoulder, hands over hearts, holding American flags, and totally silent."

We may have been a town where everybody knew everybody and most of us were related. But when the world came to our door, and innocent people were suffering unspeakable loss, they were cared for with all the love of friends and family. That is the spirit of my small town — the true spirit of America.

~Susan Kimmel Wright

48

A Ship in the Harbor

Under my skin, I'm just like you.
~Keb' Mo', blues musician, 1996

I find love notes scrawled on scraps of paper hidden around the house — under a desk lamp, behind a photo, slipped in a book, in drawers. They're always dated and he never lets on that there's still one to be found. I'm as gleeful as a kid running through sprinklers whenever I find one, and this treasure hunt has been going on for more than fifteen years.

I always hoped that my Prince Charming would be tall, dark, and handsome, but I never expected him to be black. I'm white, raised in Orange County, California, in the 1950s and 1960s. I had a happy childhood and youth, but by no stretch of the imagination could it be called culturally diverse. I had white neighbors, white friends, white teachers, and I listened to white music, mostly The Beach Boys, while I whiled away summer days with my friends on the white sands of local beaches. My life was a blend of *Father Knows Best* and *Gidget*, insulated from the social and civil injustices that were prevalent beyond my world.

My college years were an explosion of new experiences, socially, intellectually, and politically, and yet, for the most part, my social circle remained white. Then I moved to Los Angeles. Languages exotic to my ears, people who looked nothing like me, and mouthwatering aromas of Thai, Korean, Chinese, and soul food stimulated my senses.

I settled in an ethnically diverse neighborhood. Years passed. My neighbors Bill and Annie invited me to their Super Bowl party.

Bill had told me about a friend of his, Richard, who he wanted me to meet. I agreed to come by. As Bill greeted me on the day of the party, I scanned the room wondering which of his friends was Richard, when a tall, dark, handsome man with warm brown eyes, a wide grin, and a shaved head stepped forward, extended his hand, and grasped mine firmly in his. He said, "Hello, I'm Richard." To borrow a line from the film *Jerry Maguire*… he had me at hello.

He was a black man raised in Jackson, Mississippi, and I was a white woman raised in Orange County. What could we possibly have in common? The card he sent me a few days later set the tone for the months and years to follow. On the front was a ship in a harbor with the words, "A ship in the harbor is safe… but that's not what ships were made for." Indeed, over the past fifteen years, we've ventured into new waters and explored uncharted lagoons. We've weathered rough seas. It's taken courage, mutual respect, open hearts, and an abundance of love and laughter, and I'm thankful every day that we were both willing to take the risk.

Last month Richard surprised me with a birthday party. It was a casual backyard gathering, a barbecue reminiscent of my childhood, yet endearingly different. My heart swelled with love as my teary eyes beheld my dearest friends. They were black. They were white. They were gay. They were Christian. They were Buddhist. They came in their Mercedes. They took a bus. They were the faces of the people I love most, especially the man with the strong handshake, the wide grin, the shaved head, and the hidden love notes.

~Karen Howard

49

Memorial Day

No duty is more urgent than that of returning thanks.
~James Allen

t was Memorial Day 2009 and I was flying out of Dallas/Fort Worth, bound for Seattle to film a segment of *Disappeared...* a Discovery Channel episode based on a quickly written book I'd crafted for a client.

Several military troops were making their way through the terminal after disembarking their flight. Some would be connecting to other flights while others were now home.

It saddened me to see our troops walking through the area without a single civilian stopping to say "thank you!" It was, after all, Memorial Day.

Approaching my designated waiting area, I thanked several of them as we passed.

I took a seat next to a pretty, young woman dressed in fatigues. She was busy working on an e-mail or a text, probably telling someone stateside of her location and that she'd be seeing them soon.

As I sat there next to this guardian of peace, I thought about how just a few hours earlier I had walked out to the pasture to feed my horses. Looking up into the beautiful clear Texas sky, there was nothing but blue sky.

There were no fighter jets overhead, no sound of exploding grenades or sniper fire — just the peaceful sound of freedom! Freedom to go about daily life without the threat of being gunned down by enemy fire.

I wanted to convey my thanks to the warrior sitting next to me, so on a scratch pad I wrote a note of gratitude and thanks. I can't recall the exact wording but it went something like this: "I don't know your name or what your background is or where your future will take you but I want to tell you how very proud of you I am for risking your life to keep me safe here at home. Thank you for your service to our country! God has blessed you because you are here and you're alive. May you live your coming years in the same peace you've provided for others."

I folded the paper in half, then again, then gently nudged her arm. She looked a little uncertain when I handed it to her. I gave her a smile, and then opened the book I had with me.

In my peripheral vision, I saw her carefully unfold the paper and read the message. As she finished, she sat for a moment in silence, perhaps recalling events in Iraq. Then she clutched the note to her chest as she bowed her head. Tears fell on the tablet she'd been using. She turned to me and said, "Thank you so much! You don't know how much this means to me. I'll keep this for the rest of my life. It will be in a pocket of whatever I'm wearing. It means that much to me."

It was a breathless moment. A moment I'll never forget.

I fought back my own emotions and responded, "I do know how much it means and that's why I had to write it."

As I stood, after hearing the boarding announcement, she rose as well and gave me a hug before I got in line for my safe trip to Seattle.

~Jan Sydnam

We Are One

We are one, after all, you and I, together we suffer,
together exist and forever will recreate each other.
~Pierre Teilhard de Chardin

My job as a senior manager for a Fortune 500 company allowed me to travel across the United States. The people I worked with in Los Angeles liked to joke that something strange happened every time I came to town. Like the time the transit workers went on strike and Southern California turned into one huge parking lot. Or when the Oscar statues went missing and miraculously reappeared in a Dumpster, found by a homeless man. So when I flew to California on Sunday, September 9, 2001, I wondered what headline would greet me once I arrived.

During an uneventful flight, the pilot announced football scores to help fill the time on the six-hour trip. Traffic was light as I drove to the hotel in my rental car. I'd made plans to have dinner with a friend.

"Did you feel the earthquake?" she asked when she picked me up.

"There was an earthquake?" Being from Florida, I'd never experienced one and never wanted to. Mother Nature gave us hurricanes so California could deal with the earthquakes.

"4.2 on the Richter scale. You should have felt it." She rattled off the statistic as if it were a commonplace event.

"Thankfully, I missed it," I laughed. "But I guess now I'm covered for my crazy news event for this trip. It's officially behind me."

I'd made this trip so many times, I had the work routine down pat. Being on East Coast time and wide awake at 4 a.m., I got up early, made calls back to Florida, ate breakfast and headed to the office before everyone else. I became hungry for lunch at 10 a.m. and wanted to call it a day by 3:00, so it was not unusual for me to be heading out of my hotel room by 6:15 in the morning.

That Tuesday morning, I picked up the remote control to turn off the TV when a breaking news banner came on. I stopped to watch.

"It appears a small plane has flown into the World Trade Center," the news anchor announced.

I sat down on the bed. The news camera fixed on the smoking building when the second plane came crashing through the other tower. Scenes of fire, plumes of smoke and horror gripped my heart. I couldn't move, watching the events of the morning unfold, helpless to do anything. Soon the news came of another plane hitting the Pentagon. The United States was under attack.

When I finally tore myself away from the television, I had no idea which way to turn. I hadn't had breakfast, but didn't feel like eating. Plenty of work would be waiting for me, but nothing productive would be accomplished today. I headed to the office, where I could find comfort with friends.

At the office, we watched the news. We cried, we hugged whether we knew each other or not. The barriers between the many different departments in the workplace disappeared.

The next morning when I arrived at work I found a note on my desk.

Prayer circle at 10:00 in the parking lot.
Please come.
Everyone welcome.

The sky displayed a brilliant blue with a few soft, white puffy clouds floating by. People poured out of the building, from the executives to the warehouse workers, the salesmen to the janitors. The sun gently warmed us as we gathered in a circle, filling the parking lot from one end to the other. Hands grasped without hesitation. Our heads bowed as we observed a moment of silence. When our eyes opened, tears spilled down faces of every size, shape and color. Linked hands turned to comforting hugs. At that moment, we were one.

With airplanes grounded, my trip was extended indefinitely, so I tried to settle in as best I could. Every morning I woke up wondering when I'd be able to go home. I went to the mall down the street to pick up a few more clothes and stopped at the bookstore looking for something new to read. Nothing appealed to me. A favorite ice cream parlor couldn't even tempt me. My hotel room became my refuge.

"Linda, would you like to go to a movie tonight?" my friend Patty asked. "You need to get out. We both do."

"I don't know. Should we be out having fun?" I sounded depressed even to myself.

"We can't let the bad guys win. Let's try to get back to normal, whatever that's going to be."

The movie was *Moulin Rouge*, starring Nicole Kidman, and dinner was a big fat Mexican burrito at my favorite local restaurant. The combination of the two distracted my racing mind at least for one night. I slept better than I had since I arrived in Los Angeles.

Invitations began to come from all over. Every day a different lunch crowd wanted me to join them. A co-worker asked me to a family barbecue on Sunday afternoon. The barista at Starbucks now called me by name.

Ten days later, I flew back to Florida, relieved when the plane landed safely. All the familiar sights and sounds welcomed me. Grateful to breath the warm, moist Florida air, I got in my car and drove the road out of the airport.

The song "Proud to Be An American" by Lee Greenwood came on the radio. I sang a few lines before the tears started pouring out. My chest heaved with hard, heavy sobs. I was free and I was home. This despicable act of terror would live in my psyche forever but it would not define me and it would not defeat any of us. We are American and we are one.

~Linda C. Wright

Our Victory Garden

*Out of infinite kindness grow real love and
understanding and tolerance and warmth. Nothing
can take the place of such an enduring asset.*
~Branch Rickey

Our 100-year-old historic neighborhood in Muskogee, Oklahoma is, I suppose, typical of neighborhoods all over America. Neighbors wave at each other when we're out and about and we sometimes visit over the back fence, too. We call out greetings when we gather on our front porches to watch the sky when the tornado sirens sound. Or we sit on our porch swings and enjoy a free concert when Jermaine is visiting his mother and playing his tenor sax for her.

Occasionally we gather for a neighborhood association meeting or one of our fall garden parties that give us a chance to talk about our concerns and share some good barbecue. We had gathered for such an event just a few days after the September 11, 2001 terrorist attacks, although I wondered, along with the other officers of the association, if anyone would come.

Would anyone want to picnic under the 100-year-old oak tree or enjoy the music of our local blues band or sit on lawn chairs and blankets and chat amiably with each other about grandchildren, the weather or their own fall gardens? We set up the grill for the hot dogs and iced down the soda (we call it pop in Muskogee) and waited. A street maintenance crew set up barricades at each end of the block to keep out through traffic. Soon a long, shiny red fire engine pulled up to the curb in front of the garden. We had invited the fire department to present fire safety materials to the kids — something arranged long before September 11th. How could we know that we had invited our new heroes?

Then it happened. Slowly people began to gather. At first it was a tiny trickle of neighbors who lived on the same block as our garden. They brought blankets and potato salad and brownies and pictures from the last neighborhood gathering.

Kids started scrambling over the fire engine — their first time seeing one so close. Then the trickle of people became a stream and the stream became a flood as those who remembered the party left to knock on the doors of other families to remind them to come.

We are fortunate in my neighborhood to have a wonderful mix of colors and cultures. Soon white grandmothers were scooping up African American babies to tickle and cuddle and the Asian American kids were playing tag with the Native American kids. Fathers helped their toddlers up the steps of the fire engine that now looked like a strange new creature with dozens of arms and legs of every size, shape and color sticking out of it. The firemen patiently explained the different apparatus and let the kids turn on the lights (but not the siren).

The hot dogs were about done so the district's president gathered folks around our makeshift stage and asked for a moment of silence in remembrance of September 11th victims and heroes. We wiped the tears from our eyes. One of our community's own residents had lost a son in the Pentagon attack. It hit home. It hurt. It made us stop and appreciate the simple pleasure of sharing hot dogs, potato chips, coleslaw and cake with family, neighbors, friends and heroes of our own.

After we'd eaten more than we should we relaxed on blankets and lawn chairs and listened to Shy Willie croon the blues. Sad songs about love and loss fit the mood that settled upon us with dusk's shadows. Then Olivia — a two-year-old, blond pixie — stood up on her family's blanket and began to dance.

She scrunched her eyes tightly shut, chocolate cookie crumbs freckling her mournful little face, and she swayed to the music as if she deeply felt a sadness that she couldn't possibly have understood. We gently laughed at her earnest, soulful dance, but we knew what she was feeling. We felt it too.

I looked around our community garden that we had worked so hard on through the summer. It had taken months of effort. The city had razed a burned-out, abandoned house, leaving the foundation stones for our use as boundaries for our garden beds. We had planted shrubs and flowers, mostly donated items from gardens in the neighborhood. It still had a long way to go to be completed but we were pleased with our progress.

Sitting there among my neighbors that evening, I thought of the victory gardens my mother told me about from World War II. People grew vegetables as a patriotic necessity — their way of helping with the war effort. We had planted flowers in our little garden, but on this evening it became our victory garden because something even more wonderful was growing there.

Families made up of every race and age, faith and background had gathered and shared a special moment. It seemed like the worst of times, but in that moment we were victorious over intolerance, violence and hate. We might have been sad and a little frightened, but we were united as families, neighbors and citizens. And if in gathering with our children that evening, we taught them tolerance and unity and who our real heroes are, then that was our victory.

~Jonita Mullins

52

A Taxing Topic

I like to pay taxes. With them I buy civilization.
~Oliver Wendell Holmes, Jr.

once believed that "beware the Ides of March" related to income taxes. In the early 1950s, when the tax deadline was March, my father acted as if it were the worst day of the year. Why he put off his computations until the very last minute still puzzles me. Once the dreaded return actually had been dispatched, my parents would debate how they'd spend their expected refund.

"Maybe it's time for an automatic washer," my mother would suggest, ladling cream gravy over my father's favorite chicken-fried steak. Maybe she'd hint that we all needed new shoes.

"No, no. The Chevy needs a new carburetor," he would respond, smearing margarine on his corn. Or perhaps he'd complain that his mower blades were so worn out that they left our lawn corrugated.

My father enjoyed helping me with my math homework, so it couldn't have been totaling up the columns of figures that irritated him so. Nonetheless, on tax day he always acted peeved.

At the last possible minute, he would sprawl at the kitchen table, glare at his W-2 form, flip through the pages of the IRS booklet, and gnaw at his yellow pencil. My mother would plop a plate of oatmeal cookies, fresh from the oven, at his elbow, and hover with a coffee pot.

"Dang government robs a man blind," he'd growl hours later, slipping his completed forms into an envelope. He'd grudgingly affix a three-cent stamp, glance at the clock, and then toss the packet to me. He would never waste gas driving to the post office when he had a preteen daughter lingering nearby, eager for a chance to be helpful.

"Don't just shove it in the mailbox! The Slauson office only stays open until 6:00. Be sure to get the envelope postmarked or they'll subtract interest for a late filing!"

"Don't worry, Daddy. I'll ride my bike."

And I'd fly down West 59th Place, pigtails flapping in the breeze, musing on my father's baffling attitude.

Later, as a newlywed, I witnessed my husband act just like my father, practically frothing in panic come income tax day, now April 15th. Though Bob had a whole month more to fume and fidget, he still waited until the deadline was nigh. Then he'd slouch on the couch, sigh, and slowly hunch over the coffee table to spend the next several hours scratching away with his pencil.

Though I brewed coffee, I didn't bother baking cookies. By now I'd studied enough anthropology to wonder if this income tax angst simply was a crisis of manhood, some secret long-standing initiation rite handed down from father to son, akin to thrusting a hand into a glove filled with bullet ants or hurtling from a 100-foot tower while land diving in Vanuatu.

"You know, I'd be glad to do the taxes. I can add and subtract," I offered. Bob had clutched his papers and forms to his chest, mouth agape, staring at me as if I'd proposed he trade his gray flannel suit for my bolero-sleeved dress.

"I'm the head of the household," he blustered. "This is a man's job."

Scrupulously honest, Bob fretted about tax cheats and never claimed a dishonest or questionable deduction. Still, he treated me to heated diatribes over the legality and immorality of the 16th Amendment, outlining most of what the IRS and the federal courts now term "frivolous arguments."

Years later, single once more, I finally filed my own taxes. I'd prepared for the worst, laying in a supply of chamomile tea and peppermint lozenges. To my astonishment, the process proved relatively pain-free. Weeks before the deadline I simply sat down, totaled up the figures on my calculator, and sent off the completed form.

To celebrate, I phoned my father.

"Guess what? I just filed my taxes and I'm getting enough on my refund to take a trip to the Bahamas."

"What did you have to pay the preparer?"

"Not a cent. I did it myself."

At least a minute elapsed before he replied. "You probably made a lot of mistakes. Don't be surprised when the IRS knocks at your door."

Eventually I learned that it's not male or female outlooks, per se, that causes anxiety. Rather it's a matter of basic attitude. My second husband had no qualms about delegating me to handle our paperwork. Nor did Ken ever fret about parting with a buck, if he felt that it was well spent. I always paid the bills, so it felt natural to fill out our joint taxes. Ken gladly barbecued a rib eye for me on tax preparation day, served with a glass of Shiraz.

"How'd we do this year?" he'd ask.

"We did fine. We paid enough to keep the nation's highways paved and to ensure that hospitals will remain open for our veterans. We're not getting much back, but we don't have to send any more in, either."

"I'll drink to that," he'd say, tilting his glass before digging in to his steak.

When I became widowed several years ago, I pored through my tax forms and learned I'd be able to file a joint return that subsequent year, claiming my late husband in figuring the standard deduction. I didn't have to prorate.

"How generous," I thought, electing the simple 1040A rather than itemizing.

Even so, because of earnings from my freelance writing and editing, I had to enclose a check for the U.S. Treasury. Fortunately, I'd allowed one of my tiny annuities to accumulate in a savings account all year to cover this anticipated bite.

I stuck the envelope in my roadside mailbox and flicked up the red metal flag so the carrier would be certain to stop and collect it. Then I strolled back to my house, reflecting on how curiously comforting figuring my taxes always has proved for me.

I consider myself blessed. I've lived abroad, working in developing countries. I'm grateful that I roamed the world, from Mongolia to Mauritius, protected by my American passport. I'm grateful that when I retired I drove from Washington, D.C. to Washington State on relatively well-maintained highways. I'm grateful I don't live in a dictatorship. I'm grateful I can continue to support my country, even on income tax collection day.

April indeed may be the cruelest month for some. Me, I'm thankful to be able to pay for the privilege of living in America.

~Terri Elders

53

Flying with Spirit

It is the love of country that has lighted and that keeps
glowing the holy fire of patriotism.
~J. Horace McFarland

s anyone here flying with Spirit?" I asked the small group of travelers who were waiting for our town shuttle to take us to the Orlando airport. I had recently retired to Florida and was unfamiliar with that airport. So I was relieved when a young woman named Chris said she, too, was flying on Spirit and also going to Chicago.

It was two days before Thanksgiving, not long after the tragedy of 9/11. It seemed that all America was still in shock, in a state of sadness, fear and depression. The government was cautioning that we should expect further terrorist attacks and that there would be heavy security at all airports.

I was more than hesitant to fly. I was scared. I was leery of being in an airport, much less on a plane. But my son and his family from Australia were in the States for only a short time. So being with them over the holidays was extremely important to me, especially on this Thanksgiving when life seemed so precious. And so, after weeks of indecision, I prayed for safety and braced myself for whatever was to come.

Six of us boarded the shuttle and immediately began wondering what the airport security would be like. A young man sitting behind me said he was prepared to be questioned, scanned and his luggage searched as he had experienced this on the first leg of his trip.

My stomach felt queasy. But thankfully, whatever fears I had were one by one put to rest as the day progressed.

I stepped onto the plane and was unable to pass an attendant who was blocking the aisle to talk with two young boys who were probably six or seven years old and flying alone. "You do know this is a non-smoking flight, gentlemen," she said with a very serious look of concern. "Neither of you have cigarettes, right? You don't smoke, do you?" The boys giggled, and the attendant smiled and stepped aside to let me pass.

Chris was seated at the window across the aisle from me, and a petite, middle-aged lady named Tina sat next to me. We chatted briefly before one of the flight attendants took the microphone and welcomed us aboard. In closing she said, "We'd like to suggest that you say hi to the folks around you today. Get to know each other a little bit, because for the next three hours we are all going to be a family."

Tina and I smiled at each other and nodded in agreement. She then told me about her daughter, Kerry, a Navy communications expert. Right after 9/11 Kerry had been deployed to the Middle East and was unable to disclose her final destination. Tina and her husband, of course, were terribly concerned for their daughter.

On one occasion Tina had taken a package to the post office to be sent overseas. "A care-package for the holidays?" the postal worker inquired.

"Yes," Tina said. "It's for my daughter who is in the Navy and has been sent to the Middle East."

The worker flashed a look of concern. He weighed the package, and the amount due was a bit over $25. Smiling at Tina compassionately he said, "I'd like to do something to help the cause, Ma'am. This package is free for you. I'd like to pay for it myself."

I had a big lump in my throat when Tina finished her story. Just then an attendant announced that Rodney, a young passenger, was going to sing a song for us. There was no holding back my emotions as the child's sweet voice began singing "God Bless America." When the song ended, Rodney received a big round of applause, and Tina and I laughed at each other as we wiped away our tears.

Next, one of the attendants announced that a young future airline attendant was in training and would be performing her first duty. She then handed a basket of candy to an adorable little three-year-old girl who proceeded down the aisle passing the basket to each row.

As Tina and I continued to share, we laughed often. At one point, a dignified looking attendant approached us with a very stern expression on his face. "There will be no laughter on this flight. Is that perfectly understood?" he said with a British accent. Then he winked and continued down the aisle talking and laughing with passengers on each side. When he returned to the front, I asked, jokingly, if he were going to sing for us. "Maybe I will," he said with a grin. From then on, whenever he walked past, I asked if it were time for his song. "Later," he'd say.

"Yeah, right," we'd respond.

About fifteen minutes before landing, to our amazement, the British attendant announced that he had been requested to sing and was about to honor that request. He then broke into the melody of "This Old Man, he played one..." with:

We love you. You love us
We are faster than a bus
Hope you liked our hospitality
Marry one of us and fly for free

When the laughter subsided, the attendant who had welcomed us at the beginning took the microphone and said, "I hope you've enjoyed your time with us today. We want to thank you for all of your kind comments. In this time of uncertainty and stress we need and appreciate them. We hope you all have a wonderful holiday. And please continue to wear your USA shirts, your pins of the flag and other patriotic symbols. Wear them proudly to show our unity. We are a family. We are one. God bless you."

Again we clapped. And again I felt a lump in my throat. I smiled over at Chris and she pointed to the window. Outside on the horizon was a line of merging colors — vivid orange, indigo and maroon. The folks on that side of the plane started motioning to others to look. From around the cabin came "oohs" and "ahs."

Then suddenly, in the center of those radiant colors so near to us, the golden sun appeared in all its brilliance to illuminate the heavens. For a brief moment a hush came over us all as we took in the magnificence of this last phase of our journey. It was as though God were, indeed, giving a final blessing to this awesome adventure.

The fear and pain of 9/11 that had traumatized and numbed us had, on this flight, been replaced with a warm sense of camaraderie and an overwhelming feeling of pride and unity.

~Kay Conner Pliszka

54

What American Spirit Means to Me

We may have different religions, different languages,
different colored skin, but we all belong to
one human race.
~Kofi Annan

W hen I was a teenager working part-time at a home goods store in San Antonio an incident occurred that took away my innocence. It was a spring day in Texas. I remember it as if it were yesterday. A middle-aged woman came through my cash register line because she knew I was bilingual. She was holding a can of Drano. "Can you explain the directions to me?" she asked me in Spanish.

"Of course," I said.

There was a man behind her who was obviously in a hurry. In retrospect, I probably should have waited on him first, but I did not and I got an education that day.

I translated the directions for the woman and rang up her purchase. She thanked me and said in Spanish, "My husband passed away two months ago. He used to do everything for me. I miss him so much."

She and her husband had been in the store many times. I had heard about their son who had been drafted a few years earlier. I could see she was fighting back tears so I squeezed her hand and wished her a good afternoon, silently saying a prayer for her.

Then, I turned my attention to the male customer next in line. As I began to ring up his purchases, he said, "Damn Mexicans, they should all go back where they came from."

It was 1970, the Vietnam Conflict was raging, but I had lived a fairly sheltered life in the south side barrio where I grew up. I never witnessed a flag burning or bra burning protest. Harlandale High School, which I attended, had a junior ROTC program and patriotism prevailed. The poor, brown, black, or white families in our school district thought their American duty was to support the President of the United States.

The customer's words shocked me. My instincts took over; I knew what he had said was not nice. Somehow, with tears in my own eyes I defended the old woman. "Her husband just died. Three years ago, her only son was killed in Vietnam. She is an American," I said.

Clearly flustered the man took his change and left quickly.

Four years later, I surprised my parents by enlisting in the United States Air Force. My maternal grandparents had been born in Texas in the 1890s, yet the fear of never quite belonging hung over me. I have no regrets. The decision to enlist transformed my way of looking at the world.

Before I enlisted, I had very little personal interaction with Caucasians, or Anglos, as they are called in Texas. My high school only had a few dozen white kids whose families hadn't yet fled to the far north side. In elementary and junior high I could count on one hand the number of Anglos in our school. Of course, the teachers were mostly white.

I used to believe white people were somehow gifted with a heavenly supremacy. There's an old movie where the famous actress says of her parents something like, "They think I pee perfume." That's sort of what I thought about Caucasians — if not perfume, then certainly their urine did not smell. I am not totally sure how I came to that belief. Maybe it came from the nuns in Sunday School pounding into our young minds the wickedness of darkness and Satan, or, perhaps from my own culture where a light-skinned baby received more oohs and ahs than a dark-skinned one.

In the Air Force, my first profound experience occurred in basic training. Fifty women; black, brown, white, from all walks of life and all fifty states, Guam and Puerto Rico ate, slept, and showered together for almost two months. I remember the big open shower. In the beginning, shower curtains provided some privacy. Later on, we discarded the flimsy curtains, as they were difficult to keep clean and dry for daily inspection.

I became aware for the first time that although our skin color came in various shades of white and brown, we were all young and equally human. All of us got homesick, we hurt, we cried, we laughed, and we all wanted so much to make it through basic training.

I rose in the ranks to Chief Master Sergeant and I was addressed as Chief Holmes. Now, I am a grandmother. And, I hope my young grandchildren will understand America is not perfect. Bigotry and intolerance exist. I sometimes think of the angry customer, but I prefer to focus on the remarkable people I have met along my journey through this game called life.

To me, undoubtedly the spirit of America is displayed every time a young person decides to serve his or her country. But, serving our country can also mean taking care of your children, volunteering at a soup kitchen, or showing up for work every single day. Most of all, the spirit of America is exhibited when we embrace other cultures, when we show compassion to the poor and the illiterate, when we welcome recent immigrants to our dream. We are all Americans.

~Sylvia Garza Holmes

55

Touched by a President

*My faith demands that I do whatever I can, wherever I
am, whenever I can, for as long as I can with whatever
I have to try to make a difference.*
~President Jimmy Carter

T he auburn sun began its descent behind the oak trees on Main
Street and the parade was winding down. I sat on the curb
clenching my stomach as I watched the high school band
march by. The cotton candy had stained my tongue and I could
still feel the gritty sugar on my lips.

I had known for months that he was coming to our small town
in Idaho. I began to ponder what it must be like to be him. To have
his life. Was it scary to be the President? Did he always know he was
intended for power? Did he ever doubt himself? This might be the only
time in my life I would get this close to greatness. Somehow I knew
deep down inside, like you know when you are in trouble, that if I
got to see him it would change my life. Everything would be different.
Everything would be special. I would be special... changed.

My mom waved from down the street where she and my aunt
sat in lawn chairs. "Are you okay, honey?" she shouted with her hand
cupped to one side of her mouth.

"Fine, Mom," I replied, while suppressing my tummy ache.

The sound waves from the brass trumpet made my lips tickle and
I could feel the vibrations in my chest from the bass drum. I could
hardly tell the difference between the drum's beat and the thumping

in my chest. All of which only increased my anxiety. The President would be proceeding down Main Street soon. I was fearful I would get swept up in the crowd and would be unable to see him. I didn't want this opportunity to pass me by like so many others. I was ten years old and I had been waiting a long time for something spectacular to happen to me.

The marchers began to disappear around the bend at the end of Main Street like a snake slithering back into its den. Confetti fell slowly in the empty street and it reminded me of snowflakes gliding to the ground in winter. The street had gotten quiet. Only the faint beating of the bass drum was heard.

My cousin plopped herself next to me on the curb and said, "Do you think we will be able to see him from here?"

"I don't know," I grumbled. I told my cousin she was on her own when he arrived. She gave me a nudge and I could see the reassurance on her sweet face. She had been listening to my rambling for weeks about what would happen if we saw the President. She had been my trusted companion for many years and understood me more then anyone in the world.

In slow motion, a black limousine rounded the corner at the east end of Main Street. The chrome grill sparkled in the last remaining rays of sunlight. A shot of light reflected off the windshield and blinded me for a flash. But I could hear the tapping of shoes jogging alongside the limousine. The trotting began to get louder and louder.

"It's the President," yelled a voice from behind me.

I sprang from the curb and I was catapulted toward the Secret Service. The men in suits ran alongside the vehicle, protecting its precious cargo, and apparently not seeing me as a threat.

Thousands of balloons were released. It was as if a dam had been liberated and the street was gently flooded with a tide of red, white, and blue. The balloons bounced off my knees as I fought my way toward the limousine.

I was not alone. I could feel the mob at my ankles. The adrenaline rushed over me and gave my muscles the push they needed to lead the mob toward the President. All of us had the same mission.

As I approached the side of the limousine the window slowly rolled down to reveal the smile I had seen on TV so many times. It was him! President Jimmy Carter. He reached his hand out and I instantly grabbed it and ran along with the limousine. His hand was soft and his eyes were friendly. He winked at me! The President of the United States had touched my heart and soul with one simple wink. And, then the moment vanished. His hand released from mine, and I dropped back and watched the limousine continue its journey down Main Street.

I stood in the aftermath and savored the experience. He had been a state senator, then governor, and now he was the President. In my ten years of life, I had never been so inspired. Anything was possible. Anything could happen. I had been touched by the President and forever changed.

~Hetie Burt

56

Electing to Serve

Those who expect to reap the blessings of freedom,
must, like men, undergo the fatigues of supporting it.
~Thomas Paine

On Sunday, September 9, 2001, my brother-in-law returned to New York City after visiting my husband, my four children, and me in West Virginia. My oldest child began his first year of college out of state during my brother-in-law's visit. Our life was quiet, normal.

On Tuesday, September 11th, after my three younger children left for school, I turned on the morning news to see the impossible: a plane hitting the North Tower of the World Trade Center. My husband and I grew up in Brooklyn, a short subway ride from the World Trade Center. I watched the buildings rise bit by bit until they towered over the other skyscrapers in the city.

I called my husband to check on where my brother-in-law's office was. As we talked, I watched the second plane hit the South Tower.

Eight of my cousins worked in the financial district in Lower Manhattan. But I did not know exactly where.

My next phone call was to my seventy-five-year-old mother, living alone in Brooklyn. She was closing windows to keep out the ashes. My aunt's Staten Island telephone buzzed a busy signal for hours. I learned later that as Mom and I talked, our family members and friends ran, then trudged, through the debris to leave Manhattan.

I also had several friends who worked in the Washington, D.C. area, and cousins living in Pennsylvania. The principal and vice principal of my children's school, at a conference in Washington, D.C., had run from the Capitol Building, on the heels of the building's security guard. The guard had ordered bystanders to run; then he ran. Friends of ours, returning from Europe, were stranded in Canada for several days.

This attack affected so many people in my small world, all over the country. Within a few days, I was defiant. I went out. Salespeople thanked me as I walked through the stores in several malls. "If we stay home, they win. We can't let them win," I said.

I hung an American flag in a front window of my home. I placed a 9/11 decal on my car window. I wrote a thank-you note to local firefighters after they put up a display of solidarity with the people of New York.

Later, I learned that three of my cousins had indeed been at a breakfast meeting in the South Tower when the first plane hit. One cousin, remembering the 1993 bombing, forced the other two to leave the building. It collapsed as they walked away. I could be strong because the loss, though great, had not cut as deeply as it had for other Americans.

Still, shopping and hanging flags did not satisfy the need that I had to express my love for my country. I began to receive recruiting calls from several branches of the military, the result of taking two language courses at a local college. Military service was not a viable option for me.

Then in 2002, a friend sent an e-mail asking for primary-election poll workers. That was something I could do! Once my husband and I worked out childcare, I called Voter Registration and was accepted.

Thirteen years have passed since I first worked at the polls. I have assisted at four polling places and met hundreds of voters in my county. Many poll workers have served far longer than me, like Myna who has worked the polls for more than thirty-five years. She carefully taught me election law, while warmly greeting voters whom she had known through her many years in the precinct. Myna always dresses in red, white, and blue on Election Day, down to her sneakers, and even painted her house red, white, and blue inside and outside. Bill wisely navigated us through difficult situations with a smile. Mary Lou and Desper kindly welcomed me and treated all the poll workers like family, bringing special treats to help us through the long day. Some poll workers made significant sacrifices. Phyllis missed one year due to a grave illness, but served with us the next year even in her weakened state. Corrie served as a poll worker on her day off from driving a county school bus during the week. Tiffany, a single mother, used her day off from the county prosecutor's office to work at the polls.

Many voters thank us for serving, but it is an honor. The fourteen-hour days, the detailed paperwork, and the frayed tempers when the lines are long are a small price to pay for the opportunity to serve my country in a way that makes our country different, in a way that makes our country enviable. The citizens of the United States can vote for those who will make policy and see it through, according to the voice of the people. We can oust those who are incompetent or work against the interests of the country in a bloodless revolt. We do not live under the thumb of tyrants who would destroy what they do not understand: the right to freedom, the right to speak up about our future.

The scars of 9/11 are still with me. When I watch the memorial services each year, I remember that horrific day, pray for the families that suffered great loss, and give thanks that I didn't lose anyone. And then I prepare to volunteer on Election Day, the way that I serve and honor my country.

~C. F. Williams

57

The Cap

*It doesn't take a hero to order men into battle. It takes
a hero to be one of those men that goes into battle.*
~General Norman Schwarzkopf

About fifteen years ago, I happened upon a catalog that sold military clothing, medals, and other related memorabilia. On a whim, I bought my father a World War II cap. At the time, I didn't realize how this inexpensive hat would provide comfort to him in the most challenging and solitary time of his life, after my mother passed away nineteen days before their sixtieth anniversary. My parents were World War II sweethearts. They married in June of 1942, and my father began his World War II journey just three months later at the age of twenty-one.

My parents were each other's sidekicks. Although our family is very close and we all live in the same general vicinity, Dad was forced to do some things on his own. One of those things was going out to breakfast, at the local diner, by himself.

The World War II cap became a conversation piece, a reason for a handshake, a wave, a nod, a salute, a tip of a hat, a simple yet sincere thank you, eyes meeting eyes, shared silence, and so much more. The hat has allowed strangers to have a reason to approach my father. Instead of my dad feeling lonely or lost in his own thoughts, the hat has allowed him to know that he is appreciated. In many instances, instead of sitting alone, a complete stranger pulls up a chair and sits across from my father. They share war stories over a cup of coffee or talk about their loved ones who served or who are currently serving. Many of these strangers are young people in their twenties and thirties who want to hear the accounts of World War II firsthand. How many years are left to hear these stories from the greatest generation to have ever lived?

I'm writing this story just three hours after going out to breakfast with my dad. A young man appeared at our table, looked directly into my dad's eyes, and gave a firm handshake. Not a single word was exchanged, but the young man's eyes told a story. He was saying thank you in his own way—silence—but I could tell that somehow my father was a link to a time or a person in this man's life. I didn't have a chance to say thank you to the man for coming over, and anyway, it felt like a sacred moment not to be interrupted by words.

My dad has been honored for his World War II service many times at this little diner a few miles from his home. Dad will go to pay his check and be told that someone took care of it. Or a note will appear thanking him for his service. Once a small child walked over to his table with a crayon drawing of an American flag. During these times, my father doesn't feel alone.

One time in particular, my father met a group of young men who were pilots and performed stunt shows in Atlantic City, New Jersey. They had stopped at the diner on their way to a show and noticed my father sitting at the table. They asked questions and they listened as he shared stories from the war. My father told them about his great grandson who aspires to be a pilot one day. These young pilots got my father's address and a few days later stopped over at his house with all sorts of autographed pictures, pins, and words of encouragement for Tyler to follow his dream.

This past summer, a friend of the family ran into my dad. Our friend is a photographer for a program called the Warrior Watch Riders. This organization consists of a group of men and women (many veterans themselves) on motorcycles who greet soldiers returning from duty. The Warrior Watch Riders escort the soldiers to their homes. For those who have served in the past, they share a picture (a "mug") and a hug.

Our family friend put the word out to the Warrior Watch Riders and ten days later thirty motorcycles roared down my street. Warrior Watch Riders, along with their friends and family, took time out of their lives to honor the veterans who are so precious to me. My father, my uncle, a close friend — all World War II veterans — my two brothers — Vietnam veterans — and my son-in-law — an Iraq veteran — were all acknowledged. This occurred the weekend just after July 4th — a weekend when most adults are lounging by the pool or heading to the Jersey shore. Many of the Warriors crossed the bridges from Pennsylvania to surprise three men in their nineties who fought in a war more than seventy-three years ago. The old men tried valiantly to hide their tears.

In the past fifteen years, I have learned so much about my dad. The cap has allowed me to listen in on conversations. I learned that my father served twenty-eight months, that he flew 155 missions "Over the Hump" pushing supplies out the back of a plane when the co-pilot gave the signal. He volunteered for this mission because it paid fifty percent more. Over one thousand planes were lost trying to complete that mission.

So if you happen to read this and you are that thirtyish young man who shook my Dad's hand today — thank you from the bottom of my heart. Thank you to the tiny children who walk over and say thanks or draw a picture on their placemats. Thank you to the youth who are inspired to learn more about this generation. Thank you to the adults who have served and who have not been recognized nearly enough. How can anyone ever thank a man or woman who is drafted or enlists in a war? You put your life on hold, and it takes years to build your life back when you return.

Please look for those caps and muster up the courage to go over and say hello. My dad is lucky he has generations of family members in his life, but for some of these men you may be the only person they talk to on a particular day.

Search for the caps!

~Nancy Norton

Small Gestures

Sticks in a bundle are unbreakable.

~Kenyan Proverb

I was so tired. I just wanted to sleep. The blackness that engulfed me was slipping away. I tried to hold on to it, but the pounding in the distance was pulling it away from me, like a rope slipping through my fingers. This pounding was different than the pounding in my head. It wasn't pain... it was sound.

I fluttered my eyes and focused on the source of the pounding. The mirror on the back of my bedroom door was shaking. Boom! Boom! Boom!

"Get up, you guys!"

It was my husband's best friend, who was in town for my brother-in-law's wedding. My brain, pulsing from too much champagne at the reception the night before, could not make sense of what he was saying. He was mumbling something about the towers.

"The twin towers. We were attacked."

I followed my husband, who was just as confused and hung over as I was, into the living room.

We turned on the TV.

This was not a movie. This was the news. They didn't do special effects on the news, so it had to be real. How did this happen? What was sprinkling out of the windows? Papers? People? Why would they jump? Why would they show that on TV?

It was a live broadcast, that's why.

The three of us stood frozen in the middle of the living room. My champagne addled brain slowly soaked in the realization that this was happening.

Then, the unspeakable. The towers collapsed.

My thoughts raced to my family. I tried to call my parents back in Colorado to tell them we were okay. I couldn't get a signal. I tried the landline. Again... no signal. I knew they would be worried.

I thought of my husband's family. They had all come to town for the wedding. Were they all right?

My husband and I got dressed and headed for the hotel where they were all staying. Once everyone was accounted for, we piled into my mother-in-law's room. We sat together: some on the bed, some in chairs, some on the floor.

There was nothing we could do, so my husband and his brother and I headed for the restaurant where the wedding had been held the night before. There were things that needed to be picked up. Our bodies kicked into autopilot and took us to The Boat Basin Café.

The Boat Basin Café is an outdoor restaurant that overlooks the Hudson River. Last night's wedding had been a joyous occasion, which now seemed like a lifetime ago. We boxed up the few items we needed and then we sat there in silence. Not sure why. We didn't really know what else to do.

I looked out by the river and saw a fireman walking toward us.

It seemed strange to see a fireman, in his gear, walking all alone, six miles up the Hudson River from the World Trade Center. He hopped the barrier to the patio of the Café. As he got closer, I could see he was covered in soot. Not black soot, like from a fire. But tan soot, like from a beach. He sat down at a table, stared straight ahead for a moment, then put his head in his hands and began to sob. A waitress brought him a Coke and put her hand on his shoulder.

We sat, stunned, with our eyes fixed on him, and said nothing.

Suddenly, the morning's events were solidified for us. One person began to clap. Then another. And soon, we were all clapping. It seemed a bit trivial, applauding for this man. But what else could we do?

We returned the box of items to the hotel and found ourselves back out on the city streets. The three of us decided to eat. The diner we chose was not our usual Upper West Side gathering place. It was a few blocks from our apartment and was packed. We sat in the one remaining booth.

The kitchen was visible from our table. The cook was working hard, trying to fill bellies with comfort food. The waiter was running around, tending to the overflow of people. When he finally got to us, he said the other waiters couldn't make it into the city for work. So it was just him.

Having been in the restaurant industry for years, the three of us understood his stress and could have cared less about the "service" we were getting. Nobody seemed to care. It was enough to just be together. I saw someone get up from a table and get their own water. My brother-in-law made more coffee and my husband helped deliver plates of food to other tables. I sat and thought of that fireman.

The next couple of days were spent in a fog. We tried as best we could to get on with our lives. Our apartment, all the way on the Upper West Side, still smelled of smoke. I walked to work as the trains weren't running and the streets were filled with tanks instead of cabs. I hardly recognized once familiar neighborhoods, as the sides of buildings, telephone poles and scaffoldings were all plastered with the faces of the missing. And yet, people continued to gather at the restaurants where my husband and I worked, sharing their stories with one another.

That was all we could do. Be together.

On the first anniversary of 9/11, a moment of silence was declared. I found myself thinking of that fireman who sobbed in front of a bunch of strangers in a café. I thought of the waitress with her hand on his shoulder and the applause he received. I thought of the people in the diner who happily shared the shift of a lone waiter. I realized these small gestures were colossal. They meant something. They connected us as human beings and served as the foundation for our healing.

~Suzanne Herber

★ The ★ Spirit of America

That American Can-Do Attitude

Never tell people how to do things. Tell them what to do and they will surprise you with their ingenuity.
~General George S. Patton, War as I Knew It, 1947

59

The Alliance Singers

It always seems impossible until it's done.
~Nelson Mandela

Joined together by fate, The Alliance Singers came into being from the aftermath of September 11, 2001. During the first forty-eight hours that followed that horrific event, I started making phone calls to my neighbors. I felt the need to "do something." But what? No one knew what was happening — except that we needed each other to lend support to the families waiting to hear the fate of their loved ones and the fate of our country's future.

Two days later we managed to pull together a group of local residents and formed The Alliance of Neighbors, an all-volunteer organization to establish emotional and financial support for the families and the community. But we still needed a forum in addition to the street fair we had planned. The director of The Count Basie Theater in Red Bank, New Jersey offered us two nights to hold a benefit concert yet there were only weeks to prepare. Putting on my managerial hat, I became one of the founders of the organization, concert producer, and street fair director. It was the most flying by the seat of my pants I'd ever done!

Once word got out, music icons Bruce Springsteen and Jon Bon Jovi were the first to sign up, followed by Felix Cavalieri, Joe Ely, Joan Jett, and Kevin Smith — to name a few. While scrambling to cover all the details, I was faced with another last minute challenge when music director Gary Tallent urged: "We need backup singers for these acts. I know YOU can sing, so see if you can pull ten more people together for rehearsal — for the day after tomorrow."

Slightly panicked, I ran to the first place I thought of: The Pilgrim Baptist Church, where I pleaded with musical director Jesse Moorer to "gather some voices (and they have to sound good with mine) and be at my house tomorrow night at 7:00." This was to be the first meeting of many.

As promised, the singers appeared and raised their voices in harmony for the various performers of the concert and became what is now known as The Alliance Singers. Our concert was also broadcast live on Comcast and we raised a million dollars for assistance to the families and established an educational fund for the survivors' children.

Weeks after the successful concert madness, I received another phone call. This time it was Terry Magovern, Springsteen's tour director, requesting a smaller group from the original to appear with Bruce for a week of holiday concerts at Convention Hall. I called Jesse again, and he arrived at rehearsal with Antonio Lawrence, Michelle Moore, and Antoinette Moore to join in the festivities where we performed with Bruce's guests Bruce Hornsby, Elvis Costello, and Sam Moore of Sam and Dave. "Soul Man" almost literally brought down the house because Convention Hall was in such a state of disrepair! It was electrifying and also hilarious to have Danny DeVito as the show's MC.

Months later, on a snowy Sunday afternoon, I was once again called by Terry, who asked if the singers wouldn't mind working on some new material with Bruce.

Then another stunning moment arrived in June when I was phoned by Springsteen's management company informing me that the four cuts they recorded earlier that year would be included on Bruce's next album, *The Rising*. The management company wanted to be sure all of our names were spelled correctly. Trying to act cool — as if this sort of thing happened to me every day — I could barely control my excitement! This was to become a Grammy Award-winning album.

I had studied music at the University of Miami and Carnegie Hall, auditioned for dozens of shows, and cut an album that got some recognition, but I still had to keep my day job in publishing. But this? This was the validation that someone — and not just anyone — recognized my talent in this very tough, competitive business. The songs are "Mary's Place," "My City of Ruins," "Let's Be Friends," and "The Rising." Some of these tracks are also included in *The Essential Bruce Springsteen* CD. The film *Jersey Girl* also featured the entire track of "My City of Ruins."

More concerts with Bruce ensued, including an acoustic version of "My City of Ruins" for the *Today Show,* where Matt Lauer exclaimed, "They lit up the room!"

Invitations for additional performances followed as the opener for The Garden State Film Festival, The Red Bank Jazz Orchestra in a live performance on NPR, and a private concert for the entire cast and crew of the HBO Series *The Wire.*

A few years later, I received a phone call one afternoon from the producer of *The Daily Show with Jon Stewart.* She asked if the backup singers from *The Rising* would be interested in doing a bit on the show — that same day! We scrambled and made our way to New York and subsequently appeared on four additional episodes, earning an Emmy nomination and garnering us the title of "Official/Unofficial Gospel Choir." When Jon wrapped up his tenure as host, a special called *The Best of The Daily Show* featured us again as the fans voted one of our bits as "Best Smack Down."

We decided to cut a song to use as an audition piece, and to see if we could get some airplay. A spiritual from the early 1800s, "Wayfaring Stranger" was our first recording as a solo group. Its unique jazz-gospel spin on this timeless classic made it hip, smooth, and very "cool," which earned us a Top 75 position on the International Gospel Train Radio Charts.

Life can bring you the most incredible experiences. Five people who had never worked together — some of us hadn't even met before 9/11 — had some remarkable experiences together. Jesse and I often joke that we are the poster children for "you never know."

When fellowship and compassion meet with determination, remarkable things can happen.

~Corinda Carfora

60

Giving Back to the World

*Dare to reach out your hand into the darkness, to pull
another hand into the light.*
~Norman B. Rice

Sometimes, the big moments in life don't go as planned. When I told my family in late 2003 that I was joining the U.S. Army, no one said a word. But their eyes seemed to say, "You're going to be a *soldier*? Our Robyn is joining the *service*?"

Finally, my grandfather broke the silence. "Yes!" he said. "That's my granddaughter!"

Then my grandmother chimed in: "Well, it's about time!"

In hindsight, the response from the rest of my family was entirely reasonable. Given everything I'd been through, it was only natural they'd wonder about my decision. They'd spent years worrying about and protecting me — thinking of me as "sweet, little Robyn." So I'm sure it wasn't easy to hear I might be putting myself in harm's way.

But let me back up a bit.

I grew up in a postcard-perfect coastal town in southern Maine. It's the best-place-ever for kids. Everyone knows each other and everyone is always ready to help. My dad was a teacher and my mom, a trained nurse, stayed home to care for me, my older sister and younger brother.

We were muddling along just fine until I was about four years old. One day my arms and elbows began to mysteriously ache and swell. It went on for a few weeks, so my worried parents hustled me off to the doctor. He ran some tests, didn't like the results and immediately referred us to a specialist. There were more exams, more tests.

Finally, one of the doctors delivered the news: "Yes," he said, "it's cancer. Leukemia."

I was only four, but I remember it vividly. At some level, I think I even understood what it meant — or could mean.

The next two-and-a half years were a painful blur of medical procedures and hospital visits. While my friends were playing outside and learning to ride bikes, I was dealing with chemotherapy and radiation treatments. I couldn't keep food down, and my hair fell out. People asked if I was a boy or a girl. I hated that.

I knew I needed the treatments, but that didn't make it easier.

Then, when I was six, we were contacted by the Make-A-Wish Foundation. I was eligible for a wish, they said, and they wanted to know what mine was. I thought as hard as a six-year-old can and settled on two things: a phone call from Winnie the Pooh and a trip to Walt Disney World for my family.

Well, I got my phone call, and by January 1988 I was headed to Orlando and a place called Give Kids The World.

Give Kids The World is a wonderful organization. A nonprofit resort for kids with life-threatening illnesses, it hosts thousands of families every year, giving them the vacation of a lifetime. It provides them with a place to stay, it feeds them and entertains them. It even supplies complimentary passes to Orlando's theme parks. And there's never any cost to visiting families.

Give Kids The World was founded by a hotelier and Holocaust survivor named Henri Landwirth. Landwirth created Give Kids The World for one purpose: to ensure that no child's wish would ever go unfulfilled.

My time there was both magical and healing. It was an amazing experience filled with laughter and happiness — which, to me, are some of the most powerful medicines on earth. Two months after my visit, my cancer went into remission. I don't think that was a coincidence.

Fast-forward sixteen years. I'm out of high school and working. I'm healthy, things are going well, but I don't feel quite *right*. I want something more. I want to make a *difference*.

I began to think about the people in my life and I realized that, beside my parents, there were three who I wanted to emulate: my grandparents and Henri Landwirth.

My grandparents, I found out at some point, had provided tremendous financial support to my family during my illness. I'm not sure we would have made it without them. Henri created a magical place for seriously ill children. I'm not sure I would have gotten better without him.

Then I discovered something else they had in common. All three had served in the U.S. military — my grandparents in World War II and Henri during the Korean War. At that moment, I knew I wanted to serve my country, too. It would be my way of giving back to them and to so many people who had helped me along the way.

In February 2004, I joined the Army and began training as a munitions specialist. It was tough, mentally and physically. You have to push yourself. But cancer, strangely, had made me stronger, both mentally and emotionally.

Two years later, I was preparing for a deployment to Afghanistan when I was contacted by a representative from Give Kids The World. The Village was celebrating its twentieth anniversary, he said, and he wanted to know if I would come down and make an appearance.

Henri, he told me, was no longer running the Village, but he'd be there, and they wanted to surprise him with my visit. So, ten days before leaving for Afghanistan, I was back in Orlando to honor a man and organization who had sparked within me a desire to serve.

Backstage, dressed in my fatigues, I thought about what I would say and tried to compose myself. Over the years, I'd occasionally checked in with Henri, but he didn't know I'd joined the Army. Onstage, they were showing images of my visit from 1988. Then I heard my cue: "This is where she started, and here she is today."

I stepped onstage to greet an astonished Henri Landwirth. "You gave me the happiness and hope to survive," I told him. Then we both dissolved into tears.

Less than two weeks later, I was off to Afghanistan for sixteen months. I spent another five years in the military, leaving in December 2011. I'm now working as a mentor to a young man with autism, but I'm considering a return to military service. It's the best way I can think of to show my gratitude, to make a contribution. It's not something I would have planned all those years ago, but I honestly wouldn't change anything I went through. It made me who I am.

~Robyn Rothermel

Home Run to the Moon

*Don't tell me the sky's the limit when there are
footprints on the moon.*
~Paul Brandt

I married into a family of baseball addicts so we were thrilled when the California Angels built a new stadium in Anaheim on property adjacent to where my husband worked. We'd no longer have to drive to Los Angeles to see a game. We would have our very own team.

My husband Roger and our six-year-old son Jim attended the opening day game at Angel Stadium on April 9, 1966. I didn't go with them as I was about to have our second baby. The local newspaper printed an opening-day photograph of the massive crowd in the area where my men sat. Although I couldn't see their faces specifically, I could make out their forms in the picture. A couple of weeks later, our son Bob was born, so now we were raising two young baseball fans.

At Roger's suggestion, his employer purchased four season tickets for business entertaining. Roger spent much time checking out seat locations at different times of day for sun and shade, and he finally chose great seats behind home plate, just under the edge of the overhead tier. Protected from rain, out of the sun, yet with a sense of being in the open air. Perfect. The company's clients loved those seats, and our family got to enjoy them, too, when they were available.

There was one game I didn't want to attend, however. "I'd really rather stay home and listen to the broadcast of the moon landing," I said. "I don't want to miss it." History would be made that day. We had watched the launch several days earlier, and followed the progress reports since then. The landing would happen that afternoon.

"Honey," Roger said, "there won't be anything to see. It'll just be the TV news teams with mock-ups and diagrams."

I knew that was true, but I still wanted to be home to see whatever might be shown. I knew it would be exciting, even emotional. I wanted to savor it alone. I pouted a bit.

"Aw, come on Mom," nine-year-old Jim begged. "Let's go." Behind him, three-year-old Bob nodded vigorously. For him, going to the game was more about having ice cream in the miniature batting-helmet bowls. He had a growing collection of colorful helmets with the American League team colors and logos.

I couldn't resist three sets of pleading blue eyes. I gave in.

My spirits improved as we arrived at the ballpark. It was a perfect California summer day. But there was something different in the stands, a charged expectancy that quickly caught my attention. There was chatter coming from all around us as we went to our seats. Transistor radios!

"Oh, I wish we had one!" I couldn't understand the words, but from every direction, it was apparent the radios were all tuned to the same station.

As the game progressed, the electronic scoreboard in center field displayed all the game details, and occasionally an update on the progress of the moon landing.

The game continued. The minutes ticked down toward the landing. The noise of the crowd diminished. The transistor volume increased till it seemed to be one voice filling the stadium.

On the field the umpires had stopped the game that no one was watching. Rival players stood side by side, eyes fixed on the scoreboard. Both dugouts emptied as players emerged onto the field. The crowd, too, rose to its feet as the countdown dropped to seconds. My throat throbbed. The stadium fell quiet. Really quiet. Thousands of spectators seemed to hold their breath as one. Even the commentators were speechless — for once.

Total silence.

The back of my neck tingled. I knew the tears were coming.

Static.

"Houston. Tranquility Base here. The Eagle has landed."

Another second of total silence, and then the stadium erupted in a roar — cheers, laughter, tears, embraces, back-slapping, congratulations — joined by tens of millions of others across Southern California, across the United States, across the ocean, and across the world.

That Sunday afternoon in July was nearly half a century ago, but just thinking about it, reliving it, I feel the excitement, the pride, the thrill that causes my throat to tighten and my tears to form. This was America at her best — all experienced at a ball game I nearly missed.

~Lois Hudson

Made in America

There is nothing wrong in America that can't be fixed
with what is right in America.
~President Bill Clinton

"Open, you stupid tuna can!" I shrieked, banging it with the malfunctioning can opener. My husband Jake raced into the kitchen to see what had turned his sweet-tempered wife into a screeching madwoman.

My eyes blazed fire — or hunger. I held out the offending object. "This worthless can opener stopped working just like all the others, and it's only a few months old. I'm sick of fighting to open a can."

Jake shot me a condescending look. "Give it here. I'll open it."

His stance emanated confidence. I placed the implement of evil in his outstretched palm.

He put the opener on the can and rotated the handle half a turn. The opener slipped off and sent the can skittering across the counter. "Hmm, I must not have gotten it on tight enough," Jake said.

He tried again.

The can slid off the opener and plopped onto the laminate floor. Jake swooped it up with the speed of a falcon dive-bombing a mouse.

I crossed my arms and with superhuman effort restrained my "I told you so." Years of marriage had taught me this wasn't the appropriate time to gloat.

Besides, I still wanted my tuna.

"I hate this cheap foreign made stuff," Jake grumbled as he battled the opener.

Each attempt resulted in the same thing: a multi-punctured can sliding across the kitchen counter in a spray of fishy water.

Like players in an air hockey match, Jake and I took turns blocking the can's escape.

After multiple tries his jaw was clenched so tightly I couldn't tell if he was swearing under his breath or speaking in tongues.

We stood sweaty and panting in the kitchen. We'd turned can opening into an aerobic activity.

"Why'd you buy such crummy junk?" Jake fumed. He held up the opener, which was now jammed on the can.

I glared back. "It's a name brand, just like all the others. I assumed they'd work."

Just then the can opener came undone. The dented tuna can flew across the kitchen. Tuna water sprayed a wild arc throughout the room.

Jake threw the opener in the trash. I think I heard it laughing.

"What about my tuna?" I asked.

Jake's jaw muscles twitched. "Go buy a better opener," he said, wiping tuna flecks from his shirt.

I left my husband on cleanup detail and headed to the store.

In the housewares aisle utensils gleamed under the fluorescent lights like knights in shining armor. I grabbed the first can opener and flipped it over. The tiny "Made in China" letters mocked me.

I picked up the next big name brand. Sure enough, "Made in China." I worked my way along the offerings. All made in China.

One lone opener beckoned. I saw the price tag and muttered, "Holy mackerel, this one's twice the price of the others."

I lifted it and realized it weighed substantially more than its competitors. A bold "Made in America" graced the package front, right next to the Ten-Year Warranty.

The handle opened and closed effortlessly. The wheel mechanism glided smoother than an Olympic figure skater.

I put it in my basket and headed for the checkout. But then my inner voice, the one that likes to save money, piped up: "Don't get that. It costs more."

An hour earlier I'd been one step away from chain-sawing a tuna can.

Now I hesitated to spend more for a better product.

A mental image formed as I vacillated in the aisle.

I pictured a father working in a U.S. can opener factory.

The factory closes because I keep buying cut-rate inferior products.

The dad can't find another job. His wife can't support the family on her income. They lose their home, and the children are devastated.

All dire scenarios. But at the risk of sounding unpatriotic and selfish, I still wanted to open my tuna can.

"Stop being so chintzy," I chided myself. "Buy this can opener and help that dad keep his job."

I bought the American made opener, much to my husband's delight.

Food cans trembled before its mighty onslaught.

Jake and I decided we'd buy American made goods to support our countrymen who were supporting their families.

Now we enjoy "Made in America" benefits.

Our higher quality products function better.

We're helping American families.

And we can open any tuna can in the house.

~Jeanie Jacobson

63

How Baseball Saved Me

Success is one percent inspiration and ninety-nine
percent perspiration.
~Thomas Edison

can't walk, can't use my hands, and can't talk understandably. Those are a lot of "can'ts." Focusing on what I can't do doesn't help anyone, though. My mother taught me that as long as I worked hard I could accomplish many things, despite the birth accident that affected my physical skills. She was right — looking beyond my limited physical skills enables me to realize I can do what is important in life.

Not being able to communicate is my biggest and most frustrating disability and it has been a problem my whole life. When I began school, the teachers were focused on what I couldn't do instead of what I could do. They assumed that my intelligence was impaired because I couldn't speak to them. Mom had to supplement my education at home.

About a year after I started school, the district bought an electric typewriter with adapted access called the POSSUM, which stands for patient-operated selector mechanism. Every parent of a child with some difficulty handwriting wanted his child to use the "Possum." I was always at the bottom of the list since the teachers thought I wasn't as smart as the other kids.

Using the Possum was cumbersome. It had a large chart with all the keys of a traditional IBM electric typewriter. The user would hit the first switch and hold it down until he reached the column that contained the desired key, and then he would hit the second switch to go up to the desired key. To print it, the user had to hit the first switch again. Eventually, the other kids found faster communication methods, so the Possum became mine, slow as it was.

Then I made a breakthrough. I had always liked art, but I couldn't use my hands. One day, one of my friends lent me his head stick so that I could paint. I convinced Mom to buy me one so I could paint at home. Little did I know that purchase would open up a new world for me, as we discovered that I could use my head stick to type. At first, my neck was so tired that I was lucky to type one correct keystroke per minute, but at least I was getting something on paper.

With practice, I became faster and more accurate with my head stick, but no matter how hard I worked I got poor grades, because I couldn't finish all my homework. I wanted to drop out of school. Mom wouldn't allow this, but she knew I needed an outlet where I could be a normal high school kid. But where?

Luckily, Coach Sellers was coaching the junior varsity baseball team, and they needed a statistician. Everyone knew I was a rabid Dodger fan, so he asked me if I would like to be a statistician. I jumped at the opportunity. For the rest of my high school career, I was the statistician for the junior varsity and sometimes for the varsity baseball team. Baseball gave me a purpose and a sense of belonging. Baseball saved me. I stayed in high school, graduated, and went on to college.

Baseball has been a constant in my life since I was seven. Growing up in Los Angeles County, it seemed natural to become a Dodger fan. During my childhood, the Dodgers were rarely on the television, so I developed my listening skills while listening to their games on the radio. These listening skills ended up helping me in school, and I learned all about baseball statistics from those games.

While at Pasadena City College, I began a Dodger journal where I jotted down my thoughts and opinions about my favorite team. Since I didn't know how to look for a job and Mom couldn't afford to send me to a four-year university to finish my degree, it looked like I had nothing to do after my graduation.

I wasn't a person who could sit around and watch TV, though. I kept on writing in my Dodger journal every day. About a month after my graduation, I realized that I wanted to be a baseball journalist. From July 4, 1993 to October 6, 1995, when my family moved to rural Texas, I never missed a game.

When we moved, I figured that I would become a Houston Astros fan. After discovering I couldn't get the Astros on the radio or get an occasional televised game, I used a little of my disability money to pay for satellite TV so that I could continue watching baseball. Every time the Dodgers were on ESPN, TBS, or WGN, I watched them and wrote in my Dodger journal. Two years after we moved, we got a little money, and Mom helped me buy an improved computer that enabled me to go on the Internet. The first website I went to was the Dodgers' and I discovered I could listen to the games on the computer! Then I found that AOL had a group of Dodger fans that I could join. The leader ran a website devoted to the Dodgers, and I began writing for her Dodger Zone.

After a season, I decided to begin my own website named Dodger Place. There, I spent an average of fifty-five hours a week writing game reports, commentaries, and player profiles. I regularly read the *Los Angeles Times* and although I regularly disagreed with their assessment of the Dodgers, I never wrote a journalist.

However, in December 2000, I felt compelled to write Bill Plaschke, because it was obvious he wasn't watching the same team as I was. He compared Darryl Strawberry, a known drug abuser, to Shawn Green, an upstanding young man who had a poor performance. He wanted to keep the catcher who never performed well in a Dodger uniform instead of giving a rookie catcher named Paul Lo Duca a chance, and so on. I could have called him an idiot, but it wouldn't have enlightened this misguided sportswriter who needed to concentrate more on the Dodgers if he was going to write about them. I sent him a 1,200-word article explaining my position and telling him that I thought he was misguided.

To my surprise, Bill wrote me back trying to begin an argument. I refused, but I did ask him how he became a sportswriter. Unfortunately, in my response I had an equipment malfunction and I spelled the word "dream" without the "r." Bill probably only wrote back to me then to tell me about the typo, but that missing "r" started a dialog that continued. In trying to explain to Bill why an aspiring writer made such a blatant typo, I revealed my disability to him. That eventually led to Bill making the long trip from Los Angeles to my new home in Texas, and my career as a sportswriter was launched. On August 19, 2001 the *Los Angeles Times* ran an article that Bill wrote about me. It was hugely popular. For the first time in my life, people called me an "inspiration." I am no inspiration. I have achieved what I have through hard work and Bill's willingness to help a young writer get started.

Three days after the article appeared, MLB Advanced Media hired me to write a weekly column about my favorite team. It has now been fourteen years and I still work for them, but I am looking for other writing opportunities, too. In 2015 I published my first novel, entitled *Vengeance*.

Baseball, hard work, and a stranger who became a supporter, changing everything for me. It's truly the American "deam," I mean "dream!"

~Sarah Morris

64

Grounded

Remember the hours after Sept. 11 when we came
together as one! It was the worst day we have ever
seen, but it brought out the best in all of us.
~Senator John Kerry

"Delta Two-Fourteen, Denver Center. Climb and maintain flight level three-four-zero. Expect scattered light chop." With those words I started another morning shift at the Denver Air Route Traffic Control Center. It was 6:05 a.m. Mountain Daylight Time, on September 11, 2001. The skies over central Colorado were filling with aircraft crisscrossing the Rocky Mountains and the seven surrounding states that I and my fellow air traffic controllers managed.

It was about forty-five minutes later when an America West Airlines pilot queried me about some type of aircraft event. I hadn't heard anything and replied as such, but told him I'd check it out and get back to him. Another pilot keyed in about hearing something strange as well. Right after this brief radio exchange I was relieved from my radar control position for a break. With the pilots' comments fresh in my mind, I walked down to the lunchroom to see if anything was being reported on the television.

The cafeteria was packed but eerily quiet. I made my way around the edge of the crowd to see the television screen. What was displayed explained the shocked silence in the room: the North Tower of the World Trade Center was smoldering with flames shooting out of the windows near the top floors.

"What the hell happened?" I asked the guy standing next to me.

"A jetliner crashed into it. Can you believe that?" he replied.

I didn't respond, stunned by what I was seeing. Suddenly a gasp filled the room as the South Tower was struck by a second airliner careening into the side of the building. My thought was to get back to the control room and see what was happening and how, if at all, I could help.

Entering my area of specialty, I relieved the controller who was at the console. The frequency was filled with chatter, speculation, and uncertainty. Word was filtering through the airwaves and from the airline company dispatch offices that two aircraft had been hijacked and crashed into the World Trade Center. Having just witnessed the second explosive crash, I briefly explained that indeed, there had been two incidents involving aircraft and the Twin Towers.

A second controller sat down next to me, as was happening at each radar screen down the aisle. There was a sense of emergency, yet in our sectors of airspace, nothing out of the ordinary was happening. We felt the need to take action, but whatever that was, wasn't clear to us. Word from the Operation Manager's watch desk was only to stay vigilant, keep doing our jobs, and stay calm. Then, the assistant controller handed me a flight strip, a piece of paper normally used for flight plan information. This one was filled with words that confirmed what I had witnessed. I was instructed to read it on frequency to the pilots.

I did so, telling them that an incident involving several aircraft and a breach of the national airspace system, as well as national security, had occurred and that everyone was to begin planning an alternate destination for their flight. This statement only raised more questions from the pilots. Remaining vigilant for any flights that appeared off course or non-responsive to my control instructions, I relayed again that the possibility existed that flights might not be able to land at their intended destinations and that alternate plans needed to be made.

Over the next twenty minutes information was brought to our attention that two more aircraft had indeed crashed: one into the Pentagon and the other in a field in Pennsylvania. My mind raced with the possibilities of losing one of the aircraft under my control. I scanned each data block and aircraft trajectory. Everything appeared normal.

The assistant controller next to me was handed a second flight strip, which he read. Under his breath I heard him say, "You've got to be kidding me."

"What?" I asked.

He simply handed me the paper and told me I needed to read it to all aircraft on frequency. I read the note first to myself, not believing what it said. I drew a deep breath, trying to steady my voice and myself.

"Attention all aircraft: Due to national security measures and a threat to the national airspace system, all flights are to be grounded." For the first time in my thirteen years of work, my voice cracked, the enormity of the morning's events taking over my emotions. A second deep breath allowed me to continue: "Prepare to land at the nearest airport that can accommodate your aircraft. I say again, you will be instructed to land and expect a clearance to the nearest airport shortly."

I un-keyed the frequency and slouched back in my chair. What the hell was going on? This couldn't be happening. A comment from a pilot snapped me back to the moment at hand.

"Denver Center, this is American Two-Twelve. Did I hear that correctly? We are being forced to land? We've got too much fuel on board to land right away. Where are we supposed to go?"

Behind me several controllers were collecting data on what aircraft were in the skies, including their departure and landing points, to better determine the most effective way to clear the skies of all aircraft. For the first time in aviation history, there would be no one flying over the contiguous United States. Ground-to-ground phone calls were being made to airports concerning parking availability, runway configurations and capability.

One by one I cleared each flight to its new destination, often with some pushback and obvious concern by the pilots. I passed along what information I could, but understandably that was kept to a minimum. The work behind the scenes to coordinate the changes of destinations, accountability of each flight, monitoring their progress continued. Never before had I witnessed such a large-scale effort by so many to bring a life-changing event to conclusion.

By approximately 10:45 a.m. MDT, all 4,000 flights that were in the air across the country had landed without further incident. The National Airspace System had been cleared of every flight.

Emotionally drained, I left work and watched the remaining events of 9/11 play out via the news media. For the next two days we sat at our radar screens, staring at nothing. It was nearly as stressful as working a busy sector.

On the morning of September 14, 2011, a single engine Beech Bonanza airplane, bound for Southern Texas, departed from the Loveland/Fort Collins airport, the first private aircraft to be allowed in the air. Commercial flights had resumed in limited capacity the previous day.

In the fall of 2013, I met the pilot of that Beech Bonanza aircraft while serving as his fly fishing guide in Northern Colorado. We've remained friends ever since.

~Dean K. Miller

65

STS-136

The space program is not only scientific in purpose but
also is an expression of man's insistent determination
to do the nearly impossible — to explore the unknown,
even at great risk.
~Harold Urey

grew up a mile from NASA right after the Cold War, during the heyday of the space shuttle Endeavour program. My dad was an engineer at the Johnson Space Center.

Starting in preschool, I was programmed to be a space nut. We colored pictures of astronauts, shuttles, and rockets. We read books about the planets. We made solar systems out of construction paper. Mars and Jupiter seemed like places I might actually visit someday, like Moscow or Japan. We took field trips to Mission Control and the Neutral Buoyancy Lab, the giant pool where astronauts trained underwater for zero gravity. We touched moon rocks and took a class picture with the Saturn V rocket. We met Sally Ride.

In elementary school, we had school assemblies to watch shuttle launches from Cape Canaveral. Becoming an astronaut was a real career goal, like becoming a teacher or a doctor. My friend's dad was an astronaut. He came to Career Day at school and told us about his job, like it was any other ordinary job.

My sophomore year of high school, the first component of the International Space Station was launched into orbit. I volunteered at the newly built Space Center Houston, guiding visitors through the

Hall of Spacesuits. I knew more about Apollo astronauts than I did about U.S. Presidents.

It's hard to fully describe what it was like growing up at that particular time in that particular place. Space, or the idea of space, was everywhere, from billboards and car dealerships to restaurant menus and Little League team names. Even though I was just a kid, I felt like I was part of the NASA tribe of geeks and dreamers, banded together by our need to reach the stars. When the first *Toy Story* movie came out, Buzz Lightyear's catchphrase summed up the culture of Houston: "To infinity and beyond!"

My childhood memories evoke an impression of America, not the real America, but the ideal version of what we all believed America was or could be. It didn't matter that I was the first U.S. citizen born into my family. It didn't matter where my family came from. Houston in the 1990s was a melting pot forging incredible new alloys from which we could build anything we put our hearts and minds to.

The spell only wore off in my twenties, when I finally accepted that I probably wasn't going to Mars. I probably wasn't even going to the moon. Possibly not even into orbit around the earth. I felt like Buzz Lightyear in that heartbreaking moment when he finds out he's just a toy. He's been programmed with a fantasy, the world around him is make-believe, and he can't actually fly.

I was twenty-seven in 2009 when my first daughter, Sonya, was born. Four weeks later, we moved over 1,000 miles from Houston for my husband's new job. I was moving on, and my home city was moving on, too. Just like me. Houston and I decided to be practical, work the jobs we could get, and raise good families with the resources we had.

Now when we visit my parents every Christmas, my old neighborhood isn't the place I remember. Johnson Space Center is a tourist destination. They give tram tours to the old Mission Control.

On July 8, 2011, a week before Sonya turned two, NASA launched STS-135, the last mission of the American Space Shuttle Program. I cried when I watched the webcast in my living room that morning, whispering the countdown along with Cape Canaveral, as if I were at an assembly in my elementary school cafeteria, watching on a TV one of the teachers rolled in on a cart.

As the space shuttle Atlantis left the atmosphere, I saw an important part of my childhood shrink from view, something intangible and profound that I wouldn't be able to share with my daughter. For her, becoming an astronaut would be like becoming a superhero, an exciting thought, but highly unlikely — unless the commercial space industry really takes off. Sonya's grandmother bought her an orange astronaut costume for dress-up and Halloween. It looked like the one on display in the Hall of Spacesuits from 1994, when NASA astronauts started wearing bright orange instead of white or silver.

Sonya loved that spacesuit. She wore it to the grocery store. She wore it to bed. People would ask her what she was supposed to be. "Attronot," she'd say.

The week after the launch of STS-135, while the crew was still in orbit inside the International Space Station, I won a prize in an online give-away. The customs form on the shoebox-sized package that arrived in the mail listed the value of the enclosed item at $19.99. It was from a company called Makedo in Australia. I'd won a kit of blue plastic rivets, a cardboard saw, and two sheets of stickers that looked like cartoon buttons, switches, and gauges.

My husband found lots of cardboard. We went to work building a rocket ship in our living room with the help of those blue plastic rivets. The rocket was a hexagonal tower with a porthole in the door. In fat Sharpie, I wrote STS-136 down the side.

My daughter was so excited. She got into her astronaut costume and played inside the rocket with her stuffed animals. I pretended to be Mission Control, but my radio transmissions were quickly tuned out, so I left my daughter to play in her own world. That rocket towered in our living room for months. Parts of it started to cave in, but I was reluctant to get rid of it. In a strange way, the sight of it was reassuring. I liked seeing it in the corner by the window. The cardboard spaceship represented something intangible that I wanted to give my daughter, something vague but specific I wanted to pass on. A way of feeling, a way of looking, a way of being that's hard to put into words.

The prospect of me going into space now seems as unlikely and far-fetched as jet boots, invisibility capes, and time travel. But I want my children to dream of wild adventures and limitless possibilities just like I did. Sonya talks about designing jet boots with her friends at school. She draws herself with her sister Leena and her brother Arjun in rocket ships blasting off to galaxies far, far away. These things make me smile, because it reminds me of myself at that age.

But it's not really about going to space — it's about the dream of something that's beyond our reach, something that might be hard to achieve, but something we really believe in. Something that keeps us awake at night, something that makes us feel alive each day. Something that makes us better in the pursuit of it. The America I grew up in was shaped by individual know-how and team ingenuity coming together into something much greater than the sum of its parts. I want my kids to feel like they're part of something great and worthwhile, too, just like I did when I was a kid.

~Mitali Ruths

66

Welcome Home, Troops

The willingness of America's veterans to sacrifice for
our country has earned them our lasting gratitude.
~Jeff Miller

When my Corcoran, California high school class of 1965 graduated, our celebrations were tempered by the expectation that many of the young men would either be drafted or volunteer for the military. Thirty-six answered the call, leaving behind families, girlfriends, and college plans in order to serve our country.

They joined the Army, Marines, Air Force, and Navy, and dutifully went into an unpopular war. One of our classmates, Stephen Gaymon, was fatally wounded shortly after arriving in Vietnam. The rest came home from war to an ungrateful nation. Many also suffered from post-traumatic stress disorder, a little known condition at that time.

As a result, when it came time for our fifty-year class reunion, my classmates and I on the planning committee wanted to do something extra special to show our gratitude to the members of our class who served our country. One of our committee members, Pat, suggested that we honor our veterans with a special ceremony and give them ribbons with their name and service branch written on them. "I will design and make them. It would be a blessing to do this," Pat said.

The tribute was planned as a surprise for our veterans, but as the date of the event drew near, most of our military guys had not registered. It was important for them to be there. We called each one of the veterans and made a special appeal to them to attend. One veteran, Richard, told me, "I forgot all about it and wasn't planning on coming." Once it was explained that we are going to honor those who served our country, Richard agreed to come. Registration of veterans jumped significantly. All but a few committed to attending, and those who could not were disappointed.

The ceremony would be the highlight of our evening. The appointed hour came and classmate Andy walked up to the podium, along with the two others who would pin the ribbons on the men's shirts. The audience grew quiet as Andy announced, "Tonight we want to honor our veterans by giving them a gift of appreciation. When your name is called, please come forward and stay until everyone is standing."

The names of those unable to attend were read first in a slow cadence to ensure every name would be heard. The room remained silent as the names of the four deceased veterans were called and their ribbons were accepted by family members or friends. Andy finally announced, "Stephen Gaymon gave his life and the ultimate sacrifice for our country."

Then each veteran who was in attendance heard his name called and went up to have his ribbon pinned on his jacket. It was startling to see how many of our classmates served. In the end, twenty-five men stood side by side. We all got misty eyes. We knew that special group of men at the front of the room shared a bond the rest of us could not truly understand.

Then Richard stepped forward and reached for the microphone. With the following words he stole the hearts of the audience: "This is long overdue. When I came home from Vietnam, I was spit on and cursed at. Tonight we are finally welcomed home." Richard turned toward his fellow veterans and said, "Welcome home, troops!"

The audience was silent for a moment before erupting into a grateful standing ovation as patriotic music played in the background. We had welcomed home our own. It almost felt like our high school graduation ceremony was finally complete.

~Penelope A. Childers

67

To My Sister Whom I've Never Met

*Freedom is never more than one generation away
from extinction... We didn't pass it to our children in
the bloodstream. It must be fought for, protected, and
handed on for them to do the same.*
~President Ronald Reagan

I am an American woman, whose thoughts have often turned to you, my sister of the world, my sister whom I've never met. I'm so blessed to be living in a land where freedom prevails for males and females. Yet you, living somewhere else in this universe, do not share the same advantages. Sometimes I wonder why I am so lucky. I am no more and no less than you, my sister whom I've never met. But sometimes I have to remind myself not to take my good fortune for granted. That's when I think of you.

Last Sunday I kneeled in church, my hands clasped in prayer. Then I rose and without fear I sang a hymn out loud. This fundamental privilege is denied to you, my sister whom I've never met. Your belief in a higher power, if you have one, must be concealed in your soul under the threat of persecution or worse.

In my grateful heart I prayed to God that you might know the same right to religious worship of your choice as I enjoy in my great country of America.

"It's not fair," I used to grumble as I walked to school, noticing my classmates riding in their parents' cars. "Why should I walk when others ride?"

My attitude was quickly adjusted when I thought of you, my sister whom I've never met. Would you gladly walk for blocks, no matter what the conditions, if you could go to school? Or is education prohibited to you because you are a girl?

When I woke up on the morning of my twenty-ninth birthday a question briefly crossed my mind: "Am I an old maid?" I shook it off as I showered in warm water, got dressed, locked the door to my own apartment, and went to a job I loved.

I thought of you, my sister whom I've never met. Must you, as a single woman, live in your parents' home regardless of how old you are? Is it permitted for you to live alone? If a marriage has not been arranged for you by a certain age, does your culture consider you an old maid? Are your parents disappointed? Does it make you feel like a worthless burden?

After work, my girlfriends invited me to a bistro to celebrate my special day. We chatted and laughed, sipping wine.

Could you ever experience the simple pleasure of stepping out of your home without having to be escorted by a male relative? Are you allowed to enjoy carefree moments in a public place with female friends? Could you even have a glass of wine?

When male friends joined our cheerful group I thought of you again, and again when I kissed a boy goodnight.

Would that be forbidden to you?

American women have that right to freedom. They may go where they please, may congregate with friends, regardless of their gender, for the delight of friendship.

I thought of you on my wedding day as I stood next to the man I loved, a man I had chosen, not one chosen for me. We had previously discussed the number of children we might have. Would we want boys or girls or both? Nothing was certain but it was not forbidden to have more than one. And he was considerate of my wishes.

Were you happy on your wedding day? Were you filled with tenderness and affection when you stole a glance at your husband-to-be from under your veil, as I was when I gazed at mine? Did you love him? Did you even know him? Or were you filled with fear and dread?

Were you limited to the number of babies you could produce? Did they have to be only boys? If you gave birth to a girl, would you be able to keep her? To make such a decision would certainly be unbearable!

I thought of you when I went to vote. The line extended into the rainy street. The wait was long and I was irked until my thoughts turned to you, my sister whom I've never met. Would you have dismissed such petty inconveniences as the lines and the rain if you were allowed to vote for a candidate of your choice? Or can't you vote at all because you are a woman?

I thought of you last night when I ordered a meal and my hamburger was overcooked. The bun was dry and the latte was weak. I was about to complain when an inner voice stopped me: "The latte's weak? Well, la-di-dah! How entitled can you be?" I wondered if you had anything at all to eat last night.

I grieved for you when I read the papers and watched the news reporting about the girls abducted into slavery or worse. I prayed your parents never had to deal with such anguish. I hoped you were untouched from such torment and suffering.

Last night noises awoke me several times — the harmless noises of my snoring husband. Though at first I was annoyed, I resisted the urge to whine.

"Turn to your side, honey," I gently nudged him. The sounds soon subsided.

What keeps you awake, my sister whom I've never met? Is it bombs flying overhead? Is it war, gunfire or terror in the streets?

I said a silent prayer for you and pulled the covers over my head. Then I counted my blessings and gave thanks that I am an American woman.

~Eva Carter

D.C. on a Dollar

*Twenty years from now you will be more disappointed
by the things you didn't do than by the ones you did do.*
~Mark Twain

Baltimore was off my radar. I had never been there, never planned to go. But then my documentary was accepted into a women's film festival. I arranged to share a room with another filmmaker to cut the expense of attending.

I was the first to arrive at our hotel in Baltimore, so I checked in for us. "We are splitting the room," I explained to the woman at the reception desk. She nodded, took my card and ran it.

While I was out scrounging for breakfast, I tried to use my debit card. Insufficient funds. I checked my balance—all $400 I had was frozen in my account. The hotel had taken all $400 as a deposit and put a hold on my card. This left no money for food, taxis, or anything. I complained. I cried. There was nothing they could do for two business days.

My screening was early in the morning. The auditorium was completely empty. No one was there. Who would want to sit through a ninety-minute documentary on women in prison first thing Friday morning?

I'd always wanted to go to Washington, D.C. and I wasn't about to waste the opportunity: This was the closest I would get for a while. I had $30 on an old credit card I was paying down, a checkbook, and one dollar in cash. I used the last bit on my credit card to buy an

Amtrak train pass to D.C. When I arrived in the city, I used my one dollar for a bus pass.

First, I went to the Library of Congress. I studied the perfectly sculpted stone faces guarding the doors and walked in. Books, murals and sculptures were everywhere.

I visited The Capitol and the White House just as it started raining. With no umbrella or raincoat, I hopped and skipped from one free landmark to the next, only stopping to take a sip from a drinking fountain. The sun disappeared behind rain clouds over the Eisenhower Executive Office Building, where the Vice President has his office.

I strolled through the Smithsonian Gardens and visited the Washington Monument. I walked along the war memorials to a statement etched in stone: "Here We Mark the Price of Freedom." Standing above it was a wall covered in gold stars, souls lost in World War II. Each star represented 100 American deaths. The next monument stood for the soldiers of the Vietnam War. Thousands of names carved in stone. I wondered how many fought with my father. He never spoke about his war experiences.

As a little girl, I would wake up early in the morning to listen to the tapes my father sent my mother. The tapes consisted of him talking to her, plus sweet performances of early Beatles songs accompanied by a single guitar. On those tapes he still had his voice. I grew up listening to his speech get weaker and then disappear from the poison of Agent Orange. My parents now insist that they hate the Beatles.

The Monument lit up into a glowing beacon standing guard over the dead.

The rain returned and soaked through me as I slowly climbed the Lincoln Memorial. President Lincoln sat in front of me like a giant. I stood in front of him, feeling small and hypnotized. The lights at his feet turned up to him like proud servants. I read his speech: "Four score and seven years ago our fathers brought forth, upon this continent, a new nation… that this nation, under God, shall have a new birth of freedom — and that government of the people, by the people, for the people, shall not perish from the earth."

I checked my watch — I was almost late for the walking tour of

Lincoln's Assassination. The group met in front of the White House. I wrote a check to the student leading the tour, and he took it without reservation. He enthusiastically led us from one house to the next, colorfully describing the events of that night. The first attempt on the Secretary of State William Seward's life, including a clever intruder, a misfired gun and a stabbing while he was safely encased in a neck brace. The second, a drunk coward who gave up and went to sleep instead of assassinating Vice President Andrew Jackson. And finally, we stood outside Ford's Theatre, closed for restoration, and listened as a pistol through a peephole and a cheerful president collided. The small group of strangers standing outside the theater grew quiet, our smiles and questions dimmed as we turned to the house across the street where he passed away slowly, his tall legs hanging off the edge of a bed.

As his life came to an end, so did the tour. We all stood there in silence as our tour guide waved farewell and left us there. After a few minutes, we slowly broke apart and returned to wherever we came from.

My train returned me to Baltimore, where a taxi driver took a carbon copy of my credit card in exchange for a ride to my hotel.

I did all that with my one dollar. I know it was a bit crazy but I saw the opportunity and I took it. It was so worth it. I felt like I completely immersed myself in D.C. that day, getting a quick but meaningful tour of our nation's capital. It made me proud.

~Vita Lusty

69

A Hundred Feet of Hope in a Thousand-Year Flood Zone

When the world says, "Give up," Hope whispers,
"Try it one more time."
~Author Unknown

T he water in the living room was still waist-deep. Furniture scattered everywhere like two people had been wrestling for hours. The stench? Well, some things are better left unsaid.

But you could hear it coming from upstairs: the unmistakable mews of frightened cats. Cats desperate for food, water, veterinary help, and, most of all, the loving embrace of their family.

There we were in Georgetown County, South Carolina, responding to the "thousand-year flood" that had devastated the Palmetto State in October 2015. American Humane Association's Red Star Rescue team had traveled all over the state in the past few days to rescue animals and help pet owners get the supplies their furry friends so desperately needed but couldn't get because roads and stores were still closed because of the deluge.

As the team relocated from the capital city of Columbia in the middle of the state to this coastal community, we began hearing reports that there were animals trapped in homes. When the floodwaters started to climb higher and higher, desperate families were forced to evacuate. Many didn't know what to do with their pets, and left them behind with a supply of food, hoping their separation would be short.

This flood, however, was different. Folks in South Carolina who'd lived there for generations had never seen rising waters quite like this. True to the term, it might be another millennium before such an event happens there again.

Fortunately, my team knew what to do.

Many of my fellow Red Star team members had been on countless deployments to help animals in disaster situations around the country. The staff is the best-trained group in the country to handle emergency situations involving animals. Our corps of volunteer responders is a group of highly trained Americans from all walks of life — from secretaries to firefighters to animal control officers to animal lovers of all types — who take off work and deploy at a moment's notice whenever and wherever animals need them. We couldn't do our work without them; they are true heroes.

We loaded up our two 50-foot Lois Pope Red Star Rescue Vehicles, outfitted with everything our team needs to rescue, shelter, care for, and even transport animals. "One hundred feet of hope" was soon on its way.

Then it was time for us to outfit ourselves: flood zones are dirty and real health hazards. Think of all the gunk, motor oil, and other detritus that builds up on roadways, parking lots, and in sewers, and imagine that all getting mixed up in floodwaters. Not the kind of place you'd like to take a dip. Any bit of it on your skin could cause an infection.

Animals who have been exposed to floodwaters are susceptible to illness, and if one of them were to scratch or bite us, the bacteria on their claws or teeth could pass on to us. So we were in full-body suits to keep ourselves protected.

Utilizing a brand-new boat purchased specifically for this deployment, we ventured out into the waters that covered the streets and yards, unsure of what we'd find.

We found animals stranded in homes. The ones who were in good enough shape were left to "shelter in place," meaning they would be safe there and we would continue to check-in on them and give them food and water until the waters receded enough for their families to come home.

***

Just a few weeks before this deployment, I had come on board as the national leader of this historic team, celebrating its 100th birthday in 2016.

Clearly, I had some big, big shoes to fill.

American Humane Association's Red Star Rescue program was born on the battlefields of Europe in 1916. Our organization's president received a letter from U.S. Secretary of War Newton Baker urging America's first national humane organization to travel across the pond and care for the horses involved in battle. The Great War, as it's now known, was the last major global conflict to employ an equine cavalry, and the casualties were piling up.

American Humane Association served as the equivalent of the Red Cross for animals, and even before our boys saw action, the Red Star team was caring for 68,000 horses a month who were wounded in battle.

Once the war was over, our team turned its efforts primarily (but not exclusively) to the home front, and became America's leading disaster response team for animals.

During the past century, Red Star has been involved in virtually every major disaster relief effort, from Pearl Harbor to 9/11, Hurricane Katrina, the Joplin, Missouri and Moore, Oklahoma tornadoes, the Japanese and Haitian earthquakes, the Mount St. Helen's eruption, and Superstorm Sandy.

Our team also responds to major animal cruelty cases and hoarding situations, helping to give animals in abusive situations second chances at life. Over just the past ten years Red Star teams have saved, helped and sheltered more than 80,000 animals.

When we're not responding to help animals in need, our team educates communities and pet owners so that whenever Mother Nature unleashes her fury, Americans everywhere are prepared to protect their best friends.

* * *

As we made our way through the waters we got word of forty-six cats trapped in a home, seeking escape from the deep water. Gingerly, we made our way into the home where we could hear the cries of the cats emanating from the upper floors.

To the cats, the sight of our team, wearing biohazard suits with helmets and carrying nets and crates, was not comforting. Their whole world had been turned upside down by the flooding, and all of a sudden the first people they saw were complete strangers dressed like aliens from outer space.

It took quite a while, but we were able to catch most of the cats (some had escaped to the roof, so all we could do was leave them food and water to shelter in place). Before they could be taken to our temporary shelter, they had to be decontaminated from their exposure to the floodwaters.

As is the goal with all deployments, we were able to reunite the cats with their owners once the crisis had ended.

Grateful families look at us as their pets' saviors. But to us, it's just another day in the life of American Humane Association's Red Star Rescue team, and the dawn of a new century of saving animals in need.

~Randy Collins

Editor's note: To learn more about the Red Star Rescue program or to support their lifesaving efforts, please visit AmericanHumane.org.

★ The ★ Spirit of America

Our Proud New Citizens

People come here penniless but not cultureless. They bring us gifts. We can synthesize the best of our traditions with the best of theirs. We can teach and learn from each other to produce a better America.

~Mary Pipher

70

Giving Kids the World

How wonderful it is that nobody need wait a single
moment before starting to improve the world.
~Anne Frank

The call that changed my life was ostensibly about tennis. A friend needed a fourth for a game at Bay Hill Club near Orlando, and she invited me to join her. I was exhausted — I'd just returned from a months-long assignment in Paris for the Walt Disney Co. but my friend was in a bind.

So when she assured me she wasn't trying to set me up, I agreed to play. It turned out to be one of the most important decisions I ever made.

Now I should tell you that I firmly believe that if you keep an open heart and an open mind, everything happens for a reason. And it's clear to me today that each step I had taken up to that point in my life was preparing me for the journey I was destined to make.

You see on that warm, summer morning, I met a force of nature named Henri Landwirth. During the match, Henri teased me. He taunted me. He could be frustrating, but he couldn't be ignored. When the game was over, I was intrigued but not entirely sure what to think of him.

The next day Henri, a Central Florida hotelier, called me. Soon, we were meeting for lunch. Within a year, we were married.

By the time we'd met, Henri had lived an incredible life. He had grown up in Belgium with his parents and twin sister Margot. He had a happy childhood, but it was cut short by the horrors of the Holocaust.

When the Nazis came to power, Henri and his family, who were Jewish, were rounded up by soldiers. His father was killed almost immediately, and the rest of the family taken to concentration camps. Henri spent his teen years there, separated from his mother and sister. When the war finally ended, Henri learned his mother had been killed. Miraculously, his sister survived, and Henri found her living in Poland.

Hearing his stories was overwhelming. I'd been a history major in college and thought I knew about World War II. But the facts and figures were dry and clinical and couldn't compare to Henri's vivid first-hand accounts. The atrocities became real — as real and dehumanizing as the prisoner ID, "B3434," tattooed on Henri's forearm.

I was dumbfounded by Henri's life story, but what impressed me most was how he'd responded to the experience. He would never forget the brutality he saw, but he would not let it defeat him. After the war, Henri made his way to America — with virtually nothing — and, after serving in the Army, became a successful businessman.

He ran and later owned a collection of hotels in and around Central Florida. Through his industry connections, he met and forged friendships with people like Senator John Glenn, Art Buchwald and Walter Cronkite. By any measure, this smart, hard-working Belgian immigrant epitomized the American Dream.

But for Henri, financial success meant little if you didn't use it to help others. And so, at an age when some business owners might have been contemplating retirement, Henri founded a charity to serve children with life-threatening illnesses and their families.

It was called Give Kids The World, and its premise was simple: If a child with a life-threatening illness had a wish to visit Central Florida and its world-famous theme parks, Give Kids The World would provide accommodations, meals, local transportation, and just about anything else the family needed. Its goal was to give these families the vacation of a lifetime — all at no cost.

Henri created Give Kids The World after hearing the story of a little girl named Amy. She had leukemia and wanted more than anything to meet Mickey Mouse. A wish-granting organization began making plans to send her to one of Henri's hotels — he often hosted wish kids — but before the arrangements were complete, Amy's time ran out.

When Henri learned what had happened, he was beside himself. It all seemed so unfair, so unnecessary. So he made a vow to children with life-threatening illnesses everywhere. Never again would a child's wish go unfulfilled because of scheduling constraints. Never again would time simply run out.

"Though I never knew her," Henri later wrote, "Amy's death became the catalyst for building Give Kids The World…."

Henri often told me he saw himself in the eyes of children like Amy. He knew what it was like to lose all hope, to see your happiness stolen. From the terror of his own childhood came the empathy to help children facing their own nightmares.

After seeing the impact Give Kids The World had on families, I knew instantly I wanted to be part of it. So in 1993, I left the Walt Disney Company to help run Give Kids The World.

Working side-by-side with Henri, our life revolved around the Village. I watched in amazement his endless determination and laser focus.

We spent every waking moment strategizing and building relationships. Every expense was scrutinized — right down to the Post-It notes — to ensure as many resources as possible could be channeled into services for our guest families.

As we worked, the Village grew. We added villas and attractions. Thousands of families came to visit us each year. Our goal remained the same — to create the happiness that inspires hope.

The Village and its mission came to define me, and I absorbed everything I could, knowing eventually I would be entrusted with carrying on Henri's legacy. It was a daunting realization, so I asked him one day to dictate to me his vision for the future. It would be my roadmap, my north star.

That map turned out to be several pages long, but it boiled down to two things: Never turn a child away, and always do what is best for the children. If we uphold those principles, we will never stray off course.

I have tried to live by those words every day since becoming CEO and president of Give Kids The World in 1995. With the help of countless donors and corporate partners, we have now served more than 144,000 families from all 50 states and 75 countries. Henri stepped back from day-to-day operations several years ago, but he remains intensely committed to and passionate about GKTW's mission.

In many ways, the success of the Village is a uniquely American story: founded by an immigrant, built with hard work and based on the proposition that there is no higher calling than serving others.

I wake up every day grateful to be part of it — and astonished by how a simple game of tennis shaped my life. If you're open to what life presents — if you fasten your seatbelt and go along for the ride — you never know where you'll end up. For me, I've found what I was put on earth to do.

~Pamela Landwirth

71

My All-American Family

*It is the flag just as much of the man who was
naturalized yesterday as of the men whose people have
been here many generations.*
~Henry Cabot Lodge

W e were getting ready to head from our house in the suburbs to Hart Plaza in downtown Detroit, where both of my parents would take their oaths and officially become U.S. citizens. "Do I really have to wear this shirt?" I asked with a frown.

"Yes, we are all wearing red, white, and blue," my mom answered firmly. "Let's go. We're going to be late."

My mom had carefully selected clothing for each member of our family to wear for the ceremony. She wore a sleeveless, knee-length dress with bold red, white, and blue stripes running vertically from neckline to hem. My dad was dressed in a navy suit with a red, white, and blue patterned tie. And for my little brother and me, my mom had picked out matching T-shirts with "USA" emblazoned in big red, white, and blue letters. As a shy, self-conscious eight-year-old who was just beginning to pay attention to the latest trends, the last thing I wanted to wear that day was a corny "USA" T-shirt, especially in public.

But I didn't have a choice. This was an important day for my parents and we were going to be patriotically color-coordinated, even if my mom had to force that shirt over my stubborn little head herself.

My parents emigrated from the Philippines in 1972, settling in

Detroit. Like most Filipino immigrants during that time, my mom had come to the United States to work as a nurse. My dad found work in a factory shortly after they arrived, then stayed home to take care of me after I was born. Eventually, he found a job as a salesman for a large floral wholesaler. The stability in their careers not only allowed my parents to build a much better life than they would have had in the Philippines, but also enabled them to provide financial support to their family back home.

In Detroit, my parents found a thriving community of fellow Filipinos; most of them were nurses, though some had immigrated to work as doctors or engineers. When I was five, my family moved from a small, two-bedroom city apartment to a newly constructed three-bedroom house with a huge yard in a suburb bordering Detroit. Many of my parents' friends had moved to the same town and we were one of four Filipino families on our street.

While I enjoyed having friends and neighbors who shared our culture, I spent my elementary school years longing to fit in with my classmates, who mostly came from what I thought of as "All-American" families. They had roller skating parties or magicians and pizza for their birthdays. The highlight of my birthdays was usually the *lechón*, a whole roasted pig with a shiny, red apple wedged between its teeth—a sight I worried would "totally gross out" my American friends, so I never bothered to invite them to my parties. And while my friends' moms did carpool, baked cookies, and took them to the mall to buy cool outfits after school, my mom was usually working the afternoon shift at the hospital and didn't come home until midnight. In those earliest years, I wasn't really proud of my Filipino heritage and I spent a lot of time wishing I could magically become part of a normal, All-American family.

So, on that hot July day in 1984, when my red, white, and blue-clad family arrived at the outdoor amphitheater where the oath-taking ceremony was about to begin, I could feel all eyes on us as we made our way down the steps toward the front of the crowd. To make matters worse, my mom insisted that we sit in the first row of seats. She wanted us to have the best view of the stage, though my embarrassment about standing out too much made me feel like we might as well have been *on* that stage.

Before we could get settled in our seats, a Channel 7 news reporter approached us, followed closely by a cameraman.

"What a beautiful family! Can we interview you for our evening newscast?" the reporter asked my mom.

"Of course!" she replied with excitement.

I didn't pay attention to what was actually said during the interview because I was so transfixed by my mom's face, as tears of joy fell from her eyes. She was the happiest I had ever seen her. I turned to look at my dad and was surprised to see that a reporter for an AM radio station had approached him for an interview. My dad's face beamed as he spoke into the reporter's handheld tape recorder. All of a sudden, I felt like we were celebrities! As I watched both my parents being interviewed and then scanned the crowd, seeing thousands of happy faces anxiously waiting for the ceremony to start, my feelings of self-consciousness and embarrassment quickly melted away. My family didn't look embarrassing or corny at all. We — along with everyone else around us — looked like proud Americans. As I sat through the ceremony and witnessed my parents take their oaths, I could sense how deeply honored and privileged they both felt to be there.

A few years later, I was watching the Channel 7 news when a segment about upcoming Fourth of July celebrations came on. The next thing I knew, I was looking at my own family on the television screen! The news station had re-used footage from my parents' oath-taking ceremony for the segment. There we were — the four of us, in our red, white, and blue attire — proudly waving little American flags. As I watched my slightly younger self in that moment replaying on TV, it suddenly occurred to me that, for my family, being American wasn't about blending in and doing the same things as everyone else. It was about being proud of who we were and where we came from, and feeling grateful and fortunate for all of the freedoms and opportunities that we have as United States citizens. All it took for me to finally understand this was seeing one very special, very proud All-American family on TV.

~Ronelle Frankel

72

American Boots

*Some people dream of success... while others wake
up and work hard at it.*
~Author Unknown

As a kid visiting my grandparents, I was always intrigued by a very old pair of worn leather boots with missing laces that were kept just inside their back door. They certainly weren't footwear my grandmother would wear and they were too small for my grandfather. I never saw anyone put them on.

Those boots stayed there though. In the summer, when the doormat was covered with sandals and sneakers, they were there. The doorway would be surrounded with rubber galoshes and heavy shoes in the winter and the old, worn boots were there too.

Finally, one day when I was about twelve, I asked my grandmother about the boots. I remember she and I were sitting at the kitchen table — me with a glass of chocolate milk, her with a steaming cup of spearmint tea, and a plate of oatmeal raisin cookies between us. I looked over at the back door; there on the mat were my red sneakers, my grandfather's steel-toed work boots, Grandma's shiny black shoes — and the old boots.

"Grandma," I asked. "Whose old boots are those?"

"Those are my father's boots, dear," she said.

"But, you said your father died before I was born," I replied.

"Yes, he did," she nodded and slid the plate of cookies closer to me.

"So, why do you still have his boots?" I took another cookie.

"They're really worn out."

Grandma sipped her tea. "Those, my dear, are the first pair of shoes my father bought after he got to America. And he wore them his whole life. He called them his American boots."

"Do you wear them sometimes?" I asked.

"Oh, no," my grandmother shook her head. "They're not to wear. They're just a reminder."

"A reminder?" I asked. "To remind you to put shoes on before you go outside?"

Grandma laughed. "No, dear, I'm pretty good about remembering to put shoes on. You see, when my family came to this county in 1904, we had nothing but the clothes we were wearing and a few dollars my parents had managed to save before we left Germany. My father found us a place to live, got a job, earned a living to support his family, and eventually bought a house. Then, years later, I asked my father if he had ever imagined, when we were leaving the port of Hamburg years ago, that he would get to that successful point—owning his own home, with two married daughters and a grandchild on the way."

"What did he say?"

"He said he could indeed imagine it because his secret was steps—tiny little steps, always moving forward. My father knew he could make it because he thought America gave a friendly kick in the pants to everyone who came here. He believed that no matter how your homeland had hindered or impeded you, once you got to America, you'd feel that little kick in the pants that would make you take a step forward. He always joked with my sister and me that if we ever needed a kick to get going, he'd be glad to help us with his American boots."

"And what he believed is true," continued my grandmother. "My father started with nothing, but he acquired a trade, learned to vote, budget money, and get a mortgage. So, after he passed away, I always kept his old American boots right by the back door so I see them every time I go in or out. That way those boots can remind me if I need a little kick in the pants to keep me going."

Nowadays, by my own back door, among my sneakers and flip-flops, I have those old, worn American boots tucked in the corner.

It's a friendly reminder that I will always keep moving forward, even if I occasionally need an American kick in the pants to get me started.

~David Hull

73

Election Day

*Voting is the expression of our commitment to
ourselves, one another, this country and this world.*
~Sharon Salzberg

Vincenzo Gramenzi, my maternal grandfather, was born in 1887 in Piano Piccolo, a tiny village high in the hills of Abruzzi, Italy. His parents were *contadini*, tenant farmers who worked the land for the wealthy *padrone* in exchange for rent and a small portion of the crops they grew. Life was hard and there was little opportunity for improvement. Only landowners had the luxury of pursuing an education, advancing their social standing, or having a voice in their government. The only thing the *contadini* could look forward to, and the only thing they could offer their children, was more of the same hardscrabble existence. But my grandfather was an industrious young man who dreamed of a life where he could benefit from hard work and have the opportunity to steer his own destiny. Fortunately for him, fate intervened in a very unexpected way.

One day, his older sister Grazielle — the only girl in a family of nine children — went out to buy wine and never came back. My grandfather later learned that she and her boyfriend, a young man the brothers didn't approve of, had run off to America to be married. Although this incident caused a major family scandal, my grandfather secretly kept in touch with his sister. Through her letters, he learned about a country where he could pursue his dreams — where a person's future was not limited by the circumstances of his birth. He made up his mind that somehow he would find a way to join his sister in America.

Grazielle offered to sponsor him if he could manage to get to a place called Philadelphia. Defying the odds, he scrimped and saved until he finally scraped together enough money to buy a passage in steerage on the Verona, a trans-oceanic freighter. And so, on a day in early spring, my twenty-four-year-old grandfather left his family and the land of his birth and never looked back. He took with him only his dream of a brighter future and a battered suitcase holding his few possessions. The voyage was long and difficult, but he was sustained by the vision of a land of unlimited opportunity that awaited him at his journey's end.

When Grandpop arrived in the United States in April of 1911, he dove headfirst into the melting pot and set to work becoming a "Merigan" (American). He moved in with his sister and brother-in-law and took a job as a plumber's apprentice in order to learn a trade. He struggled to master English, this strange new language that sounded so different from the round, musical tones of his mother tongue. A few years later, after saving every penny, he was able to move to New Jersey and a place of his own. There he met and married a pretty young girl from the neighborhood who went on to bear four daughters and five sons (four of whom later distinguished themselves in battle during World War II). My grandfather now had nine more reasons to want a better life. After much hard work and sacrifice, he started his own plumbing business, a legacy he would eventually pass on to his sons. And on January 9, 1923, Vincenzo Gramenzi officially became a citizen of the United States of America. Now he could even have a voice in his government. He would actually be allowed to vote. His dream had become a reality.

On Election Day, my grandfather set aside his trademark denim overalls and plaid flannel shirt and put on a dark suit, button-down shirt and tie. He had purchased these items especially for this momentous occasion. He donned a porkpie cap and walked proudly to the polls to cast his ballot. A non-smoker, he even bought a single cigar to smoke on the way home. Back at his house, he poured himself a small glass of anisette and drank a toast to his new country. For this one day, he was transformed into something more than Vincenzo the Plumber. He became Vincenzo Gramenzi, American Citizen, an important part of the democratic electoral process. To him, the right to vote was a sacred honor that deserved special recognition. He was to repeat this Election Day ritual without fail for the next fifty-five years, until Alzheimer's stole him away from the voting booth.

I was about five years old when I first became aware of Grandpop's Election Day tradition. Surprised to see him in his suit, hat and tie, I asked him why he was so dressed up. He sat me on his lap and, with a twinkle in his eye, explained that today he was going to "pick-a da presidente," a man named "Icenhower." I can still remember the pride in his voice as he explained to me, in his broken English, how important this was and how honored he felt to be a part of it.

My grandfather's story isn't much different from that of millions of other immigrants who came to the shores of America "yearning to breathe free." But it is a uniquely American story, one that bears telling, especially at a time when the average voter turnout in a presidential election is not much more than fifty percent. Maybe we need to be reminded that not everyone is fortunate enough to have a voice in a government "of the people, by the people, and for the people." This precious right was hard won.

So, each Election Day, I think of Grandpop. And if my life seems too hectic to take time out to go to the polls, or if I'm not really crazy about any of the candidates, or if I think that my single vote is too insignificant to matter, I picture him in his dark suit, tie, and porkpie hat. And I go "pick-a da presidente" or senator or governor or mayor or zoning board member because I understand that the right to vote is a priceless gift that must never be taken for granted — an invaluable lesson I learned at my grandfather's knee.

~Jackie Minniti

74

Chicken Soup for the Soul

The Pilgrim's Wife

*The land flourished because it was fed from so many
sources — because it was nourished by so many
cultures and traditions and peoples.*
~President Lyndon B. Johnson

t was only the third-grade Thanksgiving play but it was my first one and I was excited. I had my heart set on the main role — the pilgrim's wife.

The only drawback was that I had recently arrived in America from Czechoslovakia and my English was not that great. But since no one else appeared to be auditioning for the role, I was hopeful.

The day of the tryouts, I had butterflies in my stomach. I so wanted this! As others tried out for various roles and read the script in front of the room I mouthed the lines along with them.

Rudy was cast as the lead male pilgrim. When Mrs. Rosen asked who was interested in the role of the pilgrim's wife, my hand shot up. Two seconds later, Colleen Nelson raised hers. Had I known Colleen would audition I never would have bothered.

Colleen was a ginger-haired beauty with piercing green eyes and creamy skin, with just the right number of tiny freckles dotting her perfect nose. Even at the tender age of eight, she knew she had power.

I was taller than all the kids in class except for two boys who had been left behind. I had a massive head of dark-brown hair with a mind of its own. My skin was so pale, I thought I looked like a ghost.

Colleen read the lines from the script with ease. When she was done, she gave the class and the teacher a dazzling smile and sat down.

How could I compete with that? I walked nervously to the front of the room and stood next to Rudy. He read his lines, which gave me my cues. Then it was as if I were transformed. My nervousness disappeared. I BECAME the pilgrim's wife. I felt it. I knew I was good! I didn't need a script. I knew the part by heart.

But my accent was so severe. When I sat down, it was with a heavy heart. I wondered if my English was even understood.

The roles were announced the next day. Yolanda and Juan were cast as the Pilgrim couples' children. Jacob and Dorothy were to play the lead Native Americans. To my surprise, I was cast in the part I longed for — the pilgrim's wife. Everyone congratulated me, except for Colleen. I heard her voice from across the room: "How could SHE play a pilgrim? Didn't pilgrims come from England? She can hardly speak English. Besides, actresses are supposed to be beautiful. And she's not!"

I was noticeably hurt. Other kids tried to console me and voiced their objections but Colleen's anger had no end. "You're all sticking up for her because she's an IMMIGRANT!" She made the word sound so ugly.

I started crying and so did she. The teacher called the class to order.

Mrs. Rosen began: "This is America. That's what made this country great — immigrants. You may have been born here, or maybe your parents were, but take a look at yourselves. You are all a blend of many nationalities, religions and races."

We looked around and it was true. We noticed what had never crossed our minds before. There was as diverse a mixture of people in that room as could be. There were Vietnamese, Latinos, Africans, Irish, Italians, Asians and Poles. There were Christians and Jews and Muslims sitting side by side in a classroom and never giving their differences a thought. It was a regular United Nations — which we had taken for granted.

Mrs. Rosen addressed Colleen gently: "Where are you from, Colleen?"

"I was born right here in Queens, New York," she answered smugly.

"And your parents?" Mrs. Rosen continued.

Colleen wavered: "I think they're from Brooklyn."

"Well, before Brooklyn I know your parents came from Ireland. They were Irish immigrants."

"But… but," Colleen stammered.

Juan spoke up. "I'm from Mexico. But I am an American."

The teacher went on, "We are all Americans now. But most of our parents or grandparents or great-grandparents were immigrants. It's the diversity that made this country so unique, so exceptional. Why do you think America attracts people from all over the world? It's because America is a special place where all men are created equal."

The lunch bell rang and the class was dismissed. As Colleen headed for the door, Mrs. Rosen put a hand on her shoulder.

"May I have a word with you, Colleen?"

I left, disappearing into the girls' room to wipe my face and collect myself. Then I went to the lunchroom and sat away from the crowd, opening my lunch. But I was not very hungry.

A few minutes later, Colleen entered the room. I opened a book and pretended to read, not wanting to face her. But she headed in my direction.

"Can I sit here?" she began cautiously.

"Sure," I shrugged, still staring down at my book. She sat opposite me.

"Eva, I don't know where to start." She started tearing up. And so did I.

"I don't know why I said those hurtful things. I guess I was jealous because you did the part so well by heart and I had the script in front of me and I still messed up.

"And Mrs. Rosen's explanation about immigrants is so true. Most of us are immigrants or our ancestors were, unless we are Native Americans. And it was the immigrants who helped make America what it is today."

She continued, as both our tears started flowing freely: "And you ARE beautiful. I love your naturally curly hair and you have skin like porcelain. You don't have these stupid freckles like I have."

We both leaned over the table and hugged. The rest of the kids in the lunchroom were looking at us with wonder and amusement.

But we didn't care.

The Thanksgiving play took place in the school auditorium and all the classes and parents attended. I played the pilgrim's wife and the play was a big hit.

Colleen was an extra, playing a Native American girl. But what I loved the best was that at the end of the show, Colleen led the entire cast of twenty onto the stage, holding hands.

Then she stepped out of the line and, like an angel, sang, "God Bless America." It didn't matter that the song was written well after that original Thanksgiving took place. What mattered was that the spirit of America was within all our hearts that day.

Colleen and I — the child of immigrants and an immigrant — are still friends today. And America is still the greatest country in the world, made up of people of all religions, nationalities and races, from all over the globe.

~Eva Carter

75

My First Real 4th of July

*America, for me, has been the pursuit and
catching of happiness.*
~Aurora Raigne

For thirty-eight years I celebrated the 4th of July as an imposter. I watched the fireworks, sang the national anthem, and barbecued with everyone else. Most people had no idea I was faking it.

Born and raised in Canada, I moved to the States at eighteen when I married an American. For most of my thirty-eight years here, my resident alien status brought the question from friends: "So what are you waiting for?" My response usually included a twinge of guilt. I'd lived here and taken advantage of this bountiful nation for longer than some lifetimes. But I'd contributed as well, I would argue. I had a social security number and paid taxes. Then my mother died, and my family ties to Canada all but disappeared. So what was I waiting for?

That answer came on 9/11/2001, the day everything changed. For the first time I felt a powerful allegiance to the USA and an unexpected burst of patriotism. I was ready.

I soon discovered that decision was the easy part of the naturalization process. Overwhelmed with Form N-400 instructions, government and history lessons, and the long list of documents I would need, I dragged my feet for months. Thanks to the persistence of my husband, who spent hours gathering information, I finally sent in my application and received an interview date. I took this as a reassuring sign — it was also the anniversary of the day my mother passed.

But as the date approached, I started to get cold feet. I protested the direction the U.S. was taking toward war and it seemed Canada and most of the world agreed with me. Even if I followed through with the process I was too late to have a voice in the upcoming presidential election. Some of my friends were posing a different question: "Why now? If I were you I'd move back to Canada."

Was I making a mistake? I could cancel my interview and remain in green card limbo but I knew I would forever regret the missed opportunity. After living here for more than half of my life, leaving my family and friends was out of the question. I finally put emotion aside and proceeded.

When I arrived at work the morning of my appointment I had to choke back tears. My co-workers had decorated my desk with balloons and red, white, and blue streamers. They cheered me on when I left early that day. I was nervous as my husband and I took the long drive to the INS building south of town. After all these years, what if I didn't pass the test? Would I be shipped back to Canada?

A smiling Immigration officer greeted me on time and invited me to sit at the desk across from him. He guided me through ten simple government and history questions prompted from his computer screen. Minutes later he congratulated me on a perfect score. An hour later, I took my place in line at the swearing-in ceremony with nearly 200 people from thirty-four different nations.

Since that day, life hasn't changed much on the outside. But the proud faces of so many new Americans at the ceremony changed me forever inside. I was humbled by the jubilant cheers from their families and friends. These brand-new citizens, many dressed in the clothing of their countries of origin, understood what it meant to be part of a country that embodies the freedom I'd always taken for granted.

That year my 4th of July celebration wasn't much different. I still ate too much barbecue and stayed up too late watching the sky explode with color. However, something surprising happened a few days after I became a citizen. I opened the mail and found a summons for jury duty. As a new American citizen, I felt proud and elated. I was able to follow up my first real 4th of July with my very first civic duty. And it was a privilege to serve.

~Maureen Rogers

76

Straight Out of El Cajon

*I love talking in an American accent. Even though it
hurts my face after a few hours.*
~Rebel Wilson

"Where are you from?" It's a question I am frequently asked, and it probably has something to do with my accent. When I tell them I live in Southern California, most people have the same response: "No, you aren't from there. You're from somewhere else."

Everybody takes wild guesses, and they suggest that I'm either from England or Boston. A few seem to think that I'm from Texas. Only a couple of people sense that I might be from the Southern Hemisphere and settle on either South Africa or New Zealand.

I don't know why anybody would think I'm from New Zealand—I've been there several times and I sound nothing like them.

In Southern California, it's tough living with this accent. It's "foreign" to this part of the world. When I go to the drive-thru window I have to wait to hear the server's accent before I order. I've come to realize that not everyone can understand the twang that I put on my words, and it's more important to my daughters in the back of the car that they get their order without me having to give elocution lessons on the correct pronunciation of the number-eight combo meal.

Over the years, I tend to go back and do business with those people who can understand the accent. We may be speaking English, but American English is a lot more truncated than my English.

My supervisor has to send my reports back occasionally. What he calls typing errors I call the correct syntax. Words like "colour" and "odour" have the correct number of vowels in my opinion.

"Hey, let's make a new language where we drop every second vowel," may not be recorded in the annals of the pilgrims at Plymouth Rock, but it's how I explain the spelling differences.

"You are not from around here," people say.

Why can't I be from around here? For a small dot on the map twenty miles east of San Diego, my hometown has its share of celebrities. An Olympic Gold medalist, no less than twelve major league baseball players, two NASCAR drivers including a six-time champion — don't tell me where I can't be from; I love my hometown.

"You have an accent."

Everybody has an accent. You have one, and even I can sometimes pick which country or state you're from.

"Oh, but I was born here."

What difference does that make? I stand in silence for the national anthem; I love our servicemen and women, those at home and overseas. I adore our liberty just as much as you, perhaps even more so. Of all the places in the world, I chose to be part of the greatest country in the world. I gave up something so I could become an American.

"So, where were you born?"

I was born overseas, but you don't need to be born here to be a patriot. You just have to love your country.

"I'm confused. Where are you from again?"

With a thick Australian accent, I just smile and say, "I'm straight out of El Cajon."

~Grant Madden

How Family Comes to Be

Families don't have to match. You don't have to look
like someone else to love them.
~Leigh Anne Tuohy

M y friend Kim called to tell me that she had ten days to get ready to add two teenage brothers to her family. Kim was already a foster mother to two other boys — unaccompanied minors seeking asylum from war-torn countries — child refugees. They arrive in America without parents, not knowing the language, having endured unspeakable trauma and heartache.

Kim is white. Her boys are African. Her brother is Filipino. Her nieces are a beautiful blend of Filipino and Mexican American.

Kim and I were roommates when she read the book that started her down this path. Mary Pipher's *The Middle of Everywhere* rocked her world. Being the good roommate and nosy friend that I was, I picked up the book to see what all the fuss was about. In it, Pipher tells of her friendship with a family of refugees who had been resettled in the Midwest. She speaks of how she helped them to navigate certain aspects of life in the States that resettlement agencies had neglected to include in their orientation. Imagine residing in a country where you don't know the language or the culture and having to determine which pieces of mail are important (bills, jury summons, welfare checks, etc.) and which are junk (credit card applications, sweepstakes entry forms, political mailers, etc.).

When I turned the final page of the book, I had a renewed appreciation for how difficult it would be to navigate life in a foreign culture. I honestly hadn't thought much about refugees. Reading that book opened my eyes to a population and a struggle I'd never personally encountered. For Kim, it did much more.

Not long after we read *The Middle of Everywhere*, Kim moved back to her home state. Within a few months she was volunteering to help a refugee woman practice her English. A couple of years later, Kim was leading the ministry to refugees at her church. Then she became licensed as a foster parent. Somewhere along the way she heard about the unaccompanied refugee minor program at Lutheran Family Services in Denver. It wasn't long before Kim's family began to form.

Jacob is her oldest. He was born in the Congo and arrived in the U.S. via a refugee camp in Rwanda. He is a bright young man who works hard, is good with his hands, and played varsity soccer at his high school. Jacob doesn't even have to say charming things; his smile is charming enough to convince you to do anything he wants you to do. One of my favorite stories about his adjustment to American living centers around Daylight Savings Time. The morning after clocks "fell back", Jacob headed out the door for school. It was still dark. He shook his fist at the sky and said, "America be crazy!"

A year later, Samuel arrived. He was in elementary school at the time and arrived by way of a refugee camp in Mozambique. He, too, was born in the Congo, but he and Jacob were from different tribes so they spoke different languages. Samuel learned English very quickly, but he also managed to communicate well by acting things out while he was learning. An observant little guy, one of my favorite quotes from him is, "In Africa, food comes from trees. In America, food comes from boxes."

Next Saturday there will be two more members added to the family, biological brothers from the other side of Africa, who will learn the quirks of living in America. They will learn about Daylight Savings Time and household pets, pre-packaged meat and pizza delivery, birthday cakes and American football, snow and camping. People from different parts of the world who are now strangers will share a roof, a bathroom, a dinner table, and become a family.

There are places in the world where Kim's family wouldn't exist, where her family's story wouldn't be possible. There are countries where Kim would have never learned to read simply because she is a female, where Mary Pipher's book would have never been written because it mentions weaknesses in our government, where orphanages stand in the place of foster homes, and where refugees are not welcome. But Kim lives in America, where people like her, in past generations, have created a society in which she can make a difference for generations to come.

~Tiffany Marshall

Home Sweet Home

Everywhere immigrants have enriched and
strengthened the fabric of American life.
~President John F. Kennedy

had taken the day off from school so I could head to the United States Citizenship and Immigration Services (USCIS) building in Newark, New Jersey to be sworn in as a citizen. Before leaving my house to drive to Newark, however, my mother and father made sure that I was dressed respectfully. I wore a gray suit jacket, khaki pants, black belt, white button-down shirt, red tie, and black dress shoes. On the way to the USCIS building, I pondered about many things. What was I missing in my Language Arts class? Did I get an A on my Algebra II mid-term? When would I be able to make up my Sports Medicine test?

The importance of what was about to happen never hit me.

An hour after leaving my house, we had arrived. My appointment was not for a while, but it was good to be early. My parents and I proceeded through the security checkpoint at the USCIS building and made our way to the room where I would fill out paperwork and wait to be called.

For me, the wait was one of the best parts of the entire process. There were people of so many different ethnicities and cultures in the room with me. It was fascinating to be surrounded by people from so many walks of life.

After about an hour, my name still hadn't been called. My father went up to inquire and learned we were in the wrong room! With only fifteen minutes before my swearing-in ceremony, we rushed up to the next floor and signed in with the security guard. Two minutes later, one of the employees closed the doors.

I looked around my new waiting room and realized that everyone there was under the age of eighteen. And then it clicked. Usually the citizenship process takes a very long time. But for children under the age of eighteen whose parents are American citizens, the process is expedited.

After a quick briefing by one of the directors of the Immigration Services, a short video was played. The video depicted historical monuments, illustrated the history of America, stated the responsibilities of being a United States citizen, and ended with the singing of the national anthem. To my surprise, the director insisted that everyone join in the singing. To be quite honest, singing is not my forte. I was afraid that every window from Newark to San Diego would shatter. But due to my deep respect for my new country, I sang. Then the process began. One by one, an immigration official called everyone's name to come up and receive his or her certificate of citizenship. Since the calling of the names was alphabetically sequenced by last names, I did not have that long to wait.

"Daniel Martin Hurley, please come up."

My life had now changed forever. I was an American. I was home.

~Daniel Martin Hurley

★ The ★
Spirit of
America

American Traditions

*Tradition, which is always old, is at the same time ever new
because it is always reviving — born again in each new
generation, to be lived and applied in a new and
particular way.*
Thomas Merton, No Man Is an Island

79

By Their Side

My whole incentive when I'm at the USO is to try to
treat people like I would want my son to be
treated and taken care of.
~USO of Arizona volunteer Michelle Selby

My life is about passion. It's a passion to lead. It's a passion to succeed. And it's a passion to give people a little bit better of a day — or even just a moment — amid some of the biggest challenges of their lives.

I work for the USO in the Middle East. For a long time, I managed one of their centers in Afghanistan. Thought that war was over? A lot of other Americans do, too. But we've still got thousands of U.S. troops serving in harm's way every day. And when those men and women need a break, a nap or a place to call home, they come to our center.

The draw for me was simple. I served twenty-eight years in the Army before retiring as a sergeant major. I was used to taking care of my fellow soldiers. Now, I see some of the same guys who I served with come through our center's doors.

The USO has been around for seventy-five years. We were with troops during World War II, we went to Korea and Vietnam in the decades after that, and we were there for both wars in Iraq and the ongoing conflict where I'm stationed now. Our organization has more than 180 locations around the world and more than 30,000 interactions with troops every single day.

Ever get an e-mail from a buddy serving in a remote location? Ever

Skype with a brother or a cousin who was in the military overseas? Ever see troops in a war zone on the Jumbotron at an NFL game, or playing video games remotely against celebrities? If so, chances are we were involved.

It's still a dangerous place outside our center's doors. But inside, it's a home away from home.

The troops we serve deal with tough situations — occasionally even life-or-death choices — every day. I don't usually see the emotions they're dealing with when they walk through the door. But eventually, I see those feelings rise to the surface. I hear their voices quiver during their phone calls home. I hear their passion in the United Through Reading room, where they can record themselves reading a children's book and send the recording back to their kids in the States. And I see the high-fives and tears of joy from some of the toughest people you'll ever meet when they watch their children being born via a Skype call made from our free Wi-Fi.

I've been in their shoes. I understand the sacrifice they make. And that's why I am so passionate about being by their side when they walk through my front door.

~Pennington Walker

80

A True Blue Sky

No one can whistle a symphony.
It takes a whole orchestra to play it.
~John Maxwell

inhaled the tropical scent as I slathered the bottle of suntan lotion on my youngest daughter. My husband tossed our sunglasses, beach chairs, sun umbrella, towels, and cooler on the back of his truck.

"Hurry up, kids," I yelled to my older daughters. "We're going to miss it."

"Mom, it's the beach, it will still be there when we get there," my oldest, Alison, responded.

I smirked. Just wait, I thought to myself. You'll see.

My family and my in-laws were visiting Fort Pickens in Pensacola Beach, Florida. We couldn't wait to spend a relaxing week playing in the sun and making memories.

My fourteen-year-old son hopped on his bike. "I'll race you to the beach!"

We unloaded the truck and set up camp in the sand as the kids raced to the water.

The waves rolled in and out as the calm chirping of the shore birds mingled perfectly with the low roar of the ocean on a perfect summer day.

I glanced down at my watch, secured my sunglasses and looked to the sky. It would only be a few more minutes until the show.

My sister-in-law smiled at me. She knew they were coming. I couldn't wait to see the reaction on my eleven-year-old's face. She would be thrilled.

Rumble. VAWHOOOSH!

The incredibly loud roar interrupted the peaceful beach scene.

Several clueless people on the beach looked up to examine the cloudless sky. Thunder?

I smiled. I knew what had created the thunderous sound.

"Hey guys, look up!" My husband pointed to the sky. Immediately our four children and niece obeyed.

Within seconds, four shiny, blue airplanes appeared out of nowhere in the radiant blue sky. Flying perfectly in sync with each other, the planes raced overhead. A few moments later, two additional planes joined them, flipping, soaring, and churning above us.

"WOW!" my son exclaimed.

"Kids, meet the Blue Angels!" I laughed, pointing my cell phone to the sky to capture a picture.

"Awesome!" my youngest, Abby, squealed with delight. "Did you see that?"

"I did. The Blue Angels are stationed here in Pensacola Beach. They are practicing their maneuvers," I explained.

I loved watching the six McDonnell Douglas F/A 18 Hornet zoom past. The roaring sound, the pristine maneuvers, the precision and speed with which they moved was absolutely exhilarating. I am a devoted fan of our military and especially of military aircraft. As the daughter of an Air Force veteran, I grew up with a tremendous respect for our fighting forces. I got goose bumps as I watched the Blue Angels soar above.

Every single morning of our vacation, I would run outside at the first sound of their roaring engines. I would watch in awe as they dominated the sky above us.

I headed home from vacation with new memories and a profound respect for the Blue Angels. I would miss their daily show.

The summer months faded into fall and we returned to our normal school and work routines.

On October 30, 2015, I stood in my kitchen washing dishes when I heard a familiar roar. It couldn't be…

I ran to my back deck to see two McDonnell Douglas F/A 18 Hornets zip above the pine trees in my own back yard. The Blue Angels were in town for the Great Georgia Air Show.

Later that morning, I was out shopping with my daughter when I received a text with a photo from a teacher friend at school.

"Look who is here," he texted.

I glanced down to see a uniformed, young man in a blue jumpsuit. On his sleeve was an American flag. I quickly enlarged the photo. Printed across the young man's back were two magical words, BLUE ANGELS, right here in our little town visiting our local high school.

"They are coming to our football game tonight," Principal Allen texted me.

"Are you serious?"

As a member of our county's local Board of Education, I rushed out to greet them.

"Welcome, we are honored to have you all here with us," I gushed.

That night I stood on the sidelines watching our high school football game with three of the Blue Angel team members. It was America at its best: Friday night lights with the elite of our nation's military.

Public Relations Officer Mike Lindsey of the Blue Angels offered me tickets to the air show the next morning. A child on Christmas morning couldn't have been more excited.

The next afternoon, I stood only a few feet away from the six elite McDonnell Douglas F/A 18 Hornets which make up the flying team and the Lockheed Martin C-130 Hercules affectionately known as "Fat Albert." I was in pure Blue Angel heaven for sure, making a human connection with these brilliant super-human "angels" from my summer vacation.

The pilots loaded their aircraft as the announcer named each team member, including pilots and all personnel. I listened intently as each name was called. They were from Sierra Leone, Ireland, and almost every state in the USA. What a diverse group of young men and women.

The engines roared to life, the crowd cheered, and the pilots offered a salute to the tower as they rolled past. Music blared across the loudspeakers, adding a new level of drama and excitement as the "Angels" zoomed down the runway. Each plane lifted into the air at exactly the same time. We sat mesmerized watching as the Blue Angels twisted, dove and spun through the sky.

As we glanced out at the familiar diamond shape of the four aircraft team, one of the solo planes crept up behind the crowd. We never even heard him coming until he was right on top of us!

I was in awe at the ability of our nation's fighting force. With each twist and spin, my American pride grew. These "Angels" willingly risk their lives every day to serve our great nation. When they are not serving with the "Angels" they often fight in combat missions. The Blue Angel air show reminds us of this sacrifice.

As I watched the last plane safely return to the runway, I offered up a silent prayer for their safe return and a prayer of appreciation to these men and women who would soon return to their active field of duty.

We are free to live our dreams here in America, free to put our toes in the sand, free to frolic in the ocean, free to vacation with family, free to play football on Friday night, and free to attend public school, all because our military has and continues to defend that right for us.

Salute!

~Amy McCoy Dees

81

My Merging Mania

If you're not in the parade, you watch the
parade. That's life.
~Mike Ditka

have a real talent for zipping in and out of traffic. I slip into a steady stream of cars, nearly unnoticed. I find ways onto exit ramps like a knife through butter. Unfortunately, my strange talent has also gotten me into some embarrassing situations.

It all began when I was sixteen and started driving. In my impatience to get somewhere I inserted myself into numerous wedding processions without knowing it. It wasn't until the cars behind and in front of me started to honk that I caught on, having usually missed the first car, the one that had all the cans, streamers and writing on it. The first few times it happened I was embarrassed. But after that I just joined in, honked my horn and pretended to be part of the procession. Little did I know that was only preparation for a much greater embarrassment.

This strange ability to "merge" kept getting me into all sorts of fascinating motorcades. I began to watch for the noisy wedding processions to avoid them but then found myself graduating into funeral formations. I always seemed to miss the lead car — the hearse — and with so many cars driving with their lights on at all times of day, how was I to know? It was only the sedate pace of my fellow drivers, and the numerous cars pulled to the side of the road in a gesture of respect for the dearly departed, that finally penetrated my brain and told me that I'd done it again. I would snap on my lights and try to look appropriately bummed out.

My merging "issues" continued, despite my attempts to be more attentive, and then I truly outdid myself with the mother of all merges. It was the Fourth of July and I was visiting my parents at their campsite along the Mississippi River. We had a nice day but it was hot and humid, and I decided to drive back home in the early afternoon because severe storms were forecast for later that day. I hated getting caught in severe weather and I didn't want to weather the storm at the campsite.

Commending myself for being responsible and leaving early, I set off with my windows rolled down because I didn't have air conditioning in my fifteen-year-old car. I sat on a large beach towel so that the vinyl seats didn't scorch my legs. Each time I stopped at an intersection I squirted myself with a plant mister. My hair was a fright: the salty sweat mixed with the not-so-clean campground water in the mister, but I didn't care. It was hot!

I drew up to a stop sign in a small town and waited for a caravan of old cars to go by. The last old car passed in front of me and I saw my chance. I pulled into traffic, glad that the car club hadn't taken forever to go by. Sometimes those old cars only went a few miles an hour and these had been fairly slow but there had only been about ten to fifteen of them. I squirted myself with the plant mister and hung my head out the window a little to cool down after sitting for five minutes in the heat.

I began to notice people sitting on the sides of the main street in lawn chairs, facing the road. I glanced around nervously as I recognized all the signs of a Fourth of July parade beginning. Man, was I glad to get through that before it started.

Suddenly an air horn blast from behind me sent my bladder into overdrive. I felt a surge of panic as I looked into the rearview mirror. Clowns of every description cavorted, capered and cartwheeled behind my car followed by a swarm of Shriners on tiny motorbikes, zipping in and out of traffic, putting my merge skills to shame. A fire engine was next, lights flashing, firemen waving.

I looked ahead with enlightened eyes at the really old cars in front of me, the band banging drums and blasting horns in front of them, and the lead vehicle, the one I had missed as usual, was a police cruiser with red, white, and blue lights twirling. I had really done it this time!

I felt sick to my stomach as clowns skipped next to my car, alternately peeking in at me and throwing candy at the spectators. People pointed from the curb, laughing. I was convinced I was the object of ridicule. (I had nightmares about clowns for weeks afterward.)

There was no way to turn off until the next main thoroughfare because the alleys and side roads were blocked with the laughing lawn-chair people. Sweat trickled between my shoulder blades. I sat with my frightful clown-like hairdo in my little car with no air conditioning, going five miles per hour in 100-degree heat.

Remembering the wedding processions and funeral lineups I had been in, I did the only thing a self-respecting merge-challenged person could do.

I smiled and waved at the crowd.

~Karen J. Olson

82

Summoned to Court

Be a Columbus to whole new continents
and worlds within you, opening new channels,
not of trade, but of thought.
~Henry David Thoreau

When my jury summons came in the mail, I scowled. Why me? Five times in the past fifteen years? Though I'd never actually made it on a jury, the thought of being called for duty seemed a great inconvenience, even unfair.

I'll get out of it, I thought. I won't even have to go in. But when I called to see if they needed me, my number was called. A lottery, and I lost. I grumbled as I got ready that morning, but I told my husband I'd likely be back in time for lunch.

After making my way through the long security line and into the room of about 500 possible jurors, I told myself that with so many to choose from I'd surely be dismissed. We all filled out a questionnaire and watched a video while we waited, and it began to dawn on me that this might not be so bad after all. The video script was well written — probably for skeptics such as me — and for the first time I entertained the idea that this might be a golden opportunity to learn something.

Then my name was called and fifty of us were lined up like schoolchildren going to recess. We were taken to the courtroom. And again we were lined up by name and seated as assigned. They sure have this organized, I thought.

As we sat there, the lawyers questioned us, trying to decide whom they would choose as one of the seven jurors. There were twelve in the jury box, so I toyed with the idea that I might not be chosen, but by then I was intrigued. What would it be like to be on a jury?

After questioning, we were released for lunch so the lawyers could choose a jury. We returned to find that most of those in the box had been released for various reasons. I was Juror Number 1! Well, I thought, I'm here, so I'll do my very best and learn all I can. I was committed.

For the next two-and-a-half days I listened to the testimony from many people, including detectives and expert witnesses. It was sometimes fascinating, sometimes boring, and occasionally even frustrating. It was emotional and we kept changing our opinions as different people testified. And all the while the seven of us tried to keep an open mind.

On the fourth day, we heard closing arguments and then we went off to render our verdict. We deliberated four long hours, trying to do what was best, trying to form a unanimous decision among strangers who held very different thoughts on the matter. It was a challenge, but one we all took seriously. After all, people's lives and futures would be greatly affected by our decision.

When we came to a verdict, we were called into the courtroom, and the judge read it. It took just a moment, but we all experienced a sigh of relief, knowing we had made a good decision.

It was done. But before we left, the judge asked us into his chambers for a debriefing, and for a half-hour we chatted freely about the experiences of the past four days. This judge truly wanted justice to be done well, so my respect for him grew, and by extension, respect for the judicial system we have.

The lawyers also asked to talk with us, so we met in the jury room for an hour of fascinating discussion. The defense lawyer was nothing like he seemed in the courtroom; he was friendly and genuinely interested in why we ruled the way we did, and he affirmed our decision. The prosecuting lawyers were sharp and nice and amiable; they even told us why they chose us. It was an education far beyond a classroom or a television show, far beyond a storyline or an exposé. This was real life, and it mattered.

So this skeptic is a skeptic no more. I am proud of my country, proud of our judicial system and proud to fulfill the mandate for me to serve our community. And although we have challenges and occasionally have a flawed ruling, we have, I think, the greatest system on earth. It's a system of justice that seeks the best for all and allows citizens such as me to participate. So when a summons comes again in my mailbox, instead of scowling, I'll smile.

~Susan G. Mathis

83

As American as Apple Pie?

In hospitality, the chief thing is the good will.
~Greek Proverb

Apple season in New Hampshire — there's nothing like it. Apple picking, hayrides through the orchard, the taste of fresh, tart macs right off the tree, and the promise of home-made apple goodies to come. You arrive home with bags full of wonderful apples and the delightful task of deciding what to do with all that goodness. There are apple crisps, apple tarts, applesauce, apple cobbler — everything apple — but best of all is hot apple pie right out of the oven. It's a time of cooking and baking and sharing with friends and neighbors. What a wonderful surprise to find a freshly baked pie left on your doorstep, and if the baker chooses to remain anonymous, trying to figure out who the giver is only adds to the fun.

When one of our church's deacons asked if I thought the refugee family that had recently begun attending our church would enjoy finding an apple pie on their doorstep, I told him that was a wonderful idea. I had visions of Albert and Marie opening their front door to find a freshly baked pie on the porch and being delighted. I imagined their children enjoying the pie and thinking what a wonderful country they had moved to where people left delicious pies on your doorstep. What I never dreamed was that I could be creating a situation of crisis and fear.

Until the day I received the upset phone call in the church office. "Mrs. Edwards, this is Marie. We found a pie on our doorstep. Who would do such a thing?"

"What do you mean?" I asked.

"Well, we had no idea what could be in it. Could someone be trying to poison us?"

"Oh no, no one would do that to you here. What did you do with the pie?"

"We were afraid, so we got rid of it right away. Why would someone just leave something like that at our door without a note or anything to say who it was from?"

As I explained that the pie was intended as an act of kindness, and was meant to be a pleasant surprise and not something scary, I began to see the whole incident through Marie's eyes. When you come from a place where you can be killed for your religious beliefs, where bombs are left on people's doorsteps, where even items received through the mail must be treated with a measure of suspicion, an anonymous package of anything creates anxiety. Marie and Albert came from a place where a surprise is rarely a good thing.

I wrestled with whether or not to tell the baker of that pie what had become of her hard work and good intentions. I did make sure not to repeat that mistake in judgment again. There would be no more surprise gifts left on Marie and Albert's doorstep, and deliveries would be made in person by someone they knew and trusted. And I am more thankful than ever that I live in a country where a fresh-baked apple pie on the doorstep is just what it should be — a sign that apple season has arrived in New Hampshire, and that someone wants to share that joy with me!

~Laurie Carnright Edwards

84

Take Me Out to the Ball Game

*People ask me what I do in winter when there's no
baseball. I'll tell you what I do. I stare out the window
and wait for spring.*
~Rogers Hornsby

There was a pause, a moment of thought, and then I went for it. With the moonlight as my guide on that pitch-black Iowa night, I sprinted with the exuberance of a ten-year-old on Opening Day across the small stream of water. I galloped on to the cool damp grass on that putrid hot night, forgetting the anxiety that came with trespassing on private property well past midnight. The magic in the moonlight was palpable; I would not have been surprised had Joe Jackson himself emerged from the darkness of the cornfield.

My brother Jeremy and I were giddy; the quietness of the night, the breeze on our faces, and the smell of the sweet corn in the outfield transported us to our youth. There is something about the *Field of Dreams* movie site in Dyersville, Iowa that you can feel in your gut. It turns adults into little boys wearing oversized baseball caps who have dreams of making it to the "Bigs" someday when they grow up. With clouds rushing past the nearly full moon that night, Jeremy and I patrolled the outfield grass. We walked into the corn, disappearing into the darkness, half expecting to magically land in some sort of baseball heaven. We didn't need to be magically transported; we were already there.

Walking onto that field had been a dream of mine since I first watched *Field of Dreams* so many years ago on the eve of yet another Opening Day. Year after year, our family would gather in the living room with popcorn and put in the movie to get us in the mood for the start of the season — the official start of summer in America. Being out there on that field in the darkness of night, with only the sound of rustling corn stalks and the occasional passing car, it was apparent to me that the magic was certainly real.

After we had our fill of the field that night, we drove back to the hotel a few miles away and went right to sleep so that we could return in the morning. After breakfast, we bought a baseball glove and drove the beautiful serpentine roads of rural Iowa until we found the long gravel driveway of the farmhouse. To see the field in daylight was just as spectacular as the night before. I could visualize the entire movie — Joe Jackson cracking fly balls to the cornfield, Archie winking, Terence Mann on the bleachers.

Jeremy and I played catch where Ray tossed with his dad. We swatted home runs (from second base) to hear the ball tear away at corn leaves on chest-high stalks. I played third base while a young boy took batting practice from his dad. I smacked a deep drive (this time from home plate) off a perfect pitch from another boy and I ran all 360 feet around the base paths, sliding into home through a pile of red clay gravel. We walked the field more than once and talked to other visitors. One man, probably in his seventies, also strolled slowly in the outfield with his hands clasped behind his back. I asked him if he'd been here before. He had. Every single year since the field opened up to visitors he had made the drive from Indiana to soak in the magic.

But why? Why did he drive every year from Indiana to some empty baseball field in the middle of rural Iowa? Why did Jeremy and I visit the field? Why had it been a dream of mine to do that for so many years?

Growing up in rural Ohio, basketball was my favorite sport to play and football was my favorite to watch. However, as I got older, baseball became my favorite. It's a special sport — timeless. It transports you to your childhood, when you played it, watched it on TV, even got to go to games. Baseball has a connection beyond teams and players. It serves as a bond between fathers and children, brothers, and friends.

Now that I have three children of my own, baseball serves as a constant in our lives. Whether we are watching the Cincinnati Reds on a warm summer night, or playing ball in the back yard, baseball brings joy and laughter into our lives. My daughter Sierra, now nine, comes to me with graph paper and asks if I can help her keep score of a Reds game. My son Aidan knew the lyrics of "Take Me Out to the Ball Game" when he was two years old. Now, he is seven, and playing knothole baseball on a dusty field in Cincinnati with visions of playing for the Reds one day. I am honored to be one of his coaches; our time together on the baseball diamond will certainly be one of my fondest memories. And little Natalie, now five, has her favorite players and asks me if she can still root for them when they are traded away from her hometown Reds.

These are the moments I will undoubtedly be whisked back to some years from now, when the three of them have left our house. The sound of their laughter, the crack of the bat, watching my wife Chrissy cheer as Sierra races around makeshift bases after hitting a rocket past Daddy. How I will long to hear Aidan's grand finale of "the old ball game!" I'll dream of sitting in the bright red seats of Cincinnati's Great American Ball Park with my amazing children, eating hot dogs, and cheering on our team.

And that is why a lonely old man strolls around an empty diamond in rural Iowa every summer with visions of his father or brothers or friends playing baseball on an emerald swath of grass so many years ago.

~Aaron M. Smith

85

Grace Visits the County Fair

America is a vast conspiracy to make you happy.
~John Updike

I cry at parades. I cry when I hear the national anthem at sporting events and I cry when everyone stands up at the seventh inning stretch during baseball games to sing "Take Me Out to the Ball Game." When it comes to celebrating our American traditions, I get emotional. So it took me by surprise when a Ph.D. from China I had been mentoring became overwhelmed with sentiment at our county fair.

During the year and a half that I mentored "Grace" (the name she chose to call herself during her stay in America), I explained American life, instructed her on nuances of the "American" English language, and took her to local events to show her what makes Americans unique. When I suggested that we take her to the county fair, she asked, "What is a county fair?"

"Oh, you know," I responded, "a fair where farmers show off their prize-winning produce and livestock, and there are contests for the best jellies, cookies, handmade quilts, and woodworking projects."

A blank look swept across Grace's face. I tried again.

"There are rides and booths where you can win stuffed animals, and "fair" food you won't find anywhere else."

The blank look again.

"You really don't know what a county fair is?"

Grace shook her head.

"Do you have any kind of fairs in China?"

She shrugged. "I don't know because I am not sure what a fair is. Is this an important American tradition?"

"You bet! Okay, that settles it," I said. "You're going to the fair with us and you are going to see for yourself."

A few days later my husband and I took her to the San Diego County Fair on a bright, sunny day. Grace looked around like a child seeing one of the Seven Wonders of the World for the first time. She said nothing, but her eyes spoke for her. She was amazed. A man walked by eating a giant turkey leg. Grace stopped in the middle of the walkway. She pointed to the man eating the dinosaur-sized turkey leg. "What is he eating?"

"A barbecued turkey leg. You want one?"

She shook her head, never taking her eyes off the man and the turkey leg. "I've never seen a turkey big enough to have a leg that large. Americans sure eat bigger quantities of food than we do in China. He isn't going to eat that all by himself, is he?"

I looked at the man; he sported a significant gut and I was pretty sure he could devour the turkey leg by himself, even though it could feed a family of four.

"Yeah, probably," I said. "Come on, let's go. There's more to see."

We turned a corner just in time to watch the pie-eating contest that required contestants to devour the pies with their hands behind their backs. Grace and I laughed till our bellies hurt as contestants smeared lemon meringue and whipped cream all over their faces and hair in an attempt to win. When they called for the next round of contestants I turned to her. "You up for it?" She shook her mane of silky, long black hair and backed away, still laughing.

We wandered into the vendors' hall, where Grace spotted a booth with people trying on toe rings. She watched intently for a few minutes before she turned to me, a look of confusion crossing her face. "What are they for?"

"Just an adornment. People wear rings on their fingers, and some people wear them on their toes, too."

She grinned shyly. "May I try one on?"

I reeled back, a little surprised. She had a Ph.D. in neurosciences and didn't strike me as the toe-ring type. "Sure, take a seat in one of the chairs."

She no sooner sat than the salesman kneeled down and tried several different rings on her toes. She raised a hand to her mouth to hide her giggles as he slid each one over the knuckle. Five toe rings later she paid the man for one and walked out of the booth wearing her new ring.

"I can't wait to call my husband tonight and tell him what I did. He won't believe it."

"Why?"

"Oh, we don't do such indulgent things in China. We're not like you Americans. He will probably scold me for wasting money, but I don't care. I love my toe ring!"

We meandered through the midway to see people testing their bravery on the daredevil rides and men spending the equivalent of a car payment trying to win colossal stuffed animals for their sweethearts.

Next, we watched the baby pig races as they ran in circles, oinking their way down the track. Grace laughed so hard that she snorted and held her sides. The race ended and she heaved a happy sigh.

"I am getting hungry. Is there anything to eat here besides the big legs?"

I led her up and down rows and rows of food vendors offering pies, ice cream, warm gingerbread, cotton candy, fish and chips, fried artichoke hearts, grilled steak, falafel, fried chicken, burritos, fish tacos, fried pickles and much more. We must have walked past fifty or more vendors; none seemed to interest her.

"Find anything you like?" I asked.

"I'm not sure what a lot of it is. Americans eat food I am not used to," she said softly, sounding overwhelmed.

"Well then, it's time to try something truly American."

I led her up to a hot dog stand. "It doesn't get any more American than this," I said, pointing to the dogs. She ordered a super long hot dog, on an equally long bun. When the vendor handed it to her, I steered her to the condiments bar. "No one eats plain hot dogs," I explained. "Load up with mustard, relish and onions, if you like." She piled on as much as would fit.

We no sooner sat down than she bit into her dog and her face lit up like she was watching fireworks on the Fourth of July. "Why haven't I eaten this before? It's wonderful!" she said between bites of food, chomping down the juicy hot dog as though she were starving, mustard smeared around her mouth.

When she finished, she wiped at her eyes before tears spilled down her cheeks. "You Americans are an amazing people," she said, using one of her new words.

I cocked my head sideways.

"Every time I think I understand the U.S., I experience something new, like this fair, like this hot dog. You are an extraordinary people and America is a remarkable place. I will remember this day my whole life. Thank you for sharing your American tradition with me."

With one hand, I reached out and squeezed one of hers, while with the other I wiped at the tear running down my cheek. Seeing someone from a foreign country appreciate a quintessential American tradition was better than watching a parade.

~Jeffree Wyn Itrich

86

The Town that Taught Me Patriotism

Learn from yesterday, live for today, hope for tomorrow.
~Author Unknown

My father, who was not born in the USA, so loved America that he could not bear anyone speaking ill of it. I didn't inherit his patriotism. It took a town to instill that virtue in me.

When I first moved a half-century ago from the western part of the state to Acton, Massachusetts, twenty-five miles west of Boston, my first impression of it was that it was a sleepy little semi-rural town where not much happened. As I became better acquainted with it — especially the more I found out about its history — the more I realized how wrong I was. A lot happened there, and learning about all those things has made me a more patriotic American.

Acton people were fully present for the events that led to the establishment of the United States as an independent nation. They shed their blood and died for the ideals we hold dear. Acton's connection to those events could be seen all around, I came to find out, and that patriotism seeped into my being.

My first eye-opening experience came after I had finished some business at Town Hall and wandered across Main Street to the monument that stands on the common. As I walked around the tall granite obelisk, I saw what looked like grave markers set into the ground around it. Reading the inscription on each, I learned that they were the gravestones of three citizens of Acton—farmer and gunsmith Isaac Davis, blacksmith's apprentice Abner Hosmer, and schoolmaster James Hayward. All three of them died as a result of their actions on the same day—April 19, 1775. Their deaths were at the hands of the King's soldiers, who had marched into the countryside from Boston to confiscate arms and munitions the rebellious colonists were reported to have stored a few short miles from where I was standing.

Our first house in Acton was on High Street at the top of a rise. As I walked one day to the bottom of the hill, I noticed a sign on the house at the corner of High and Main Streets declaring that it was built in 1707. I discovered that this, the oldest house in Acton, was the home of Francis Faulkner, commander of the West Acton militia company.

On the night of April 18, 1775, Paul Revere, Samuel Dawes, and, later, Dr. Samuel Prescott, rode from Boston and Cambridge to alert the populace in the surrounding countryside that the Regulars were on the march. It is said that one of them, Dr. Prescott, alerted Captain Joseph Robbins of North Acton, leader of one of the militia companies in town, shouting "Captain Robbins! Captain Robbins! Up! Up! The Regulars have come to Concord! Rendezvous at old North Bridge quick as possible! Alarm Acton!"

With Concord just the next town over from Acton, this must have been unsettling news indeed. Captain Robbins immediately sent his thirteen-year-old son, John, to "alarm Acton." Riding up to Major Faulkner's house, the Robbins boy shouted from his horse that the King's Regulars were on the march to Concord. Upon hearing this, Major Faulkner—still in his nightshirt—leaned out his second-story window and fired his musket three times, giving the prearranged signal to his West Acton Militia Company to muster at his house. From there, they marched to the Isaac Davis homestead to join other Acton militia and minuteman companies in the early morning light to prepare their ball and powder and sharpen their bayonets before marching to Concord's North Bridge.

I was intrigued that the early history of our nation was so close to me seemingly everywhere I went in Acton. I decided to visit the

Isaac Davis Homestead in the middle of town. Although the Davis house no longer stands on the site, if you stand at the homestead, you just might hear Captain Davis say to his wife, Hannah, as he did almost two-and-a-half centuries ago as he departed with his colonial soldiers that morning, "Take good care of the children." Davis had a premonition that he might not return alive that evening, and indeed, he did not. He was the first to fall facing the Regulars across the old North Bridge. Every April 19th, in modern times, the citizens of Acton gather at the Isaac Davis homestead to march again the seven miles to the bridge where Captain Davis and his men confronted the King's soldiers in 1775.

At the hill overlooking that bridge in Concord, you might again hear Captain Davis say, as he did before the battle, "I haven't a man that is afraid to go," when he volunteered to lead his Acton company to face the Regulars in what would be the first organized, armed colonial resistance to the King. It was there, in that fateful encounter, that the three men of Acton who are now buried at the base of the town monument lost their lives.

At the Daniel Chester French Minuteman statue on the other side of the old North Bridge, visitors can see a rendering in bronze of the citizen-farmer, his jacket lying across his plow, who dropped what he was doing to defend his home, his colony, and his ideals. And if visitors then go to the next town over, they will see, in a glass case back at Acton's town hall, Isaac Davis's wooden plow, which served as the model for the plow in the famous Minuteman statue. The plow was passed down through six generations of the family and then given to the town.

Is Acton proud of the role it played in the founding and preservation of the nation? You bet it is. Today, if you go into the Acton Memorial Library, which was donated to the town by a private citizen to commemorate the Acton men lost during the Civil War, you will see a wonderful exhibit of both Revolutionary War and Civil War artifacts. Among the former are the sword Captain Isaac Davis carried with him on April 19, 1775, his last day on earth; the powder horn James Hayward carried with him that day with a hole in it caused by a ball that went through it into his body; and the blood-stained hat that Abner Hosmer wore when he was shot and killed.

In a strange twist of fate, the first Union casualties of the Civil War were also men from the area, who were killed by a mob in Baltimore on their way to Washington to heed President Lincoln's call for men to protect our nation's capital. In a stranger twist of fate, the date they were killed was April 19, 1861, eighty-six years to the day their fellow citizens died to protect our liberty and begin our march to independence.

In learning the history of the little town I've called home for so many years, I have been captivated and inspired to a patriotism I did not know I possessed. I am so glad that I have been, and glad to call Acton, Massachusetts my home.

~Larry C. Kerpelman, Ph.D.

The Spirit of a Farmer

I take my vacation on the combine and tractor.
~John Tester

One summer evening we were invited to a tractor pull. We'd never been to one before, but I knew they were loud, so I poked flame orange earplugs into my nine-year-old's ears.

"Is that really necessary?" a woman behind me asked, referring to my son's brightly colored earplugs.

"Oh yes," I replied. "I think so."

The woman harrumphed and rolled her eyes at her friend as she shook her head. I surveyed the area. When I looked back, my son was gazing at the sky with the tangerine earplugs nicely wedged into his nostrils. The woman behind me gave me an "I told you so" look. I sighed and nudged my son. Ryan turned to look at me but continued wearing the plugs in his nose.

The earthy woman harrumphed again. She was tan, comfortably soft and had laugh lines etched around her eyes. I bet she had award-winning pies in the pie competition. She had a no-nonsense, practical look that inspired confidence and complete obedience in children and adults alike. Where did she get that quality of confidence? Did she get it through genetics... age... adversity?

We waited for the event to start. Young and old men crowded the rails of the fenced-in dirt strip that was the tractor pull arena. They slapped each other on the back and shook big, tan hands as they called out greetings. Smiles creased their faces, which had deep canyons from staring into the sun and working long hours outdoors.

They lined up, boot heels hooked on the bottom rung of the fence, tipping cold long-necks of Miller beer, cowboy hats and baseball caps tipped further back on their heads for a better view.

I pulled the earplugs out of my son's nose and stuck them in his ears at the first roar of sound. He glared at me, took them out, and put them in his pocket.

HARRUMPH!

Young men fired up their tractors, which had custom paint jobs and shiny chrome pipes jabbing out of the engine, shooting flames. As each custom built tractor pulled heavier loads the noise was almost deafening. Finally, it stopped.

Abruptly, the atmosphere changed. I looked around, trying to figure out what was happening.

My friend Bonnie appeared and sat down hard next to me. "Whew" she said, "I made it!" She handed me a soda.

"What's going on now?" I asked.

"It's the best part of the tractor pull," she said.

Around me, smiles grew wider, more men clustered at the rail. The farmers in this competition drove tractors they'd used in the field all day. The engines weren't huge chrome monsters that snaked out of the sides of the tractor. These were friendly-looking tractors, bigger versions of the toys my brothers played with when we were children. The large rear tires were old friends; I'd spent hours in tractor tire sandboxes.

Huge wheels churned through dirt as tiny front tires lifted into the air. The men driving were all middle-aged and it became clear that this was a test of knowledge, balance and driving experience.

As the tractors pulled increasingly heavier loads the front ends rose up, shifted, wavered and groaned. Everyone held a collective breath as each farmer shifted his weight in tiny increments on the springy seat to see if he could pull more weight without flipping the tractor. Sweat poured off each man as he concentrated.

I thought of farmers who have been killed in the field when their tractors rolled on to them. I remembered the farm teen who, when both of his arms were ripped off in a piece of farm machinery, ran into the house, dialed 911 with a pencil in his mouth, gave his location to rescue personnel then went and stood in the bathtub so he wouldn't get blood all over his mother's rug. These were the men and women who didn't take vacations until their children were old enough to take over the farm.

I was moved to tears and glanced around self-consciously. I noticed other tears, smiles and hugs. As each farmer reached the limits of his tractor and let the front end sink slowly to the ground, the crowd went wild. With similar small self-deprecating grins each man touched the brim of his hat or gave a slight wave.

I realized that these families came together each year to give and get emotional support from others who suffered through this year's flood, drought or bug infestation. They connected with each other before going back and starting all over again. They sowed, reaped, hoped and prayed. They gathered each year to celebrate the bounty, the trials and the spirit that was farming. I felt humbled.

The harrumphing woman who sat behind me stood behind the bleachers now. The winner of the tractor pull came up and slapped her ample bottom. She turned in mock threat, her face creased with smiles and pride.

"Well, old man, you've done it again. Where's my money?" She held out her hand.

"What money?" He gave her an innocent look, palms turned heavenward.

"You're just lucky. One of these days you are going to flip that tractor and then I'll collect insurance and we'll just see who has money."

They both laughed and a tender look passed between them. Preoccupied with congratulations, they carried on separate conversations as their hands carried out a task of their own. He opened his wallet, took out a check and handed it to her without looking, busy talking and laughing. She looked down, took the check and put it into her purse, not pausing in conversation. She rubbed his upper arm and he moved off, talking to friends.

"Ah," I thought. "She gets that quality through love."

I put my arm around my son as we walked out. He smiled at me, his orange earplugs stuck between his teeth and upper lip like walrus tusks.

~Karen J. Olson

The Casserole Effect

Why did everyone send casseroles in times of crisis?
Why didn't anyone ever send brownies
and Jack Daniel's?
~Jaye Wells

Here in the Midwest, we have a hidden code we use when we want to show our love and concern for others. Whether it's elaborate or simple, homemade or store bought, the message is the same. That we care. And where I live in Iowa that means you bring a casserole.

Someone had a new baby? Bring that poor mother a casserole to give her a break! Neighbor's barn burned down? Surely a casserole will help with the expenses. Widower? He needs a good home-cooked casserole to let him know he's not alone.

Remodeling your home? Have a casserole. Loved one going through chemo? Take this casserole because I don't know what else to do to help.

Loved one passes? Here is a casserole for all the relatives who have flooded your home. We even have casserole parties, mainly to try new recipes out on friends who will be honest in their reviews.

Yet, while we joke about it and many times the casserole effect can overwhelm or overtake your freezer, it is the love and compassion the casseroles convey that will warm your heart and memories. And instill the desire that the next generation will carry on the Casserole Effect.

~C. Joy

Play Ball

A hot dog at the ballgame beats roast beef at the Ritz.
~Humphrey Bogart

"Mom..." I tried not to sound too condescending, but my displeasure was evident. "You can't wear that to the ball game."

Mom stood up straight, looked me square in the eye, and said, "Give me one good reason why I can't wear this shirt to Safeco Field." She puffed out her chest. "It's my eightieth birthday, and I can wear anything I want!"

I sighed. "The Mariners are playing Boston, Mom. Boston Red Sox fans will be wearing red."

"Your point?"

"I'm not sitting next to a woman who dresses like a Red Sox fan."

"But I look good in red."

I sighed a second time, picked up a wrapped present I'd earlier set on her kitchen counter, and handed it to her. "Open this."

"I thought we were going to wait to open presents until later — when we have the birthday cake."

"Just open it, Mom."

She tore into the wrapping like a little kid on Christmas and held up a blue and white baseball jersey with a large 51 printed on it. "Oh! Fifty-one! That's Ichiro's number! He's my favorite right fielder of all time!"

I smiled. "So why don't you wear that today?"

Mom was already folding the shirt and attempting to reinsert it into the torn wrapping paper. "I don't want to get mustard all over it, and you know I'll have to have a Major League Mariner Hot Dog with the works while we're at the ball park."

"But you don't have to spill mustard on your shirt. That's optional."

She stuck her tongue out at me.

"Just try it on, Mom."

She headed down the hallway to her bathroom. "At least you didn't get me a hat. I won't wear hats. Hats really mess up my hair."

I smiled. For the past decade, Mom and I had gone to Mariner games twice a year — on Mother's Day in May and on her birthday in August. It was a tradition I loved, and I eagerly looked forward to each game. She loved "her boys," and I loved spending quality time at the ballpark with the woman who had instilled a love of the sport of baseball in me at an early age.

"How's this?" said Mom, returning to the kitchen. She had on the shirt, along with a light summer windbreaker. A red windbreaker.

"Mother! You've got to be kidding!"

"Now you look here, young lady..." She squinted her eyes, put her hands on her hips and dramatically stomped her foot.

"The shirt is blue and white, the jacket is red. Red, white, and blue are America's colors. Baseball is the all-American sport. You've always known how patriotic I am, so quit complaining, and get in the car. I want to get there in time to watch batting practice!"

There was no arguing with logic like that, so I picked up my car keys and we headed out the door.

God bless my mother; God bless the USA.

~Jan Bono

90

Corny American Pride

This corn will teach to you, should you peel away the
husk, and be willing to open your ears.
~Anthony Liccione

've been thinking lately about the things I've taken for granted. After living two tours of duty abroad, our military family finally appreciates what we have as Americans.

I'm not talking about ethereal concepts like democracy and freedom. I'm talking about the really important things that make a tangible difference in our everyday lives as Americans.

I'm talking about Corn on the Cob.

Yes, that sweet vegetarian delicacy indigenous to this great land of ours. Native Americans cultivated "maize" for thousands of years before Europeans discovered the "New World" and the usefulness of corn as a grain, but it was only centuries ago that Iroquois shared with settlers the sweet variety of corn eaten off the cob. Unlike the settlers, Europeans never really took to eating corn straight off the cob. In fact, they are of the general opinion that corn on the cob is hog feed.

So, for many long years while stationed overseas, we went without.

It wasn't easy, because, as far as vegetables go, corn on the cob has always been special to us. Despite the fact that my father was raised at the boardwalk in New Jersey, he was always a wannabe country boy, which is why we had a garden about eight times too big for a family of four, along with a tractor, six chickens, two goats, a cat, and at least two hunting dogs.

As such, my brother and I had chores that were uncharacteristic of suburban children. We were picking green beans, tending goats, and driving a tractor when our friends were getting jobs at the mall. Also, I had the unenviable task of selling the excess eggs, puppies, and vegetables at the end of our road. Corn on the cob was my best seller, and my first real source of income.

Nearly two decades later, my husband-to-be first laid eyes on me when I was sitting rather unladylike on the deck of a beach house, shucking corn. Unfortunately, I was covered in sand and my wet bangs had fallen into an unflattering middle part. Worse yet, my belly protruded between the top and bottom of my bathing suit. It took a shower and considerable work with my curling iron, but I was able to win him over at dinner that evening, not without help from a heaping plate of delicious Silver Queen corn on the cob.

Even my children have fallen under the sweet-corn spell. Our middle child, Anna, has always been a worrier. One night, when she was about five years old, I tucked her into bed, placing her tiny hands together under mine to say our prayers.

"Now I lay me…" I began.

"Mommy?" Anna interrupted.

"Yes, honey?

"What happens when you die?"

"Uh," my mind raced, unprepared. "Well, you go to Heaven, sweetie. Now where were we?"

"Yeah, but, what will happen to my body," she specified.

As I looked into the worried eyes of my precious little girl, I could not reveal the reality of death and bodily decomposition. Panicked, I began to ramble.

"Well, honey, when someone dies, his soul leaves his body and floats up to Heaven."

"But…" I knew I had to say something, anything, that would quickly distract her from thoughts of dead bodies being buried in deep, dark graves, where they are left to rot into the dirt.

"Heaven is beautiful!" I said, but her eyes still looked worried. "And you can have anything you want," her brows were still furrowed, and, and, you can have wings and YOU CAN FLY!"

After a painful silence, little Anna finally spoke. "Can I have purple wings, Mommy?"

"Yes! Yes! You can have purple wings!" I blurted, relieved to at long last please my relentless tiny interrogator. Her eyes fluttered with visions of purple feathers as we finished our prayers.

As I stood and kissed Anna's forehead, she murmured, "Can I really have anything I want in Heaven?"

"Yep, anything," I replied, and turned to leave the room. As I flipped the light switch, I heard Anna whisper, "Mommy?" I turned, hoping this would be an easy one.

"Can I have corn on the cob in Heaven?"

"Yes, sweetie," I answered with a smile, "you can have all the corn on the cob you want."

To this day, our family still yearns for the yellow sweetness of this heavenly vegetable. In fact, we can't get enough freshly boiled cobs rolled in butter, sprinkled with a pinch of salt and cracked black pepper. My husband haphazardly chomps at the cob, leaving tufts of missed kernels. I munch methodically from right to left like an old typewriter, occasionally stopping to chew and swallow sweet mouthfuls. Due to expensive orthodontics, Anna, now seventeen, gnaws at the youngest kernels on the ends and trims the rest off with a knife. Lilly takes spiral bites around the cob like an apple peeler. Hayden, who despises all vegetables, seems disgusted by our shameless display of gluttony.

When every cob has been stripped of its golden pearls, we sit swollen, with buttered cheeks, giggling about the stuff stuck between our teeth.

We, the People of this great Nation, possess the inalienable right to enjoy distinctly American Corn on the Cob, a liberty which one should never take for granted. Give me hot buttered ears or give me death, I say! Let freedom and the dinner bell ring!

~Lisa Smith Molinari

91

Magic on the Diamond

*You don't need a ticket to see some of the best baseball
in the world; you just need to drive one of the
players to the game.*
~Author Unknown

Brrrr. It was a freezing cold night in Small Town, USA. This was the first night game of the fall season for our son Joseph's Little League team—and possibly the last. My husband Angelo had just returned from the nearby coffee shop and passed out hot coffees to shivering coaches and parents.

"If I were a betting man, I'd say this is it. Game over," one of the parents blurted.

Others nodded in agreement as they sipped their coffees. The score was 8–4, bottom of the last inning. I sensed everyone's thoughts.

"Almost time to pack it in for the season… No championship… It's November… Time for basketball and wrestling and shopping for the holidays… Too cold anyway."

Not me. I had only baseball—and this game—on my mind.

"They can do it," I countered. I could see my breath as I spoke. "It's still possible."

Okay, call me Pollyanna Mama. But, I truly did believe our kids could come back and win this thing! Then, invoking the words of the late, great Yogi Berra, I added: "It ain't over till it's over!"

The others chuckled. I knew it was a long shot… and yet I was a little older than these parents. I had lived through the 1978 Yankees—the

Greatest Comeback Team ever. I witnessed underdog Bucky Dent smack a homerun over the Green Monster at Fenway in the historic one-game playoff against the Boston Red Sox for the go-ahead run. I saw the Yankees come back to win the World Series after being fourteen-and-a-half games behind first place in mid-July — a feat no other team had accomplished in baseball history.

I believed our Little League boys could do it, too. This is America — Land of Big Hopes and Dreams. You're never too young to dream big, and these boys dreamed of being champions. They had been practicing their batting, pitching, fielding and sliding every day since March. Besides, it wouldn't be the first time they'd come from behind in a game.

Sure enough, the scoreboard began to change. The number in the "guest" column turned to 5. Then 6. Then 7.

"It's 8–7. Still want to bet?" I asked the parent.

Suddenly, everyone switched from packing it in to cheering them on.

Then… last out. Finished. Final score: 8–7. No championship. Man, this loss really, really hurt.

That parent was still impressed with my positive belief, though.

"It WAS close. They almost tied it!"

"Yeah, almost."

Actually, our boys HAD tied it, but because of a bad call in the third inning, the run didn't count. The umpire called a ball that bounced off first base a foul ball. He soon realized his mistake — it was indeed a fair ball — but instead of allowing our boy to remain on second base on his double, he made him go to bat again, where he struck out. After that, our team loaded the bases. That player on second would have scored. The game would have been tied at 8–8.

That call and that run made this loss for the championship — the end of their dream — even more difficult to swallow.

Dejected, Joseph packed his bag. We drove in silence to Grandma's house for her homemade lasagna.

"You were amazing," we told him. "You boys never stopped trying, and that's all you can ever do in life."

A half hour later, my phone beeped. It was a text from one of the moms on the team.

"Check your e-mail. We have a life."

It sounded so ominous. What did this mean... we have a life?

The e-mail was from the coach. "Game is not over. The opposing team made an illegal re-entry of a pitcher. Game will resume where we left off when illegal entry was made. Probably Tuesday."

Then those closing words — "We have a life."

We all jumped off the couch and started doing the We Have A Life Dance! Even Pollyanna Mama here couldn't believe the game wasn't over!

Just as baseball records were made to be broken, Yogi's immortal words needed to be tweaked... EVEN WHEN IT'S OVER, IT AIN'T OVER!

The Little League Team that lost — at first — had become the Little League Team That COULD still become champions!

Tuesday came and the game resumed in the top of the 6th. Our team was up, bases loaded, one out. The score reverted back to 8–4.

Suddenly, I was catapulted to 1978. I was in the stands at Fenway Park, witnessing the historic one-game playoff between the Boston Red Sox and the New York Yankees. I had that same intense feeling one experiences when an entire season comes down to one game and every single play counts.

A few cracks of the bat and our boys were rounding the bases... and...

SWEET JUSTICE! WE TIED IT! 8–8!

Bottom of 6th — the other team did not go ahead.

EXTRA INNINGS!

Top of the 7th. We were ahead 10–8. Bottom of the 7th, they tied it — 10–10.

Top of the 8th — We scored TWO BIG RUNS! 12–10.

Bottom of the 8th... Other team...Did.Not.Score!

WE WON! WE WON! WE WON!

To think. Two nights ago, the boys had thrown their gloves in their bags and packed it in for the season. Now they were living a completely different destiny. Their dreams — coupled with hard work and determination — were revived. On this cold November night, these boys embodied the American Spirit.

In small towns all across America, Little League teams play hard and dream big. Baseball fields — as vast and verdant as America itself — symbolize endless possibilities. It's on these fields our children learn the craft, play their hearts out, and never stop believing they, too, can be champions.

~Antoinette Rainone

★ The ★ Spirit of America

Seeing America from Abroad

*How often we fail to realize our good fortune in
living in a country where happiness is more
than a lack of tragedy.*
~Paul Sweeney

92

In the Key of Connection

Music can change the world because it
can change people.
~Bono

As a singer/songwriter, I've been privileged to perform in twenty-three countries. One thing I have found true in every single country, including France, Germany, Austria, Canada, Chile, Argentina, Singapore, Serbia, and the United Arab Emirates is this: they love American music.

My first solo experience was in Nagoya, Japan. Back in 1980 not that many people in Nagoya were speaking English. During my initial trip to a local Japanese restaurant, I attempted to order in English and no one understood me. Thankfully, the dishes provided at that restaurant were all artistically displayed in the window of the shop. I simply walked the waiter to the front window and pointed at the replica of the delicious bowl of udon I wanted to eat.

At that moment, a day before my grand opening at a local nightclub, I wondered: how would I entertain people who didn't understand the words I was singing? Surprisingly, my Nagoya audiences were enthusiastic, with bobbing heads and warm, appreciative applause. Sometimes, they even sang along with me on certain popular standards like "Misty" or Stevie Wonder's "You Are the Sunshine of My Life." They had memorized these familiar tunes. Never mind that they couldn't speak the language. They could sing it!

This was the beginning of several years of entertaining in various countries and before a multitude of cultures. They were all connected to America by our music. When I arrived in Jakarta, Indonesia to appear at a popular French-owned hotel, my group and I were performing jazz. A number of the local entertainers came to our shows and invited us to come to their gigs on our off nights. We obliged. Much to my surprise, I heard at least five local Indonesian female artists who sounded exactly like Chaka Khan, a Grammy Award–winning, American, R&B/pop vocalist. We also heard at least a dozen young male vocalists who copied the style of American jazz icon, Al Jarreau. My tours helped me to recognize how much our American music influences other cultures and brings joy worldwide.

In Auckland, New Zealand, while performing with a top-40 local group of musicians, I learned they were crazy about Michael Jackson's music. But what really surprised me was that in 1983 they had never heard of rap music. When I started "rapping" on stage, my back-up group of youthful, Maori musicians were highly impressed.

There was a television producer in the audience that night and he asked me if I could write a rap for the upcoming 1983 Miss Universe Contest. Of course I said yes. The result was that my rap song was used on Auckland's popularly televised Miss Universe Pageant. Consequently, I was interviewed and appeared in New Zealand's *Woman's Weekly* magazine with the caption, "An American singer-songwriter who is concerned about the image of women has written the theme song for this year's Miss Universe New Zealand contest."

They called it a song, but it was actually a "rap" written in support of the ladies and performed by Herb McQuay, a popular New York entertainer who, at that time, was an ex-pat living in Auckland with his family. That was truly a historic moment for both Herb and me! It was the first televised rap act in New Zealand and it was positive and politically important. Some of my rap lyrics stated, "Feline, feminine, look at those eyes; she's a cat, she's a queen, she's grandmother-wise. Don't misconstrue her sexy ways. Believe me you'll get put in your place. She's more than a chassis, her motor is classy." The girls modeled as the rap was spoken.

Speaking of rap, during my performance at the Grand Hyatt in

Shanghai, China, I went out one night to a disco club and there were two young Chinese men who were wearing saggy pants and rapping in Chinese. It was quite amazing to witness and reminded me how important art and music are as a representation of a country's culture.

Most of my gigs were jazz gigs. I was so excited when jazz was being celebrated by the 100th United States Congress as "… an indigenous American music and art form, bringing to this country and the world a uniquely American musical synthesis and culture through the African-American experience. It makes evident to the world an outstanding artistic model of individual expression and democratic cooperation."

I'm really proud to represent American music that epitomizes freedom. While traveling, I learned that jazz was so intimidating to some communist countries that it was banned in China during the Mao regime. It was also banned in Russia for many years. Happily, while entertaining in Bangkok, Thailand at the famed Mandarin Oriental Hotel, my jazz back-up band was made up of a majority of amazing Russian jazz players who were now settled in Thailand. They loved American music and played it exceptionally well. The only non-Russian was a Thai pianist named Joe who also played brilliantly.

During that tour, a shocking thing happened to me. One evening, while I was performing, the club manager approached the bandstand. He said that the King and Queen of Thailand were in the dining room of the hotel, upstairs, and they requested my performance. The band was not invited.

"Me?" I was breathless with excitement and awe. "By myself?"

They explained there was a pianist upstairs already. I snatched some sheet music and was whisked up to the restaurant and introduced to a Thai pianist. To my shock, he was blind. I was so nervous, my mouth was dry and my upper lip was sticking to my front teeth.

I laid my sheet music aside and prayed that the piano player could play my American standard songs in my key. The Thai gentleman behind the piano asked me, in a kind voice, "What would you like to sing?" I called out a favorite Hoagy Carmichael composition, "'The Nearness of You' in the key of E flat."

My fingers snapped out the tempo and we were off and running.

The pianist was sensitive and knew all the beautiful changes to the song. There was great applause when we finished and I was walked over to the table where the King and Queen of Thailand were enjoying their meal. I gave the traditional greeting, placing my palms together in a prayer position and bowing my head. I hoped this was the correct greeting for Thai royalty. I guess it was, because they smiled back at me. I later learned that the King of Thailand is a huge American jazz fan. The hotel manager told me he plays saxophone really well.

I've realized over the years that music, like love, binds us all together and unites us in rhythm, harmony and creativity. I'm exceptionally proud of the music that American composers, songwriters and musicians have gifted to the entire world. It transcends race, culture and religion. If copying another artist's work is a form of compliment and flattery, then we (as proud Americans) should all take a collective bow. American music is adored, played and replicated worldwide.

~Dee Dee McNeil

93

A Tradition of Kindness

For I was hungry and you gave me something to eat, I
was thirsty and you gave me something to drink, I was
a stranger and you invited me in.
~Matthew 25:35

My husband John has a close friend from Germany. In high school, they were exchange students at each other's homes; John spent six months living with his German friend's family and then his friend spent a year living with John's family. Shortly after we were married, John and I took a trip to Germany and Austria. He wanted me to see the beautiful Alps and meet his German family before we had children and were more tied down. I am so glad we took that trip! The Alps were beautiful, and his German family was delightful.

Sitting around after dinner one evening, the German father, Vati, as my husband and his friend called him, told a story that I will remember and treasure all of my life.

He explained that he served in the German army in World War II. He was only nineteen years old and did not understand all that his country and its wicked leader were doing. He was drafted and so he served as was required of him.

Toward the end of the war, in the middle of winter, Vati was captured by the Americans. Tired, hungry, and cold, he had not eaten in days, his coat was threadbare and his boots were so worn that his sockless toes were exposed to the elements.

I still remember sitting in his warm living room, along with his wife, son, and my husband, sipping hot tea, while he told his story in German with his son interpreting for me — the only one in the room who could not understand German. The story must have been familiar to his family but it was mesmerizing to me.

Vati said he saw a fellow soldier cross an open field successfully, so he tried it. He figured if that man could make it, then the enemy must not be watching the field closely. But his assumption was incorrect and American soldiers quickly surrounded him, pointing their guns directly at his head. He dropped to the ground with his hands up. I'm not sure if he even had a weapon but if he did, it had no ammo. At any rate, he knelt in the snow, unarmed, expecting to be shot in the head, where their guns were aimed. But he was not shot.

Instead, the soldiers told him to get up, keep his hands held above his head, and go with them to a nearby prisoner of war camp.

"Oh," he thought, "they are going to torture me before they kill me."

He trudged slowly over the snow-covered field, fully expecting that upon arrival he would be tortured. How he dreaded the ordeal that was about to unfold!

When they entered a clearing, hidden deep in the woods, the Americans pointed to a log on the ground near a campfire. "Sit down," one of the soldiers instructed. Vati did not know much English, but he at least understood those words. He made his way to the log and sat down, fearing what would happen next.

At least the fire felt warm. It was the first warmth he had experienced in weeks. Small comfort under the circumstances, but it did feel good at that moment.

As he waited, one of the American soldiers brought him a bowl of hot stew and a spoon. He hadn't had a hot meal in weeks. It was delicious! Then shortly after, they gave him new boots and a new coat.

Vati smiled as he said, "They did not torture me. They gave me shelter, warm clothes and food." His eyes danced as he continued,

"If I had known this is what it would be like to be captured by the Americans, I would have surrendered much earlier."

~Harriet E. Michael

94

Rediscovering America

The love of one's country is a splendid thing. But why
should love stop at the border?
~Pablo Casals

When my husband Richard and I moved to Japan seven years ago, we assured friends and family it would only be for two years at most. But then, satisfying work and a comfortable lifestyle kept us longer. As the years went on, though, and as the news broadcasts from home seemed forever negative, I felt increasingly disenchanted. Staying in Japan seemed like a better alternative than going home.

When Richard took a new job and we moved, I started teaching part-time at a nearby university. One of my classes helped students improve their essay writing skills. It was an elective course, which meant the students who chose to enroll were motivated to learn.

For their first assignment, I asked the students to write about why they wanted to learn English. Some of them wrote that they had a desire to travel and some simply wanted to learn a foreign language. Others came with a passion for music or a particular sport, and they wanted to communicate with their foreign counterparts in a common language. For one student, Kenji, it was his love of America. "Americans are amazing," he wrote. "I love their culture. I want to be like Americans."

As I read his paper, I shook my head. "Poor kid. He has no idea," I said to my husband as I set the paper on a stack of others I was marking that evening.

The semester wore on, and I saw that Kenji struggled to stay awake during class. Students do a great deal of writing when we meet, so the atmosphere tends to be quiet and cozy. While it's perfect for concentrating, it's also easy to fall asleep. I usually wake them up with a gentle touch on the shoulder and only have to do it once. They sit up in embarrassment and then carry on with their work.

Kenji, however, dozed off more frequently than the others. Once, he hit his head on the desk when the arm supporting his chin gave way. Snickers from the other students rippled around the room as I hurried over to ask if he was okay. "I need coffee," was his only reply, and I nodded in agreement before moving off, stifling my own laughter.

Kenji later explained that he worked every morning from five to ten at a McDonald's on a nearby American military base. "When I told my friend I wanted to learn English and that I loved America, he gave me the idea," he said. "I love it, but I'm so tired."

I admired his gumption.

Despite his sleepiness, Kenji blossomed as a writer during the semester. Gradually, his spelling and grammar improved, as did his ability to tell a story. I found myself looking forward to reading his work, wondering what he might tell me in answer to that day's prompt.

One of the essay topics I gave students was to tell me about an aspiration or dream. "It can be anything," I said. "A job, a trip, a fitness goal, anything at all." Before I finished explaining, I could practically see their minds sifting through ideas, searching for that one hope or ambition they held most dear.

A week later I collected their first drafts. Many of the students were juniors or seniors, and the hunt for a job after graduation loomed large. Others focused on getting married or taking a trip. Kenji, however, wrote about wanting to "change his culture." His title was "How to Become a Great Person."

I started to read with interest.

Kenji discussed his passion for America and how he learned English by watching American television programs. He wrote, too, about his job at McDonald's. Rather than describe the work, though, he wrote about the customers: "Everyone is so friendly. They always say, 'Good morning' or 'How are you?' I think this is very good. In my culture, we don't do this. It makes for a warm feeling. Now, I have many friends on the base."

He went on to describe other things he noticed, such as how Americans always woke up early. "I thought they were crazy at first, but now I see how much they get done." He then mentioned an article he read about successful people around the world and how they all get up early, too. "It's hard for me, but I'm going to try," he concluded.

Most importantly, though, Kenji reasoned that if he absorbed things he liked from other cultures and combined them with elements he liked from his own, it could only result in something positive. "If I can learn from another country's culture, I will absolutely be a great person," he wrote.

Kenji saw American friendliness as a gateway to more than success. He saw it as an integral part of being a good person. Being warm and openhearted made it possible to communicate with others and learn more about them. Waking up early allowed people to be productive. American friendliness and discipline led to amazing things and, for Kenji, sat at the heart of what makes someone great, or in his words, "very cool like Americans."

I chuckled a little, read the draft again, suggested some edits, and continued on to the next student, but Kenji's images and ideas stayed with me, interrupting my flow of thought. I grabbed his essay back out of the pile, reread it, and felt a rekindling of a love for country and culture that had long been missing.

In a way, these were such small things, but instead of focusing on the negative news coming out of the United States, Kenji's words made me think of my country in a more positive light. I thought about the people back home and the culture we weave together every day. I thought about our friendliness to strangers and the easy way we talk with others, our directness and our helpfulness to those in need, and our generosity in times of joy as well as sorrow. I thought of these and more as I sat with Kenji's essay on the table before me. All of these things combine with so many other good things to make Americans unique. We are a young country, with some of the issues that come with adolescence, but with all the charms of youth and enthusiasm, too.

"Thank you, Kenji," I wrote below my list of edits and suggestions. I sat back with tears in my eyes and smiled, and then wrote one more line. "Thank you for reminding me of what I love about my country."

~Joan Bailey

95

The Strength of a Nation

*Appreciation is a wonderful thing. It makes what is
excellent in others belong to us as well.*
~Voltaire

We were two young, first time visitors to the United States. Unwittingly my wife and I made the mistake of arriving in New York City on Saint Patrick's Day. Our first indication of a problem came as our taxi driver picked us up at the airport. Rolling his eyes heavenward he muttered under his breath when we gave him the address of our hotel. He apologized for his reaction but pointed out that no matter what route he took into the city it would be a long drive. He suggested that it would require a bit of Irish luck to make it to our hotel, situated as it was, just off Times Square.

Progress was steady until we arrived in Manhattan, and then, as predicted, we slowed to a crawl. It was not much of a problem for us as it was our first visit to the city. Everything was new. The taxi was comfortable and we were happy to be taking in the sights and sounds of the streets. We put our windows down to get a better sense of the place. We strained our necks upwards to get the best view of the skyscrapers as we made our very slow way through the towering canyons. Even the steam spiraling out of the sewer drains held a childlike fascination for us.

Thousands of pedestrians clad in green seemed to be making their way in the same direction as us. Inevitably our progress came to a halt. From somewhere up ahead came the sounds of marching music and the general noise associated with a parade in full progress. The driver helped to pass the time by giving a running commentary on every building we crawled past. The library got the most attention. He pointed out, in a heavy Middle Eastern accent, that the free lending of books was a totally alien concept in the country he had come from, as it no doubt was for us.

After making no progress at all for about fifteen minutes we decided, in consultation with the cabbie, that our best chance of getting to our hotel would be by foot, as we still had to cross Fifth Avenue. The driver didn't hold out any hope of being able to drive anywhere anytime soon. We settled the cab fare, collected our luggage, and joined the throngs of pedestrians making their boisterous way toward the parade route.

We were carried along with the crowd and arrived at a gray metal barrier at Fifth Avenue manned by half a dozen policemen. We stood clutching the handles of our suitcases and watched a number of the marching bands go by. There was even one of my favorites, a pipe band. We felt a little out of place not wearing green and we seemed to be the only ones who had thought to bring suitcases with them. Calling on my uncanny sense of direction, we walked south. It was in the same general direction as most of the crowd. It looked as though the parade was coming to an end and the spectators were beginning to make their way home.

All the streets we walked down had familiar names but their relationship to one another defied my uncanny directional skill. At last I had to admit we were lost. Now in my full male mode, I rejected the idea of asking for directions in spite of the fact that I had absolutely no idea where we were, much less where our hotel was located. My wife overruled my reluctance to ask for help and stopped two young men and a young woman walking in the opposite direction. She explained our dilemma and the young woman took the situation in hand. They introduced themselves and pointed out that we had been walking in the opposite direction from our hotel. The girl suggested that they would walk with us to make sure that we got there safely. The two young guys, who turned out to be off-duty firemen, effortlessly picked up our suitcases and we all set off toward the hotel. My wife and the young lady managed to talk the whole way while I spent most of my time just trying to keep up with the guys.

When they got us safely to the hotel they stayed to make sure that we got settled in. Unbeknownst to me the two ladies had made arrangements for the trio to meet us again the next day and show us around town. As a result we probably had the best city guides that anyone could have hoped for. The next day we were invited to their home for dinner and to meet their respective families. When we finally parted it was as good friends and with the promise to keep in touch. My wife cried a few tears when they drove us to the airport. I have to admit that when I shared goodbye hugs with the guys I could feel some emotion welling up in my throat.

I am sorry to say that as time went by we never managed to properly keep in touch other than exchanging Christmas cards once a year. It was many years later that the tragedy of the Twin Towers took place. I learned that our firefighting friends had lost their lives in the ensuing events. They had chosen to help others rather than keeping themselves safe. Their selfless actions helped many people but in the process they paid the ultimate sacrifice. My wife and I will always be grateful for having known, however briefly, such wonderful and generous human beings.

As a Canadian, I believe the true strength and spirit of America lies in its incredible people.

~James A. Gemmell

96

Privilege and Perspective

The privilege of a lifetime is being who you are.
~Joseph Campbell

'm late for a blind date. We've agreed to a drink at a bar down-town, and I have vastly underestimated how much time it will take to find parking. I send him a text: "I swear I'm here. Just might take me another five hours to park."

By the time I walk into the bar, he's been waiting for twenty minutes.

He told me to look on the bar's patio for the guy in the leather jacket. I do, and I find him easily. He is drinking a Blue Moon. He appears completely content and not the least bit annoyed at having to wait.

We hug in greeting. He only smiles with half his mouth — more of a smirk, really — but his eyes are warm and sincere, and his gaze is direct, and so I am at ease. I order my usual: a tequila sour. He puts it on his tab.

The bar is crowded for a Wednesday night. We shout over the noise.

His name is Arthur. He moved to the U.S. from Istanbul, Turkey in 2014 to complete an M.A. in sociology. His family is very well off back in Istanbul, or he wouldn't be here. He says public education in Turkey is awful — mostly religious indoctrination with a hint of basic math skills. His parents were able to send him to an elite private school instead. He's applying to Ph.D. programs now. If he isn't accepted, he won't be allowed to stay here on his student visa.

He also tells me about the full-size American flag he keeps in his bedroom in his nearby apartment.

I ask him if he's joking. He isn't. Arthur adores this country.

The more he talks about how much he loves the U.S., the more I can hardly stop myself from enumerating all its flaws. For every point he makes, a "yes, but…" immediately springs to my lips. I bite back most of them. I'm not looking to fight. Still, I can't help but let a few arguments slip out.

Everything we see is from opposite perspectives: he, the rich foreigner, privileged because of his family's wealth and status in Turkey, yet disadvantaged because his situation here is so tenuous; I, disadvantaged as someone who grew up in poverty, yet privileged because I was born here in America and can't be sent away.

He talks about how much he loves the culture here. Everything he has ever loved came from America. If he's allowed, he wants to stay here for the rest of his life.

We order another round of tequila sours and I ask him how long he's known this country was the place for him.

"I think since I was twelve. I was always home throughout my youth, playing video games, watching movies, and reading comics. Everything I liked was imported from here."

In addition to a handful of family vacations to the States, he's also spent time in England, Scotland, the Netherlands, Belgium, France, Germany, Poland, Italy, Spain, Lebanon, Bosnia, and Romania. Even with this impressive travel history, he still feels that none of those places compare to America; none feel like they could ever become home.

He thinks I am lucky to have spent my whole life here. It's hard for me to see myself as the lucky one between the two of us. I see a young man who was traveling the world with his family before he even hit puberty, while I was eating the bizarre things that people donate to food banks. But to him, I am the lucky one, because I am an American.

When we leave the bar we are still talking, and so we go for a walk. The night is crisp but pleasant.

As we walk, I ask him what his impression was of this country the very first time he visited. He was nine years old, and his older brother had taken him on a trip to California "just to hang out."

That's when he gets me.

"I remember noticing how colorful it was. In Turkey, everyone looks like a clone. Here, everybody's different. It's beautiful."

Standing next to him with my bright raspberry hair, wearing a pair of faux-leather pants, stilettos, and a fuzzy bunny hoodie, I can't argue this point even if I want to.

Arthur continues, "You can't smile at people in Turkey. You can't talk to people. Everybody's tense and distrustful. Here, you can go into a bar and talk to strangers and make friends."

He tells me he read somewhere that Turkey is the number two country in the world in terms of people not trusting each other. This is untrue. I look it up when I get home. It's actually the number three most distrustful country in the entire world. The United States doesn't make the top three for most trustful, but it does rank in the top fifteen percent of all countries.

"Here, people smile at me," he says. "It's incredible. It's like *Star Trek*."

~Allison Paster-Torres

97

Let Freedom Ring

Freedom is the oxygen of the soul.
~Moshe Dayan

was born in Canada. We lived in Toronto, about eighty miles from the U.S. border crossing, and in the 1960s much of our television was received from America. Our parents took us all through the U.S. on camping trips and we visited many beautiful and exciting destinations. American History was my favorite subject. However, it wasn't until I began living in the U.S., nearly fourteen years ago, that I fully understood the most fundamental treasure that America held — freedom. I am a Canadian, by birth, who is proudly and fiercely an American by heart.

It began with my mother. She was born and raised in England and lived in London during World War II. Suffering through "the blitz," she and her family watched as England's despair and desperation turned to confidence with the arrival of millions of American soldiers, sailors and airmen. My father was in the Royal Canadian Air Force, serving alongside British and American service personnel. Dad held (and still holds) Americans in high regard, but my mother — she openly wept in joy for all that America meant to her and her family. If anyone had anything bad to say about America (and it was the Sixties, so you often heard such comments in Canada) she would say, "You can never comprehend the marvel of a people who would come to OUR soil and die for OUR freedom." She often stated that she loved how Americans truly cherish freedom and will willingly give their lives to preserve it.

My dad taught me that in the United States a person might completely disagree with your point of view, but disagree or not, they would willingly and gladly die to preserve your freedom to express it! Freedom might seem like a strange thing to cherish, but believe me, the rest of the world desires the freedoms that Americans fought to gain and preserve. I have learned that in America I have the freedom to be as successful as I am willing to work for, or as unsuccessful as I choose to be. Sure, there are issues and problems that still plague us, but our country is predicated on freedom.

I am a musician and last year began playing at a Catholic Church in Buffalo, New York, where a vast majority of the congregation is comprised of newly arrived immigrants from around the world — including a large number from Myanmar and Africa. We celebrate our service with songs and readings in many languages. It is a celebration of the diverse cultures that have come to this great nation and embraced the freedoms that they now have. Today I see people from African and Asian nations, just as 150 years ago America welcomed Irish, Italian, German and Polish immigrants. Yet when I speak to any of these congregants who came from around the world, their pride at being American is so powerfully evident. They love their new nation, just as I love mine.

Recently I was driving in New Jersey, near the Hudson River, and I looked up and noticed that the Statue of Liberty was standing proudly in the sunlight. I was so joyful at this sight — and I said to myself, "The most beautiful woman on earth." She has welcomed so many who sought freedom and a new life. She is a symbol of that freedom and she announces it proudly every day.

As a Canadian, I cherish the relationship that my home nation has had with the United States. We stood together in World War I and World War II. Canadians served alongside Americans in the Korean War. Canada was alongside the U.S. in the first Gulf War, and has been serving in Iraq and Afghanistan. Canadian soldiers stand with the U.S. today in Afghanistan. Canada may have one-tenth the population, but we have a heart that echoes that of our larger brother to the south. When the tragedy of 9/11 compelled passenger jets to divert from American airports, many landed at Canadian cities along our East Coast and stranded travelers were welcomed and cared for by Canadians. This is a testimony to the deep respect and love that Canadians feel for the United States and its people. We — as Canadians — know that America has been our steadfast ally and friend throughout our 149-year history as a nation.

Growing up, I was taught to follow the news and current events. It always amazed me that when disaster struck somewhere in the world — earthquakes, storms, floods, disease or manmade disaster — the American relief services were the first to go in and help. I learned from an early age to love and respect Americans — and then later in life I had the opportunity to become one, and I am honored beyond words to be here. I have embraced the freedom of being who I want to be, who I feel I am called to be, with only myself to answer to and a society that simply asks me to defend the freedom of others as passionately as they will defend mine. One day, soon, I will undertake the citizenship test and become a full American citizen. I look forward to this not because of what America can do for me, but because of what I can do for others as an American!

There is good and bad in all peoples and in all nations. America is no exception. What sets America apart is a set of freedoms that are protected and intended to protect the society that upholds them. Freedom of speech, assembly and the press, to name just three. I have been around the world and those freedoms are not guaranteed anywhere as they are in the United States of America. Want to know how good we have it in America? Visit an American embassy or consulate in a poor nation, and look at the faces of those who are lined up to seek entry to the United States. What they want — well, it's what we have. We must always remember we also have an obligation to protect it and to preserve it. Those anxious faces may someday — soon — arrive and join us in upholding that obligation.

Let freedom ring. Every day. Let it start in your heart, as it beats in the greatest nation on earth. God bless America!

~Peter J. Green

98

The Sixty-Year-Old Little Girl

There are those, I know, who will say that the liberation
of humanity, the freedom of man and mind, is nothing
but a dream. They are right. It is the American dream.
~Archibald MacLeish

Like most Americans, I'm baffled by why so many people in other countries dislike America. I usually write it off as jealousy of our success, not because I'm arrogant, but because I've visited many other countries and I can see the difference. I also usually point out that most of the world dreams about living in America and very few Americans are trying to leave. Of course, the option Americans have to go somewhere else if they want to is another basic freedom denied to many around the world.

I once had a long conversation with a man in Marmaris, Turkey who thought America was too aggressive militarily and too imperialistic politically. I argued that America is the only country that ever fought wars with nothing in it for them (World War II and Bosnia, to name two), and that America is the only country that not only didn't occupy countries it defeated, but rebuilt what it destroyed. (Japan, Germany, Iraq, etc.)

I was in my early twenties the first time I encountered hatred of America. I had just graduated from college and was living and working on the farm of a friend in Aldershot, England. I had been there for about a week when her mother arrived home from a business trip and made dinner for us. It didn't take long before she launched into an all-out attack on America. I didn't immediately spring to America's defense for two reasons. First, she was over sixty and I was still young enough to be a little intimidated by aggressive older people. Secondly, I had been influenced by ultra-liberal college professors who had successfully muddled the patriotism I felt before starting college, insisting that Americans had much to feel guilty for. They ridiculed students who dared to disagree with them. This left me not only wondering if their criticisms of America were true, but also less likely to question authority, which is ironic because questioning authority is one thing most of those same professors ostensibly promoted. Apparently, they were referring to authority only outside of their classrooms.

So there I was in that English farmhouse, sharing a bottle of wine with my friend's mother and listening to her run down America in every way possible. Her speech was obviously well rehearsed, as if she had said it a thousand times. I felt like I was back in college. I can't recall every point she made that night. All I remember, and all that really matters, is how the conversation ended.

We had been talking for about two hours. Because she was a very pedantic and difficult woman to have a civil discussion with, and for the reasons mentioned above (her age and the confusion college had left me with), I let her do most of the talking. Maybe it was my silence that caused her to suddenly change, or maybe it was the wine, but she said, "Okay, so that's what I don't like about America. Would you like to know what I do love about it?"

After such a tirade, I eagerly said yes.

"I love America," she continued, "because when something goes wrong in the world, people look to America for help. They don't look into the reporters' cameras, clutching their children in their arms and barely alive from war or starvation or some natural calamity and demand help from other countries. It's always America, as if America is obligated to help everyone everywhere. And America always shows up, whether there's something in it for them or not. America leads the charge. In fact, most other countries wait to see what America will do before deciding if they're going to do anything! So despite your country's mistakes, it's still the beacon of light to the world it has always been, and it's still the greatest hope for mankind."

She went on to tell me about a faint memory she had from her childhood of her mother holding her and waving to American GIs passing through London during a victory parade the day World War II ended. One of them smiled at her and handed her a candy bar. She watched as her mother hugged him and cried into his chest like they were old friends. Other GIs played with children. There was hugging, kissing, waving and cheering everywhere.

"To say it was a happy day doesn't even begin to do it justice," she said. "It was like being awakened from a nightmare."

She talked about the nights she and her parents hid in air raid shelters, and how they sat huddled in fear, listening to the dull thuds of Nazi bombs falling on buildings in the distance, not knowing if their home, or their friends, would be there when she returned.

"So many buildings were on fire," she said, "it was like an aerial view of hell."

Her eyes welled with tears as she told this story. She even sobbed a little when she finished, as if she knew she was contradicting all of her previous criticisms, or that the weight of what she just said reduced them all to the point of irrelevancy. Then this formerly imperious Englishwoman softened, smiled at me, and asked, "Can I give you a hug?" Again, this may have been inspired by her secret love of America, or the wine, or both, but I was glad to accept it either way. We embraced for a few seconds and I went to pull away, but she held on a little longer. And in that moment, I realized it wasn't me she was hugging. She was hugging that GI who gave her candy fifty years earlier and let her and her mother know the nightmare was over.

As I have remembered that night over the years, I've wondered if her cynicism about America stemmed from disappointment in policy decisions since World War II that didn't rise to the levels of honesty, goodness and integrity personified in that GI — that soldier who was hardly more than a boy himself, and who had just witnessed mankind at its worst, but still managed to kneel down, smile warmly at a little girl, and give her candy. Maybe he set the bar too high for any country to live up to. Men of the "greatest generation" could do that. I've known a few of them. They were a hard act to follow, not only in terms of courage, but also of integrity and goodness.

Whatever it was that compelled her to traverse the spectrum from hate to love that night, that hug taught me more about America and its perception around the world than all those college professors combined. And despite the times America has stumbled, I have seen my country just the way she described it — as a beacon of light for the world and mankind's greatest hope — ever since.

~Mark Rickerby

99

The Fullness of Freedom

*We must be free not because we claim freedom but
because we practice it.*
~William Faulkner

surveyed the grocery store and tried to wrap my mind around the shopping process. A couple dozen pyramids of various canned goods and boxed items rose from the floor. Counters edged the room, with shelves of bread, meat, and cheese behind them. People queued up in long lines yelling to the clerks that manned those counters. The customers didn't seem to always leave with food, though, just tickets. Then they moved to another line. "Well," I thought, "I'm certainly not in the United States."

When I traveled to Kazakhstan with a student group for a month, I knew being immersed in a different culture would bring surprises. But I'd never thought of this. A grocery store is a grocery store, right?

The Kazakh student I'd been partnered with explained: "You get in line at the meat counter to see the goods and tell them what you want. You're given a ticket for the item, which is set aside. Then, you go to the payment counter and get in line to pay for what you ordered. Your ticket is stamped. After that, you get back in another line at the meat counter to pick up what you ordered. Simple."

At that point, I realized how different their everyday life was from mine. If they wanted canned vegetables, they were lucky if there was a pyramid of beans that day. I had about twenty different types to choose from on a shelf. They stood in three different long lines for one loaf of bread, while I got frustrated when three people were in line in front of me at the checkout where I could purchase dozens of different items at once. At the same time, I came to see why most Kazakh shopping was done at the local street markets, which were a lot like our farmer's markets, or at small shops. Much simpler, with a lot of charm and a sense of community.

As my trip continued on, I learned about Kazakhstan, while the Kazakh students we partnered with discovered things about the United States. I certainly got a fresh perspective on my country when I tried to de-mystify our culture for them. Just try explaining to someone who hasn't experienced it why we celebrate the Fourth of July like we do. "You eat outside? Why?" (I was describing a picnic.) Or clarify how our transportation system works. "On TV it looks like everyone in the United States has a car. Do they really? Why don't they take buses?" (Cars were a true luxury there. People took trains and buses everywhere.)

One moment, however, made me appreciate my nation more deeply than the others. Somehow, in the midst of a conversation with my counterpart student, the issue of visiting other parts of our respective countries came up.

"So, is it difficult to get a visa to travel?" she asked.

"Do you mean to another country?" I replied.

"No, like when you want to go to another… what do you call the smaller regions… state?"

"Oh. Um, we don't actually have to get a visa to do that."

"How do you get permission to go there then?"

"We don't have to."

"You just… go?"

"Yeah."

"But you have to get permission if you move, don't you?"

"Not even then. We just tell them where we moved to."

My counterpart shook her head trying to grasp that.

I sat across from her struggling to imagine not being able to travel around my own country without getting permission from the government. To me, what business was it of the government where I went?

To my Kazakh friend, such an idea was incomprehensible.

Right then and there, I gained a new appreciation of freedom and what it was. Oh, it was freedom from oppression, sure. I saw how, at that time, the people of Kazakhstan were still working through the break they'd experienced from the Soviet Union. Many were very sensitive to how secure their country was from another nation threatening them. Some still felt more secure when Russia was in charge, and they wanted that back. Others wanted to maintain their independence, but still realized how easily that could be lost.

That simple conversation with a fellow student, however, helped me see that freedom is so much more than just that. It is the freedom to choose. Not just to choose from fifty rather than one type of canned vegetable. But to choose to visit family in another state on a whim. To choose to live my life with as little oversight as possible.

I used to think it was a little cheesy when, on TV, I saw people kiss the ground when they returned to their home country. Candidly, though, it took everything in my power not to do that when I landed in the United States after that trip. Oh, I recognized our country's imperfections in new ways. For a while, I was irritated by the impatience of people waiting in relatively short lines. And I still long for the kind of community bond I often saw among the Kazakhs. There is profound beauty there. But I wouldn't for one moment trade it for what my country offers: Freedom that we often take for granted. Freedom that we sometimes don't even realize isn't as universal as we assume. Freedom that defines what our nation is all about.

~Diane Gardner

The 9/11 Connection

We will remember every rescuer who dies in honor.
We will remember every family that lives in grief.
We will remember...
~President George W. Bush

Observing the tenth anniversary of 9/11 was challenging for me. I wasn't on American soil. I was in Canada on a two-year work assignment with my family. I couldn't help feeling disconnected with all that was going on in the States, as our coverage was screened through the lens of the BBC and CBS.

The ten-year anniversary fell on a Sunday. That morning, I was getting ready for church. I never wear jewelry other than my wedding ring. Yet, for some reason, I was rummaging through my jewelry.

I found an antique locket, a gift from my husband a decade ago. I opened it, curious to see if there were any pictures inside. Sure enough there were two — one of my older daughter wearing a tutu, another of my son smiling broadly, trying to hold his baby sister.

My stomach dropped. I remember taking those pictures. It was the morning of September 11, 2001.

I had a three-week-old baby and three hours of sleep that morning. My oldest was four and had been up since 6:00, dressed for her first ballet lesson. I took her picture before breakfast, fearing spilt milk and absent-mindedness. My two-year-old son wanted his picture taken, too, so I propped the baby in his arms and took it.

The *Teletubbies* were on TV. I let the older two eat cereal in front of "Electronic Mommy," while I went to my room to nurse the baby in peace.

I remember little things — how blue the sky was, how much I craved coffee, how inane I found the *Teletubbies*, how perfect my baby's fingers were. Perhaps everyone can recall with such clarity the thirty seconds before learning of the attacks.

Sometime after nine, the phone rang. It was my mother.

"Are you watching TV?"

"No."

She told me about New York. I ran upstairs, still holding my daughter, and commandeered the television. I saw the towers smoking. Stunned, I sat on the coffee table and didn't move.

Hours passed. I saw the towers fall. I saw the Pentagon burn. I saw the field in Pennsylvania. Eventually, my daughter asked when we were going to ballet. I looked at her.

How could something as innocent as a pre-ballet class happen today?

I called the ballet school to see if they were still holding classes, as if the attacks where on the same level as a snow day. My old director answered, cheerful as yesterday. She didn't know about the attacks. I found myself playing the reluctant reporter.

Silence.

When she spoke, her voice was soft. Classes would go on as scheduled.

I hung up the phone. I turned off the TV. The ensuing silence was loud, almost irreverent. I buckled the kids in the minivan, kissing their heads because I could. I started the engine and rolled down the windows. The sky was so blue — no clouds, no planes. I turned on the radio, letting the news kill the silence.

I drove fifteen miles under the speed limit. No one passed me or honked. When I pulled into the parking lot and turned off the car, I could still hear the radio. Looking around, I realized it was coming from the open windows of the adjacent buildings and cars. It was my first brush with a national connection.

I wasn't just a mom in a minivan; I was an American.

I don't remember putting those pictures in that locket. I don't know what possessed me to pick it up on the tenth anniversary of 9/11.

All I know was that it no longer mattered that I wasn't on American soil; I was still connected.

~Nicole L.V. Mullis

In Hot Water

A mind that is stretched by a new experience can never
go back to its old dimensions.
~Oliver Wendell Holmes

felt like an idiot. Had I really just asked, "Is it dishwasher-safe?"
We were in the middle of the Peruvian highlands in the Andes,
in a little shack where a local artisan was selling ceramic pitchers he had baked in a wood-fired kiln, and I was asking if one
of his handmade creations was dishwasher-safe. Because I was going
to use it for maple syrup. For pancakes. And I didn't want to wash it
by hand afterwards.

You can't get more "Ugly American" than that!

The artisan and our tour guide looked at me, confused. Yes, I
could wash the pitchers. Why would I think they weren't washable?
The concept of an automated dishwasher eluded them. I realized my
mistake immediately, bought two ceramic pitchers, and reminded
myself that 90% of the world didn't use a dishwasher and had never
heard of such a thing.

This was in 2003, in an area of Peru where the vast majority of
the tourists were hikers. Most of the local residents lived in one-room
houses with no electricity and a fire pit for cooking. Toilets were holes
in the ground. Everyone had food and shelter and clothing; everyone
was friendly, and there was no crime at all against tourists. The children
were inspiring, clad in neat school uniforms and walking miles back
and forth to school each day through the steep foothills.

People seemed happy and productive and healthy. They didn't need dishwashers. No one really *needs* a dishwasher. Life was simpler, more grounded, more self-sufficient. And it made me feel spoiled, privileged, and pretty wasteful.

Ironically, the afternoon before we were to leave for Peru, August 14th, was when that huge blackout had occurred, the one that knocked out power to 10 million people in Ontario and 45 million people in eight northeastern U.S. states. We had scrambled to find a new flight to Peru on the 15th, driving from New York's shutdown JFK airport all the way to Boston, discovering miraculous pockets of electricity in Massachusetts so that we could fill our empty gas tank, and staying in Boston overnight. We managed to fly to Peru from Boston on the 16th, a day late for our tour and with renewed awareness of our dependence on modern conveniences.

I've traveled all over the world since I was a kid, from highly developed countries in Europe, Asia, and the Middle East to Third World countries in South and Central America, and in Africa. I've visited forty-two countries so far — some for weeks or months, some for just a day, and many of them repeatedly over the years. They have all been beautiful and exotic and fascinating. All of them have opened my mind and made me aware of how fortunate I am to live in the United States.

We don't have to go through armed border crossings to drive from one state to another; we can move freely about our vast territory without government interference and live and work wherever we want; we can go to college even if our parents did not; women have (mostly) equal rights; and we don't wake up every morning wondering what danger the day will bring. Nothing beats the USA for standard of living, for freedom of choice, for ease of movement, and above all, for the opportunity to prosper.

I think one of the best things I did for my kids was taking them on as many trips to Third World countries as possible. That travel opened their eyes to the same things — and they are unspoiled even though they grew up in a pretty fancy town.

I have friends who spent years attaining their U.S. citizenship. But

I was born to it, due to the hard work of my great-grandparents. They were the ones who saved up their money and boarded boats and took off with nothing in their pockets for uncertain new lives in America. I have a great-grandfather from Russia who started out selling tea from a pushcart and ended up owning a small chain of furniture stores in Boston. I have another great-grandfather, from Lithuania via England, who ran a commercial laundry in Harlem in New York City — his son went into real estate and that son's son became a Harvard-educated lawyer. All eight of my great-grandparents arrived with nothing after leaving countries that offered them no opportunity to live and prosper. Here, they were able to work hard and be rewarded for that hard work.

We are the lucky ones. We get to enjoy all the American privileges and freedoms.

And every single morning I stand in the shower and I think about those Andean highlands in Peru. I am grateful for my shower with its unlimited hot water, my clean towels, and the unbelievable luxury of the way that we live. I think about those kids walking miles to go to school as I get in my car to go to work.

My ancestors could have moved somewhere else. But they moved here. And I get to be an American. It's not something I take for granted.

~Amy Newmark

★ The ★ Spirit of America

Meet Our Contributors

Meet Amy Newmark

About Lee Woodruff and the Bob Woodruff Foundation

Thank You

About Chicken Soup for the Soul

Meet Our Contributors

Cathy Ancewicz began writing in 2013 when she joined a creative writing ministry at her church. She loves sharing her stories with her grandchildren. When she is not writing, Cathy enjoys reading, calligraphy, and pen and ink drawings. She lives in South Florida near her daughter and family.

Elizabeth Atwater lives on a small ranch in North Carolina where she and her husband Joe raise Standardbred racehorses. In her spare time, you can find her tending to her roses, curled up with a book or in her office writing.

Joan Bailey currently lives in Japan where she divides her time between teaching and writing about food, farming and farmers markets. Learn more at www.japanfarmersmarkets.com.

Jan Bono's new cozy mystery series set on the southwest Washington coast is now available! She's also published five humorous personal experience collections, two poetry chapbooks, nine one-act plays, a dinner theater play, and has written for magazines ranging from *Guideposts* to *Woman's World*. Learn more at www.JanBonoBooks.com.

Michelle Bruce is a registered nurse from Nebraska. Michelle has been married to her spouse Jeremy for twenty years. Together they raise their four teenagers. Michelle enjoys traveling, swimming, writing stories, watching her kids' sports and spending time with her numerous pets.

Carisa J. Burrows is a writer and contributor to the *Chicken Soup for the Soul* series. She lives with her husband Ralph. She thanks her parents, Gary and Carmellina, for a childhood full of memories and a lifetime of love, along with her siblings Garrett, Melina and Gina for making those memories so great. E-mail her at carisaw@hotmail.com.

Hetie Burt received her Bachelor of Arts in Horticulture from Auburn University and is currently a stay-at-home mom. She is married with three beautiful boys. Hetie enjoys writing, gardening, scuba diving and volunteering at her kids' schools. She plans on continuing to write non-fiction, children's books and articles.

Corinda Carfora is a graduate of the University of Miami. A multi-talented creative professional, she has sung backup for Bruce Springsteen, performed on *The Daily Show with Jon Stewart*, produced videos, and built a twenty-five-year career in book publishing. An avid animal lover, she also helps support Animal Care Sanctuary.

Eva Carter has spent many years as a financial analyst. She is now concentrating on creative endeavors such as writing and photography. She was born in Czechoslovakia and has traveled extensively. She and her Canadian-born husband, Larry, live in Dallas, TX. E-mail her at evacarter@sbcglobal.net.

Beth Cato is the Nebula Award–nominated author of *The Clockwork Dagger* series from Harper Voyager. Her newest novel is *Breath of Earth*. She's a Hanford, CA native transplanted to the Arizona desert, where she lives with her husband, son, and requisite cat. Follow her at BethCato.com and on Twitter @BethCato.

Sara Celi is a television journalist and published author. She lives outside of Cincinnati, OH.

A.B. Chesler is a writer and educator from sunny Southern California. She enjoys traveling, spending time with her family and friends, and finding the lighter side of life. E-mail her at achesler24@gmail.com or visit her blog at thishouseoflove.net.

Penelope Childers is a published author and enjoys writing inspirational true stories. She and her husband Larry live in Fresno, CA. She dedicates her story to her classmates at Corcoran High School, class of 1965.

Randy Collins is American Humane Association's National Director of Red Star Rescue & Emergency Services for Animals. He has a long history in emergency response including work with the Department of Homeland Security, FEMA, and the armed forces. He served in the U.S. Marine Corps for six years on active duty and six years in the reserves.

Christie Schmitt Coombs is a freelance writer and blogger who graduated from The University of Arizona. After her husband's death in the 2001 terrorist attacks, she and their three children started The Jeffrey Coombs Memorial Foundation: a foundation in Jeff's memory. Christie oversees the foundation and volunteers for several other nonprofits.

Amy McCoy Dees is a patriot at heart. A mother, historian, civil servant, and published author, she loves her country and honors all that have served — past and present. She writes American history novels for young adults/children and loves traveling into the past to discover "hidden gems" to share with her readers.

Karen DeVault earned her B.A. degree in English, with honors, from Oakland University in 2007. She lives with her husband in southeast Michigan, with two daughters and grandchildren nearby. Karen enjoys motorcycling, fishing, bicycling, running, and acting. She is currently writing her first novel.

Laurie Carnright Edwards loves living in New Hampshire with her pastor-husband Dale. She has been published in the *Chicken Soup for the Soul* series and on *Leadership Journal's* website. She is a proud mother and mother-in-law, and a graduate of Berkshire Christian College and Gordon-Conwell Theological Seminary.

Terri Elders, LCSW, served with the Peace Corps in Belize, Dominican Republic and Seychelles, as well as in the USA following Hurricanes Rita and Katrina. Her stories appear in over a hundred anthologies, including two dozen *Chicken Soup for the Soul* books. She blogs at atouchoftarragon.blogspot.com.

Josephine Fitzpatrick is a wife, mother and grandmother. She is a retired attorney who loves to write. She co-facilitates a memoir writing class at the Osher Lifelong Learning Institute at California State University, Long Beach, and has been published in *Creative Nonfiction* magazine, *The Sun*, and the *Chicken Soup for the Soul* series.

Marianne Fosnow has enjoyed writing stories and poems since childhood. She raised two children and now enjoys her grandchildren. Marianne is also interested in photography. She loves to end each day relaxing with a good book. E-mail her at fosnowmary@yahoo.com.

Ronelle Frankel loves reading all kinds of inspiring books and stories, especially in her role as an editor for Chicken Soup for the Soul. When she's not reading, Ronelle enjoys spending time with her husband and three children, going to the beach, trying new restaurants, and testing out healthy recipes.

Sally Friedman is a longtime contributor to the *Chicken Soup for the Soul* series who uses her life and experience as inspiration. The material is always there! A graduate of the University of Pennsylvania, she is the wife of a retired New Jersey Superior Court judge, a mother and grandmother.

Diane Gardner holds a Bachelor of Arts and a Master of Arts degree in mass communication and journalism. She is a full-time editor and writer living in the San Francisco Bay Area. She enjoys traveling, painting, theater, street fairs, anything chocolate, and quiet evenings at home with her husband.

James A. Gemmell is a married father of two children. Most summers he can be found hiking across Spain on the Camino de Santiago. His other hobbies include writing, playing guitar and collecting art.

Peter Green lives near Niagara Falls, NY and is the producer and co-writer of an original dinner theater show called *Niagara Falls — America's Wonder*. As a professional musician and entertainer he hosts tours of Niagara Falls in addition to performing in Niagara Falls, NY throughout the tourism season.

Award-winning author, speaker and teacher, **Lynn Hare** has published numerous devotions, articles, and poetry in Christian periodicals. She enjoys praying, playing the piano, hiking and photography. She lives in Portland, OR with her husband Tim, three adult children and a grandson. E-mail her at lynnrhare@gmail.com.

Samantha Harmon-Thompson is a self-described geek and loves life. She is a wife, and a "mom" of three dogs and a cat. Samantha enjoys baking and cooking for her parents, in-laws, husband, and her two sisters when they visit with her nieces and nephews. E-mail her at samsterbelle@gmail.com.

Cathryn Hasek is a freelance writer from North Ridgeville, OH. She is active in her local VFW Post where she is editor of the newsletter and webmaster of their VFW website. She enjoys building new websites, fixing computers, hanging out with her husband and their Beagle, and writing creative nonfiction.

Lori Hein is a freelance writer and author of *Ribbons of Highway: A Mother-Child Journey Across America*. Her work has appeared in numerous publications and in several *Chicken Soup for the Soul* books. Visit her at LoriHein.com.

Suzanne Herber received her Bachelor of Arts degree in Theatre from the University of Colorado Denver and went on to complete the three-year acting program at Circle in the Square Theatre School in New York City. She currently resides in Colorado with her husband, son, and Australian Shepherd. Suzanne is an avid soccer, tennis, and pickleball player.

Miriam Hill is a frequent contributor to the *Chicken Soup for the Soul* series and has been published in *Writer's Digest*, *The Christian Science Monitor*, *Grit*, *St. Petersburg Times*, *The Sacramento Bee*, and Poynter online. Miriam's manuscript received Honorable Mention for Inspirational Writing in a Writer's Digest Writing Competition.

Sylvia Garza Holmes is a native Texan. She enlisted in the United States Air Force in 1974. She has attended Oregon Institute of Technology and St. Mary's University in San Antonio. She and her husband have been married for forty years and live in Oregon. Sylvia spends her time writing for children and teaching English.

Following a career in fundraising at the University of California, Los Angeles, **Karen Howard** now enjoys hiking, yoga, long walks, lively discussions with her book club, volunteering at Descanso Gardens, and life with Richard and her two cats, Belle and Jedi Jack.

Lois Hudson co-authored *Ending Elder Abuse: A Family Guide*, and has been published in devotional collections. When she is not reading or writing, she enjoys photographing the beauties of northern Nevada where she lives. She is the mother of two adult sons (with their wives), and grandmother of two amazing grandsons.

David Hull is a retired teacher who has published short stories in numerous magazines and *Chicken Soup for the Soul* books. Besides writing every day, he enjoys gardening, reading, and watching reruns of *Everybody Loves Raymond*. E-mail him at Davidhull59@aol.com.

Daniel Hurley immigrated to the United States, from Ireland, when he was two years old. In his free time, Daniel enjoys exercising, spending time with his family, and being involved in local, state, and federal politics. Daniel has future plans to pursue a career in public service.

Gayle M. Irwin is an award-winning Wyoming writer. The author of inspirational dog books for children and adults, she's also contributed to other titles in the *Chicken Soup for the Soul* series. She enjoys photography, visiting national parks, and supporting pet rescue groups. Learn more at www.gaylemirwin.com.

Jeffree Wyn Itrich is the author of four books and numerous articles. She has a master's of social work and a master's of journalism. Her new blog, thegoodnessprinciple.com, shares good news and positive stories that warm the heart.

Jennie Ivey lives in Tennessee. She is the author of numerous works of fiction and nonfiction, including stories in many *Chicken Soup for the Soul* books. Visit her website at jennieivey.com.

Jeanie Jacobson is on the leadership team of Wordsowers Christian Writers. She has been published in eight *Chicken Soup for the Soul* books. Her new book, *Fast Fixes for the Christian Pack-Rat*, is on Amazon. Jeanie loves visiting family and friends, reading, hiking, praise dancing, and gardening. Learn more at jeaniejacobson.com.

C. Joy is a medical professional with a passion for storytelling. As a freelance writer from the cornfields of rural Iowa, she enjoys reading, painting and traveling. Her greatest accomplishments are being a parent to five children and grandma to two grandsons.

Although **Tziyona Kantor** has a B.A. in Journalism from BU, she catered instead. She wrote a cooking column for two and a half years. Parents of seven, grandparents of more, she and her husband have lived in Israel for thirty-five years. She is back to writing about what she loves: family, learning, Judaism, Israel, touring and even cooking.

Named by *TIME* magazine as one of the "Top 100 Most Influential People in the World," **Dean Karnazes** is an ultramarathoner and NYC bestselling author of the book *50/50: Secrets I Learned Running 50 Marathons in 50 Days — and How You Too Can Achieve Super Endurance!* He lives with his wife and family in the San Francisco Bay Area.

Multi-published, award-winning author **Larry C. Kerpelman** holds a Ph.D. in Psychology from the University of Rochester. This is his second story published in the *Chicken Soup for the Soul* series. His memoir *Concrete Steps: Coming of Age in a Once-Big City* is being published in 2016. Learn more at www.LCKerpelman.com.

Pamela Landwirth is president and CEO of Give Kids The World Village, a nonprofit resort near Orlando, FL that serves children with life-threatening illnesses and their families. More than 144,000 families have visited the Village, and Pam works tirelessly to create for them the happiness that inspires hope.

Susan Lendroth is a children's author with two new picture books slated for a 2017 release. She lives with a clueless, but cute, cat named Kitten, and if ever stranded again, would rather spring for lodgings than ask the sheriff for a spare cot in the cells.

Barbara LoMonaco has worked for Chicken Soup for the Soul as an editor since 1998. She has co-authored two *Chicken Soup for the Soul* book titles and has had stories published in numerous other titles.

Barbara is a graduate of the University of Southern California and has a teaching credential.

Vita Lusty has work appearing or forthcoming in *Green Lifestyles*, *Luna Luna*, *Penny*, *Paper Nautilus* and the collaborative manuscript *By One's Own Hand: Writing About Suicide Loss*. She is now hiding in the Joshua Tree desert and finishing her first book in a key lime house with a pack of rescued dogs.

Renae MacLachlan has been a licensed battlefield guide for fourteen years at Gettysburg National Military Park, where she received the Superintendent's Award for Excellence. She wrote *Treasures of the Civil War*, a book and exhibit for Gettysburg's 150th Anniversary. Renae is at work on a new book and lives in Gettysburg, PA.

Australian-born author **Grant Madden** immigrated to the USA in 2005 and currently resides in El Cajon, CA. By the time of publication, Grant expects to have his American citizenship. Grant's cover stories have appeared in *Sailing*, *Cat Sailor* and the *San Diego Reader*. Learn more at www.grantmadden.com.

Bridget Magee is a writer, editor, and educator. When not writing, Bridget can be found reading. She lives in Tucson, AZ with her husband, two daughters, and crazy dog, Smidgey. Her personal essays, blog posts, and poetry have appeared in several online and print publications.

Author and speaker **Mary Beth Magee's** faith leads her to explore God's world and write about it. She writes news, reviews and feature articles for print and online publications; fiction, poetry, and devotions, as well as recollections in several anthologies. E-mail her at MaryBethMageeWrites@gmail.com.

James C. Magruder is an award-winning advertising copywriter and executive speechwriter. He has had articles published in *Writer's Digest*,

HomeLife, *Christian Communicator*, and six *Chicken Soup for the Soul* books. He blogs about the writing life at thewritersrefuge.wordpress.com.

Tiffany Marshall is a freelance writer residing in Fort Worth, TX. When not at the keyboard, she enjoys books, movies, waterskiing, board games, college football, and *The Big Bang Theory*.

Dana Martin received her Bachelor of Arts degree in English from California State University, Bakersfield. She has written for *Woman's World* magazine and has been previously published in the *Chicken Soup for the Soul* series. Her current goal is to figure out God's plan for her life. E-mail her at Dana@DanaMartinWriting.com.

Susan Mathis is a published author in Colorado Springs, CO. Her first two books, *Countdown for Couples: Preparing for the Adventure of Marriage* and *The Remarriage Adventure: Preparing for a Life of Love and Happiness*, were co-authored with her husband, Dale. Learn more at www.SusanGMathis.com.

Phyllis McKinley has received multiple writing awards. She is the author of four poetry books and one children's book, an avid reader, and enjoys cooking, walking and spending time in nature. She dedicates this story, her fourth in the *Chicken Soup for the Soul* series, to her four children and five grandchildren. E-mail her at leafybough@hotmail.com.

Dee Dee McNeil has been a published songwriter and freelance journalist for nearly five decades. Her music has been recorded by icons like Gladys Knight, Diana Ross, Nancy Wilson, the Four Tops, and Edwin Starr, and her *Storyteller* CD was well received in 2015. McNeil's poetry and essays appear in numerous anthologies.

Harriet E. Michael is an author, freelance writer, and speaker. Her work has appeared in numerous publications. She has authored two books: *Prayer: It's Not About You* and *Glimpses of the Savior*. Born in Africa as the daughter of missionaries, she is a wife, mother, and grandmother. Follow her blog at harrietemichael.com.

Dean K. Miller is an author, poet, and editor residing in northern Colorado. He has published three books and his work has appeared in over three dozen print and online literary magazines. He is the creator of *The Haiku For You Project*. This is his second story published in the *Chicken Soup for the Soul* series. Learn more at deankmiller.com.

Jackie Minniti is the award-winning author of two novels: *Project June Bug*, the story of a teacher and an ADHD student, and *Jacqueline*, a middle-grade historical. She is a columnist for *The Island Reporter* in St. Petersburg, FL and is a previous contributor to the *Chicken Soup for the Soul* series. Learn more at www.jackieminniti.com.

A Navy wife and mother of three, **Lisa Smith Molinari** writes the award-winning blog and syndicated column, "The Meat and Potatoes of Life," which appears in civilian and military newspapers including *Stars and Stripes*, the official newspaper for U.S. Armed Forces. Read more at www.themeatandpotatoesoflife.com.

Sarah Morris is a writer for Major League Baseball Advanced Media and a novelist. Her first novel, *Vengeance*, is available through Amazon. She can be reached via e-mail at sarahmorris27@gmail.com.

Jonita Mullins grew up in Haskell, OK and earned an English degree from Oklahoma State University. She has published six books focused on Oklahoma history. She is a frequent speaker on history and is a passionate preservationist. Jonita owns a historic home in the Founders' Place District.

Nicole L.V. Mullis is the author of the novel *A Teacher Named Faith* (Cairn Press). Her work has appeared in literary magazines and anthologies, including the *Chicken Soup for the Soul* series. Her plays have been produced in New York, California and Michigan. She lives in Michigan with her husband and children.

Nancy Norton received her Bachelor of Arts degree from Rowan University. She has three grown daughters and teaches second grade in New Jersey. Nancy enjoys traveling with her husband and spending time with her grandchildren. She is the proud daughter of a ninety-four-year-old World War II veteran.

Welby O'Brien loves her veteran husband as they face the daily challenges of PTSD. With a master's degree in counseling, she has authored the book *Love Our Vets: Restoring Hope for Families of Veterans with PTSD*, and leads the widespread Love Our Vets — PTSD Family Support network. Learn more at www.LoveOurVets.org.

Linda O'Connell, a retired teacher and accomplished writer, is a firm believer in positively affecting others. She and her husband, Bill, have a blended family. Their four adult children, nine grandchildren, and great-grandson have given her laugh lines. She enjoys a hearty laugh, dark chocolate and walking on the beach.

Karen J. Olson is a writer from Eau Claire, WI. She graduated from the UW-Eau Claire with enough knowledge in psychology and sociology to make people-watching a job. She loves reading, walking, and all things Midwest. She especially enjoys writing humor and inspirational pieces. E-mail her at kjolson@charter.net.

Allison Paster-Torres was raised by a pack of wild libraries in South Jersey. She currently lives in upstate New York, where she is completing her MFA in creative writing.

Kay Conner Pliszka received her master's degree in Education from the University of Wisconsin–Milwaukee. Now a retired teacher living in Florida with her husband of forty-four years, Kay enjoys choir, golf, bridge, writing, editing and public speaking.

Kay Presto has stories published in several books in the *Chicken Soup for the Soul* series. She's an award-winning television and radio broadcaster, and photojournalist, covering motorsports. She has recently completed a middle-grade novel, and is currently writing several children's books. E-mail her at prestoprod6@yahoo.com.

Connie Kaseweter Pullen lives in rural Sandy, OR, near her five children and several grandchildren. She earned her Bachelor of Arts degree at the University of Portland in 2006, with a double major in Psychology and Sociology. Connie enjoys writing, photography and exploring nature. E-mail her at MyGrandmaPullen@aol.com.

Antoinette Rainone is an award-winning journalist and inspirational writer for *Guideposts*. She is currently working on a memoir about bonding with her dad during the 1978 Yankee season where she learned comebacks are possible — in baseball and life. Read her blog at findyourwingsnow.blogspot.com or e-mail her at findyourwingsnow@gmail.com.

Natalie June Reilly is an author and a proud American and Navy mom. E-mail her at girlwriter68@hotmail.com.

Cindy Richardson resides in Missouri with her husband Tom, where she teaches kindergarten. She enjoys the friendship of her three grown daughters and loves being Nana to six grandchildren. She hopes to encourage and inspire others with her writing and speaking. Learn more at cindyrichardson.org.

Mark Rickerby is a writer, voice actor and frequent contributor to the *Chicken Soup for the Soul* series. His proudest achievements are co-authoring his father's memoir, *The Other Belfast: An Irish Youth*, and *Great Big World*, a CD of songs he wrote and sang for his daughters, Marli and Emma. He's currently writing a children's book series.

Maureen Rogers is a transplanted Canadian who has lived in Seattle, WA for over forty years. She writes fiction and poetry as well as nonfiction, and her work has appeared in various newspapers, online publications and several titles in the *Chicken Soup for the Soul* series.

Robyn Rothermel is an Army veteran who served in Afghanistan. She grew up in Maine with her parents and two siblings. She survived childhood leukemia and chose to enter the service as a way to give back to all of those who helped her.

Mitali Ruths grew up in Houston, TX about a mile from NASA. She now lives in Montreal with her husband and three children, but feels even more American now that she's north of the border.

D.J. Sartell is a freelance author living in a quiet suburb outside Sacramento, CA with her spouse and teenage daughter. An animal lover who enjoys spending time with friends and family, D.J. is hoping to get exposure to further her growing writing career.

Aaron M. Smith earned a degree in journalism from Ohio University in 1998 before working as a sports editor and writer in the newspaper industry. He now works as a freelance writer and has written two books. Smith lives in Cincinnati with his wife, Chrissy, and three children, Sierra, Aidan, and Natalie.

Judee Stapp is a speaker for Stonecroft Ministries and women's events. She writes to inspire people to use their God-given gifts. She has a son in Pennsylvania, a daughter, son-in-law, and three grandkids in Minnesota, and a daughter, son-in-law and grandson in California. Judee and John live in Placentia, CA. Learn more at www.judeestapp.com.

Katelynn Stream is an Army wife of ten years to her husband, Paul. They have four young children: Isabella, Greyson, Paxton, and Keegan. She is a labor and delivery nurse and enjoys volunteering with the Army Family Readiness Group. She is the recipient of the Artillery Order of Molly Pitcher. E-mail her at katelynnstream@gmail.com.

Jan Sydnam has authored several nonfiction books since 2008. Her writing icon is Nicholas Sparks. Her true crime books are definitely hard to put down. Although multitalented, writing has been a mainstay in supporting her addiction to horses and equine competitions.

Annmarie B. Tait lives in Conshohocken, PA with her husband Joe Beck. Annmarie has been published in over twenty *Chicken Soup for the Soul* books as well as various other magazines and anthologies. Annmarie and her husband also enjoy singing and recording Irish and American folk music. E-mail her at irishbloom@aol.com.

A Western Canada native, **Elaine Thomas** writes award-winning non-fiction from her country home near La Grange, TX. Elaine considers it an honor to be entrusted with sharing and preserving the memorable stories of individuals that offer invaluable insight into life. Learn more at elainethomaswriter.com.

Lisa P. Tubbs is a widowed mother of four who lives in the Fort Worth area. She has enjoyed reading and writing stories and poems since early childhood and has had numerous publications of online content. She plans on using her knack for writing to share her Christian faith with others in the near future.

Gayle Veitenheimer is a writer and mother of four. She is married to her high school sweetheart and resides in Fort Worth, TX. Her blog, *Cross Training for Character*, can be found at www.gayleveitenheimer.com.

Pennington Walker is a retired U.S. Army Sergeant Major after twenty-eight years of service. He is a proud father of one daughter currently serving in the U.S. Marine Corps. Currently, Pennington is the USO Center Director in Dubai and prior to that served five years in Afghanistan supporting the USO Kandahar and USO Camp Leatherneck.

Arthur Wiknik, Jr. served in Vietnam with the 101st Airborne Division and has appeared on the History Channel and Military Channel. This is the seventh *Chicken Soup for the Soul* book he has been published in. Arthur frequently shares his military experiences at schools and civic organizations. Learn more at www.namsense.com.

C. F. Williams received her Bachelor of Arts degree at the University at Albany and Master's of English degree at Marshall University. She and her husband raised four sons. C. F. teaches writing in West Virginia and enjoys knitting and reading in her spare time. She plans to continue writing both nonfiction and fiction and to enjoy her grandchild.

Woody Woodburn is a national award-winning journalist and the author of *Wooden & Me: Life Lessons from My Two-Decade Friendship with the Legendary Coach and Humanitarian to Help "Make Each Day Your Masterpiece"* and *Strawberries in Wintertime: Essays on Life, Love, and Laughter*. Learn more at woodywoodburn.com.

Linda C. Wright lives on the Space Coast of Florida with her husband Richard and four-legged friend Ginger. Several of her personal essays have been published in the *Chicken Soup for the Soul* series. In her spare time, she enjoys traveling, photography and bike riding. E-mail her at lindacwright@ymail.com.

Susan Kimmel Wright grew up in Lambertsville, PA. She's written several books, and has had many stories published in the *Chicken Soup for the Soul* series and elsewhere. She dedicates her story to the people of Somerset County, PA, and the passengers and crew of Flight 93 and their families. E-mail her at kidsbookwrighter@gmail.com.

Meet Amy Newmark

Amy Newmark is the bestselling author, editor-in-chief, and publisher of the *Chicken Soup for the Soul* book series. Since 2008, she has published 125 new books, most of them national bestsellers in the U.S. and Canada, more than doubling the number of *Chicken Soup for the Soul* titles in print today.

Amy is credited with revitalizing the Chicken Soup for the Soul brand, which has been a publishing industry phenomenon since the first book came out in 1993. By compiling inspirational and aspirational true stories curated from ordinary people who have had extraordinary experiences, Amy has kept the 23-year-old Chicken Soup for the Soul brand fresh and relevant.

Amy graduated *magna cum laude* from Harvard University where she majored in Portuguese and minored in French. She then embarked on a three-decade career as a Wall Street analyst, a hedge fund manager, and a corporate executive in the technology field. Her return to literary pursuits was inevitable, as her honors thesis in college involved traveling throughout Brazil's impoverished northeast region, collecting stories from regular people. She is delighted to have come full circle in her writing career — from collecting stories "from the people" in Brazil as a twenty-year-old to, three decades later, collecting stories from the people" for Chicken Soup for the Soul.

When Amy and her husband Bill, the CEO of Chicken Soup for the Soul, are not working, they are visiting their four grown children. Follow her on Twitter @amynewmark and @chickensoupsoul. Listen to her free daily podcast, The Chicken Soup for the Soul Podcast, at www.chickensoup.podbean.com, or find it on iTunes, the Podcasts app on iPhone, or on your favorite podcast app on other devices.

About Lee Woodruff and the Bob Woodruff Foundation

As co-author of the New York Times best-selling *In an Instant*, Lee Woodruff garnered critical acclaim for the compelling and humorous chronicle of her family's journey to recovery following her husband Bob's roadside bomb injury in Iraq. Appearing on national television and as keynote speakers since the February 2007 publication of their book, the couple has helped put a face on the serious issue of traumatic brain injury among returning Iraq and Afghanistan war veterans, as well as the millions of Americans who live with this often invisible, but life-changing affliction.

They have founded the Bob Woodruff Foundation to assist post-9/11 injured service members, veterans and their families to heal from the physical and silent wounds of war. To date, the nonprofit foundation has invested more than $30 million in finding, funding, and shaping innovative programs across the country that have created positive returns for more than two million of our nation's heroes and their families. Much of this funding has come from the Foundation's annual Stand Up for Heroes concert, which enlists the aid of top comedians and iconic musicians to honor those who serve.

Woodruff has been a contributing reporter for *CBS This Morning* and ABC's *Good Morning America*. Her best-selling book, *Perfectly Imperfect: A Life in Progress*, was followed by her first novel, *Those We Love Most*.

A freelance writer, Woodruff has penned numerous personal articles about her family and parenting that have run in magazines such as *Ladies' Home Journal*, *Real Simple*, *Good Housekeeping*, *Redbook*, and *Parade*. She also wrote the foreword for *Chicken Soup for the Soul: Recovering from Traumatic Brain Injuries*.

Woodruff lives in Westchester County, New York, with her husband and four children. You can learn more at www.leewoodruff.com.

The Bob Woodruff Foundation will receive a contribution for every copy sold of this book, to help create long-lasting positive outcomes for today's veterans and their families. For more information about the Bob Woodruff Foundation, please visit bobwoodrufffoundation.org.

Thank You

We owe huge thanks to all of our contributors and fans, who shared thousands of stories about what America means to them. We loved reading all the submissions and choosing the 101 that would appear in the book. In these times, when we hear so much negativity, it was refreshing and inspiring to read these stories. Patriotism is alive and well, and these stories do a great job of reminding us why we love our great nation.

We owe special thanks to D'ette Corona, Barbara LoMonaco, and Mary Fisher, who read all the submissions. They narrowed down the list of finalists for Amy to make some difficult decisions and choose and edit the stories that you see in this volume. D'ette Corona continued to be Amy's right-hand woman in creating the final manuscript and working with all our wonderful writers. Barbara LoMonaco and Kristiana Pastir, along with outside proofreader Elaine Kimbler, jumped in at the end to proof, proof, proof. And yes, there will always be typos anyway, so feel free to let us know about them at webmaster@ chickensoupforthesoul.com.

The whole publishing team deserves a hand, including Director of Production Victor Cataldo, and our graphic designer Daniel Zaccari, who turned our manuscript into this beautiful book.

Sharing Happiness, Inspiration, and Wellness

Real people sharing real stories, every day, all over the world. In 2007, *USA Today* named *Chicken Soup for the Soul* one of the five most memorable books in the last quarter-century. With over 100 million books sold to date in the U.S. and Canada alone, more than 200 titles in print, and translations into more than forty languages, "chicken soup for the soul" is one of the world's best-known phrases.

Today, twenty-three years after we first began sharing happiness, inspiration and wellness through our books, we continue to delight our readers with new titles, but have also evolved beyond the bookstore, with super premium pet food, a line of high quality soups, and a variety of licensed products and digital offerings, all inspired by stories. Chicken Soup for the Soul has recently expanded into visual storytelling through movies and television. Chicken Soup for the Soul is "changing the world one story at a time®." Thanks for reading!

Share with Us

We all have had Chicken Soup for the Soul moments in our lives. If you would like to share your story or poem with millions of people around the world, go to chickensoup. com and click on "Submit Your Story." You may be able to help another reader and become a published author at the same time. Some of our past contributors have launched writing and speaking careers from the publication of their stories in our books!

We only accept story submissions via our website. They are no longer accepted via mail or fax.

To contact us regarding other matters, please send us an e-mail through webmaster@chickensoupforthesoul.com, or fax or write us at:

Chicken Soup for the Soul
P.O. Box 700
Cos Cob, CT 06807-0700
Fax: 203-861-7194

One more note from your friends at Chicken Soup for the Soul: Occasionally, we receive an unsolicited book manuscript from one of our readers, and we would like to respectfully inform you that we do not accept unsolicited manuscripts and we must discard the ones that appear.

Chicken Soup
for the Soul.

My Very Good,
Very Bad Dog

101 Heartwarming Stories about Our
Happy, Heroic & Hilarious Pets

Royalties from this book go to
AMERICAN HUMANE
ASSOCIATION
EST. 1877

Amy Newmark
Foreword by Robin Ganzert
President and CEO, American Humane Association

They come in all shapes, sizes, and personalities. From goofy to guard, from hero to ham, and everywhere in between, our dogs are important and beloved members of our families. This collection of 101 funny, heartwarming, and sometimes mindboggling stories is all about all the very good, very bad, simply amazing things our dogs do.

978-1-61159-956-5

AMERICAN PETS...

Chicken Soup for the Soul

My Very Good, Very Bad Cat

101 Heartwarming Stories about Our Happy, Heroic & Hilarious Pets

Royalties from this book go to
AMERICAN HUMANE ASSOCIATION
EST. 1877

Amy Newmark
Foreword by Robin Ganzert
President and CEO, American Humane Association

Our cats can be so good, and then they can be not-so-good, but boy do they give us great stories! These 101 heartwarming, humorous and completely true stories about our feline friends are sure to touch every cat lover's soul.

978-1-61159-955-8

ANOTHER KIND OF HERO

Chicken Soup for the Soul.

Miracles Happen

101 Inspirational Stories about Hope,
Answered Prayers, and
Divine Intervention

Jack Canfield,
Mark Victor Hansen
& Amy Newmark

Miracles happen every day! And these 101 true stories of divine intervention, answered prayers, healing, and extraordinary connections prove that miracles can happen to anyone at any time. You will be awed and uplifted by these personal stories of faith, prayer, and healing that show a higher power at work in our lives.

978-1-61159-932-9

MORE INSPIRATION...

Seen or unseen, angels are in our midst! These divine guides, guardian angels, and heavenly messengers help and guide us when we need it most. In this collection of 101 miraculous stories, real people share real stories about their incredible, personal angel experiences of faith, divine intervention, and answered prayers. You will be awed and inspired by these true personal stories, from religious and non-religious, about hope, healing, and help from angels.

978-1-61159-941-1

HOPE AND JOY

Chicken Soup for the Soul
for the **Soul**®

Merry Christmas!

101 Joyous Holiday Stories

Amy Newmark
Foreword by Santa Claus

This collection of 101 heartwarming and entertaining stories of holiday traditions, family, and goodwill will spread the wonder and joy of the holiday season. A fantastic holiday gift and a great way to start the season!

978-1-61159-953-4

MORE GREAT STORIES...

Chicken Soup for the Soul

The Joy of Christmas

101 Holiday Tales of Inspiration, Love, and Wonder

Amy Newmark
Foreword by Mrs. Nicholas Claus

Anyone who loves this joyous time of year will love these heartwarming and entertaining stories of family bonding, holiday hijinks, community spirit, and family and religious traditions. A fantastic holiday gift and a great way to start the season!

978-1-61159-963-3

FOR HOLIDAY GIVING

Chicken Soup for the Soul

for the Soul

Changing the world one story at a time®
www.chickensoup.com